Jesus through Jewish Eyes

$\mathcal{J}$ESUS
through $\mathcal{J}$ewish $\mathcal{E}$yes

RABBIS AND SCHOLARS
ENGAGE AN ANCIENT BROTHER
IN A NEW CONVERSATION

Compiled and edited
by
BEATRICE BRUTEAU

ORBIS BOOKS

Maryknoll, New York 10545

232.9
J58

Founded in 1970, Orbis Books endeavors to publish works that enlighten the mind, nourish the spirit, and challenge the conscience. The publishing arm of the Maryknoll Fathers and Brothers, Orbis seeks to explore the global dimensions of the Christian faith and mission, to invite dialogue with diverse cultures and religious traditions, and to serve the cause of reconciliation and peace. The books published reflect the views of their authors and do not represent the official position of the Society.

To learn more about Maryknoll and Orbis Books, please visit our website at www.maryknoll.com.

Manufactured in the United States of America

Library of Congress Cataloging-in-Publication Data

Jesus through Jewish eyes : rabbis and scholars engage an ancient brother in a new conversation / compiled and edited by Beatrice Bruteau
    p.   cm.
    Includes bibliographical references.
    ISBN 1-57075-388-1 (pbk.)
    1. Jesus Christ—Jewish interpretations. 2. Jesus Christ—Jewishness. 3. Jesus Christ—Historicity. 4. Judaism—Relations—Christianity. 5. Christianity and other religions—Judaism. I. Bruteau, Beatrice, 1930–

BM620 .J47 2001
232.9'06—dc21

                                                            2001034654

Contents

Preface

THREE MOTIVATIONS lie behind the compilation of this book—but let me say at the outset, so that there be no misunderstanding, encouraging conversion of Jews to any form of Christianity is not one of them. One might say that almost the reverse is the case: there is a strong interest in resituating Jesus within his native Judaism.

The first of my motivations has to do with Jesus himself. For some time now it has seemed to me that Christianity, as the religion *about* Jesus, is, in a number of respects, quite different from the religion that Jesus himself practiced and encouraged. That religion was, of course, his own presentation of Second Temple Judaism. To invite Jews to comment on him in this context would be a step in the direction of giving him back his own voice. We might be better able to see his particular emphases in terms of his historical culture and tradition. To put him again in a conversation with his coreligionists would be a move toward truth and justice if later developments have distorted his original intentions.

I am sympathetic to the sentiment with which Geza Vermes ends the introduction to his *Jesus the Jew:* If we can recognize that "this man, distorted by Christian and Jewish myth alike, was *in fact* neither the Christ of the Church, nor the apostate and bogeyman of Jewish popular tradition, some small beginning may have been made in the repayment to him of a debt long overdue."[1]

Jesus should have the opportunity to be known on his own terms —if it is possible to disentangle them from the theologies and institutions laid over them. Of course, we must also recognize that English-speaking Jews of two millennia later will be looking through lenses of their own, just as Christians are and have been doing. But the perspective will be different, and that may help.

The second motivation has to do with the Jewish people. Christian abuse of Jews is a long tale of shame and sorrow. The extent and per-

---

[1] Geza Vermes, *Jesus the Jew: A Historian's Reading of the Gospels* (Philadelphia: Fortress, 1973), 17.

sistence of the religiously sponsored persecution are more than one can believe. And this has been done on behalf of Jesus! Obvious injustice to them, but also injustice to him. That they should come to hate him because of what Christians have done to them is tragic. Many can't bear to hear his name mentioned!

But if he himself is not actually the cause of their multitudinous sufferings, then his memory is being abused together with them. *He is on the side of the victims, not the perpetrators.* If this is the correct view, then anything that can be done to heal this frightful wound should be done.

The third motivation has to do with the Christians. The book is not primarily for them; it is primarily for Jesus and his fellow Jews. But it is likely to be read by more Christians than Jews. At the present time, many Christians are eager to see Jesus in his original context and are interested to see what other Jews make of him and what Christians can learn from such Jewish views.

Put him on a level playing field with other Jewish teachers, without any special claims or privileges, in the give-and-take of Jewish learning and debate, and let us see what happens. There is also the context of Jewish mystics and *tzaddikim*, people of outstanding virtue and holiness, of great generosity, whose whole lives are devoted to service to others. Will Christians in search of "the historical Jesus" see something more with such Jewish help? One would think so. So for their sakes as well this discussion may be valuable.

These are the compiler's motivations for assembling the book, but it is important also that the reader know what invitation was issued to prospective contributors, what task was sketched for them, to what they are responding in writing their pieces. To this end I am reproducing here the material I sent them. I did not know what they would be apt to say, and I did not reject any because of what they said.

The responses are quite varied. Some contributors are academics and give us historical and theological views. A number are congregational rabbis who speak out of their experience with people whose lives are affected by some of these issues. Some share quite personal feelings and experiences vis-à-vis Jesus. Most of them still have difficulty "leaving Christianity out of it" when discussing Jesus. Some offer views that they hope will constitute a kind of common ground with Christians. Many begin by reminding us of what has been done to the Jewish people because of Jesus. A few remark that there is no call for them to take any particular interest in him at all; he doesn't add anything that they don't already have. Others see him as a teacher to be honored within the Jewish fold. They don't all have the same degree of scholarly knowledge, and their styles are different—some are formal, others colloquial, maybe humorous, maybe mystical. From my point of view, this is to our advantage. I wanted to see a variety of views from different sorts of people. I wanted to open a conversation in which many people could participate. I hope it will continue.

Invitation to the Contributors

THIS BOOK WILL BE A COLLECTION of pieces by Jews who are moved to take an independent look at whatever the writer chooses to isolate as "the historical Jesus," after leaving aside Christian interpretations, elaborations, theological developments, anti-Jewish and other polemics, and so on. The idea is to get Jewish views of a thoroughly Jewish Jesus, as he was (as nearly as we can tell) before there was any such thing as Christianity. Views should be personal and honest and can be offered in whatever context the writer chooses.

Historians think they now have reasonably secure grounds for sorting through the Jesus material and grading various items as historically real words and deeds, or at least as accurate representations of his mentality. Judging from this position, they can then consign other items to the class of dubious or fictitious. Archaeologists, anthropologists, and language and literature experts also make contributions to this study. There are several methods of judging, and there is a good deal of debate. This kind of search has inevitably obliged scholars and those who read them to take very seriously the historical fact that *Jesus was a Jew*. (It seems ridiculous to have to make such a point, but an amazing number of people don't seem to realize this.)

This being the case, those who have accustomed themselves to this idea naturally wonder, How does Jesus look to other Jews? (Allowance has to be made for the fact that modern Judaism is itself a reworked outgrowth of ancient Israelite religion/culture, not exactly the same thing as its parent.) But suppose you could go back to Jesus himself, before Christianity, before all those theological elaborations, when he was simply a Jew among Jews, what would he be like? Could a modern Jew imagine that, and if so, how would the view come out?

In proposing this, it is important to insist that the viewer not import anything from later Christian development. This means that the viewer will have to make decisions in going through the sources as to what is fiction, apologetic, polemics, catechetics, liturgy, and other nonhistorical material. This is where the "Jewish eyes" may have a marked advantage. The expectation is that Jewish eyes will see differently, significantly, helpfully. In particular, the editor hopes for additional light on what the historical Jesus was doing in his own proper Jewish context and whether any of that—the basic principles and maybe the general outlines of the practical application—could still be usefully applied today. For example, did he have an idea, perhaps a program, for *Tikkun Olam*, and would it work?

Another obvious thing that has to be said is that Jesus is not anti-Jewish. He is not "superseding" the Jewish religion. He is precisely immersed in it. If Jews can start to separate him, in his own historical reality, from all the dreadful things done to their people in association with his name, if they can begin to see that these injustices and horrors are not his fault, but that, rather, he too is being victimized by these distortions, then this may occasion some relief.

Therefore, this book could be seen, on the one hand, as justice to a historical figure, and on the other hand, as justice to the people and the tradition that produced him and therefore have first right to comment on him. The extreme ironies of what history has done to his memory and to his people deserve whatever corrections we can offer.

Exposure to new perspectives is usually stimulating and often prompts whole new breakthroughs and revitalization. Can a fresh Jewish perspective on Jesus, and especially on his ideas and programs if they should be found worthy, say anything to our present situation? If our proposed study should result in lifting up insights and values that in themselves still have relevance and power for our contemporary needs, then our project will have brought a helpful resource to the world table.

Acknowledgments

T HE EDITOR AND THE PUBLISHER gratefully acknowledge permission to reprint the following excerpts from previously published work:

Lawrence Kushner: *Jewish Spirituality: A Brief Introduction for Christians,* copyright © 2001, by Lawrence Kushner (Woodstock, VT:
Jewish Lights Publishing). $12.95 + $3.50 s/h. Order by mail or
call 800-962-4544 or on-line at www.jewishlights.com. Permission
granted by Jewish Lights Publishing, P.O. Box 237, Woodstock,
VT 05091.

Michael Lerner: *Jewish Renewal,* copyright © 1994 by Michael Lerner.
Used by permission of Putnam Berkley, a division of Penguin
Putnam, Inc.

Daniel Matt: Excerpt from *God & The Big Bang,* copyright © 1996
by Daniel C. Matt (Woodstock, VT: Jewish Lights Publishing).
$16.95 + $3.50 s/h.

Byron L. Sherwin: "'Who Do You Say That I Am?' (Mark 8:29): A
New Jewish View of Jesus," published by the *Journal of Ecumenical Studies* in vol. 31, nos. 3–4 (summer–fall 1994), in a longer
form.

Lewis D. Solomon: Excerpts from *A Modern Day Rabbi's Interpretation of the Teachings of Jesus,* copyright © 2000. Used by permission of SterlingHouse, Pittsburgh, Pennsylvania.

Arnold Jacob Wolf: "Jesus as an Historical Jew," *Judaism* 48, no. 3
(summer 1997).

The editor acknowledges and thanks Stanley Ned Rosenbaum for
suggesting the title *Jesus through Jewish Eyes;* Lance Edwards for a
phone conversation remark, "I want to draw Jesus into a new conversation," which became the subtitle; Drew Leder for recommend-
ing the picture on the cover; Marshall and Mark Marvelli (father and
son) of Winston-Salem, North Carolina, and Stanley Ziobro of
Pfafftown, North Carolina, for hours of technical work on the elec-
tronic version of the manuscripts; Stuart Matlins for invaluable
advice; and Michael Leach of Orbis Books, for constant help and
encouragement.

A Jew Writing about Jesus the Jew

Laura Bernstein

I can't write about Jesus.
How you entered my life abruptly at age 17
when my first love from the Moody Bible Institute
introduced me to you
and you became my second love
for a time. I learned to pray
in your name and consulted your mother
as well on matters of spirit.
My mother said worshiping you
was worse than being a prostitute.

I went off to college, my heart in a vise
my head in a crown of thorns.
For years I stopped communicating with you.
We were estranged.
I stopped praying altogether
and began paying psychiatrists
for my salvation. And became a therapist
myself, a wounded healer
still seeking, longing, aching,
not yet praying.

Decades later, rabbinical school beckoned
and I was thrust into the wilderness
of your home turf, Jehoshua—
learning Hebrew, reading Torah,
chanting psalms, intoning mystical supplications.
I called you my beloved brother
when the Amish man in the garden
asked me if I loved you.

And you came to me in a dream:
We davenned together in another garden.
Your eyes were transparent, your hands, soft.
You gave me two gifts—a scarf and a pair of socks,
garments for the journey.
To keep my neck covered?
To prevent me from getting cold feet?
On my hands the tetragrammaton blazed
like stigmata—our father's holiest, unpronounceable name.
Alright . . . All right.
I can write about Jesus.

PART ONE

HISTORICAL AND THEOLOGICAL VIEWS

1

Evolving Jewish Views of Jesus

Michael J. Cook

THIS PRESENTATION FOCUSES not on Jesus himself but on Jewish views of him and on the changes these views have undergone over time. By "Jewish views" are meant perceptions about Jesus by Jews dissociating themselves from Christian affiliation and affirmation.[1] For many centuries, such perceptions were generally disparaging. With the onset of nineteenth-century Jewish scholarship, however, a substantial reversal set in: many Jewish assessments of Jesus (as a *historical* figure) now became more positively inclined, a trend still in effect today.

Given so broad an expanse of time, it will be helpful to distill five periods for our special focus:

Period 1: During *Jesus' ministry itself (ca. 30 C.E.)*, only relatively few Jews—aside from his own followers—may have known of him, and we cannot surmise with any certainty what they thought about him.

Period 2: *From Jesus' death (ca. 30 C.E.) through the end of the second century*, we have little by way of Jewish writings mentioning Jesus. Certain *Christian* works, however, are indirectly helpful. From these we infer that Jewish appraisals of Jesus were often uncomplimentary.

Period 3: With the age of *early rabbinic literature (approximately the third through the sixth centuries)*, we begin encoun-

---

[1] Excluded, then, are views about Jesus that may have been held by his Jewish followers, by Paul, and by any Gospel writer who might have been Jewish; also views of modern-day Christians who fancy themselves Jews (i.e., self-styled "Hebrew-Christians," "Jews-for-Jesus," and "Messianic Jews").

3

tering more evaluations of Jesus in *Jewish* source material per se (some of these likely perpetuated oral traditions from the preceding era). These assessments of Jesus were usually denigrating.

Period 4:   In *the Middle Ages*, proceedings from Christian–Jewish disputations tell us much about Jewish views of Jesus, but how reflective these recordings were of the general Jewish populace is difficult to gauge. Additionally, we can examine a polemical tract entitled *Toledot Yeshu* ("The History of Jesus"); strongly denying Christian claims, this work caricatured Jesus along lines that persisted, in some circles, for centuries to come.

Period 5:   During the *early modern period, beginning in the 1800s,* as Jews emerged from generations of ghetto stagnation, a substantial change began to ensue—with many now becoming more open to assessing (the historical) Jesus sympathetically.

PERIOD 1—JESUS' MINISTRY

Jesus' ministry preceded composition of any written sources about him (Jewish, Christian, or other). Accordingly, reconstructing what Jews of his own day thought about him is problematic. Several "curtains" eclipsed the historical Jesus from the Gospel writers themselves. The same curtains impede *us* from determining how Jews had viewed him during his ministry.

- The first curtain is *chronological*: One to two generations elapsed between Jesus' ministry (ca. 30 C.E.) and the eventual completion of the four canonical Gospels (ca. 70-100). Such an extensive hiatus raises doubts: how accurately did these writings preserve not only the realities of Jesus and his ministry but also the particulars of *how and what Jews had thought about him* during that ministry?

- Second is a *geographical curtain*: Early Christianity expanded rapidly from Palestine into and throughout the broader Mediterranean arena. Most adherents of such new churches were unfamiliar with Palestine, not to mention with the milieu of Jesus' ministry. At least two or three, possibly even all four Gospels were completed within these Diaspora regions. With regard to our particular quest, geographical distance impeded an author's access not only to information about the historical Jesus but also to information about *how Palestinian Jews during Jesus' ministry had viewed him.*

- *Demography* is a third curtain: By the time of the Gospels' completion (70-100), Christian ranks had undergone dramatic alteration. Most Christians now reflected Gentile rather than Jewish extraction.[2] How did this circumstance impact the manner by which the Gospels described *Jewish views of Jesus during his ministry?* Were these recountings formulated in any way to satisfy Gentile interests (conditioned as these were, in turn, by new times and locales)?

- Some Gentile-Christians were not merely, as by definition, non-Jewish, but *anti-*Jewish as well. This conjures up an *ideological* curtain. Just as Gospel depictions of Jews could manifest or reflect overtones of bias, so also could Gospel portrayals of *how Jews had perceived Jesus* during his ministry.

Each of these curtains, considered in its own right, poses a substantial impediment for us. When viewed as combined, or superimposed, these curtains become all the more formidable! The current problem—determining how Jews of Jesus' day had perceived him—demands that we visualize all four curtains in concert: for underlying the Gospels' descriptions of these Jewish perceptions were traditions already beclouded by the passage of time, some shaped in Gentile-Christian communities geographically removed from Palestine, with many of these traditions coalescing during years of bitter ideological invective between Christians and Jews (especially from 70 to 100). The interaction of all these dynamics makes it impossible to gauge, with confidence, the extent to which Jesus' Jewish contemporaries (aside from his own followers) had viewed him positively, negatively, or even been aware of him at all![3]

---

[2] See Michael J. Cook, "The Mission to the Jews in Acts: Unraveling Luke's Myth of the 'Myriads,'" in *Luke-Acts and the Jewish People: Eight Critical Perspectives*, ed. Joseph B. Tyson (Minneapolis: Augsburg, 1988), 102-23, 152-58.

[3] What of Jews who knew Jesus through involvement in his Sanhedrin trial? The historicity of this episode is highly questionable. See Michael J. Cook, "The Death of Jesus: A Catholic-Jewish Dialogue [opposite Raymond Brown]," in *No Religion Is an Island: The* Nostra Aetate *Dialogues* (New York: Fordham University Press, 1998), 56-100; see also idem, "Destabilizing the Tale of Judas Iscariot," in *An American*

While we may not know precisely *how* Jews of Jesus' day regarded him, can we even be sure *that* they thought about him? Did not Jesus twice feed thousands by the Sea of Galilee? Did not Jerusalem turn out en masse to greet him on Palm Sunday?[4] Yet such traditions, along with repeated Gospel assertions that Jesus' fame had spread far and wide,[5] also happen to match the usual mold of Hellenistic tales of wonder-workers. Some religious elements in the Mediterranean world advanced sagas (termed *aretalogies*) that routinely aggrandized a hero's fame, words, and deeds, often so as to attract new believers or adherents. Early Christian traditions might likewise have embellished Jesus' fame in line with conventions prevailing for other charismatic figures of that time.

Should we nonetheless persist in accepting the Gospels' statistics at face value—suggesting that Jesus was indeed well known to Jews of his day—then we would still need to explain the dearth of early sources (aside from New Testament writings themselves) that mentioned him. The early-second-century Roman historian Suetonius, for example, alluded to a disturbance instigated by a certain "Chrestus" (*On the Life of the Caesars,* "Claudius," 25). While he could have had "Christ" in mind, Suetonius dated him to the year 49 C.E. (Jesus died around 30) and placed him in Rome. More likely, then, he was referring to an incident involving not Jesus himself but Christian missionaries who, by preaching "Christ," had provoked a commotion—possibly within Rome's Jewish quarter itself. Suetonius's contemporary Tacitus, meanwhile, confirmed that "Christ" was executed while Pontius Pilate was Roman procurator (governor) of Judea (26-36) (*Annals* 15.44).[6] Yet by Tacitus's day, the Gospels were already long in circulation. Thus, he could well have drawn this knowledge from exposure to the Gospels themselves or at least from passing acquaintance with information in them—rather than from direct recourse to independent official records about Jesus (such as in Roman archives per se).[7]

Rabbinate—A Festschrift for Walter Jacob (Pittsburgh: Rodef Shalom Press, 2001), 114-47.

[4] Mark 6:35ff.; 8:1ff.; and 11:7ff. (and parallels); also John 6:1ff.; 12:12ff.

[5] E.g., Mark 1:28; Matt. 4:24; 9:26, 31; 14:1; Luke 4:14, 37; 5:15.

[6] Tacitus's designation of Pilate as a "procurator" is incorrect. Pilate was a "prefect."

[7] See E. P. Sanders, *The Historical Figure of Jesus* (London: Allen Lane, 1994), 49: "Roman sources that mention Jesus are all dependent on Christian reports." Tacitus's

The first-century Jewish historian, Flavius Josephus, in his *Antiquities* (93 C.E.), affirmed the popular following of another New Testament figure, John the Baptist (18.116-19). Josephus's two references to Jesus, however, must be approached with caution. His long paragraph about Jesus, called the "Testimonium Flavianum," is so adulatory and consistent with what we would expect of a *Christian* assessment that most scholars dismiss it as a reworking, even an outright forgery, by a later Christian hand (18.63-64).[8] Further along in the same work (20.197-203), Josephus describes the execution (in 62 C.E.) of a certain James—identified as "the brother of Jesus who was called the Christ." This phraseology conveys little substantive about Jesus himself. But assuming the passage is authentic, the identification of this James *by reference to* Jesus could imply that Josephus had introduced his readers to Jesus somewhere earlier in the *Antiquities*— possibly where the "Testimonium" (as a recasting or replacement?) now resides. Even this conclusion, of course, need not suggest that Jesus himself had been particularly well known to fellow Jews, for Josephus also described other figures from Jesus' era who likely had been unfamiliar, even unknown, to most of their contemporaries.

We therefore face a quandary. If Jesus were genuinely as famous as some Gospel passages allege, then why have we such minimal first- or even second-century (non-Christian) source material about him? Yet if we grant that Jesus probably was *not* widely known, then how productive or meaningful can be our efforts to reconstruct specifically Jewish views about him from his own day?

---

error—in terming Pilate a "procurator" (see preceding note)—likewise suggests his nondependence on official Roman records.

[8] Preserving Josephus's writings, the church had opportunity to revise them. The clauses italicized here render the "Testimonium" as we have it suspect: "About this time there lived Jesus, a wise man, *if indeed one ought to call him a man*. For he was one who wrought surprising feats and was a teacher of such people as accept the truth gladly. He won over many Jews and many of the Greeks. *He was the Messiah*. When Pilate, *upon hearing him accused by men of the highest standing amongst us*, had condemned him to be crucified, those who had in the first place come to love him did not give up their affection for him. *On the third day he appeared to them restored to life, for the prophets of God had prophesied these and countless other marvellous things about him*. And the tribe of the Christians, so called after him, has still to this day not disappeared" (Loeb Classical Library, vol. 9 [Cambridge, Mass.: Harvard University Press, 1965]). Raymond Brown retains as genuinely Josephan the clause, "upon hearing him accused by men of the highest standing amongst us" (*The Death of the Messiah*, vol. 1 [Garden City, N.Y.: Doubleday, 1994], 373ff.). See also John P. Meier, "The Testimonium: Evidence for Jesus Outside the Bible," *Bible Review* 7, no. 3 (1991): 20-25, 45.

As we turn now to periods 2 through 4, we will encounter increasingly negative—even increasingly odd—descriptions of Jesus by Jews. Some of these may be explicable on the assumption that, from the start, little by way of any accurate understanding of Jesus was passed on by his Jewish contemporaries to Jews of later generations. We should of course be mindful that Jesus was a Jew, not a Christian; accordingly, the more fully he lived and spoke as a Jew, the less reason there might have been for him to be especially known or remembered by fellow Jews. Undoubtedly, the Jesus to whom Jews eventually did come to react was not as much the historical figure as the Gospels' later reconfigurations of him—conditioned as these were, in turn, by the needs of the developing church and by the complicating factors already noted: chronology, geography, demography, and ideology.

Any idea that Jesus might not have been widely known by Jews in his own day could influence our assessment of the so-called Messianic Secret in Mark, the earliest Gospel (ca. 70 C.E.): the notion that Jesus had instructed his disciples to conceal his identity until after the resurrection.[9] This motif is curious since it contradicts other traditions, in Mark itself, that assert Jesus' fame already during his ministry.[10] But the "Secret" becomes more intelligible as a Markan device to explain away an otherwise glaring anomaly, namely: if "the Messiah" originated as a Jewish concept, and if Jesus were genuinely that Messiah, then why had so few Jews ever acknowledged him? As a stratagem, the suggestion that Jesus' identity was initially hidden would render more comprehensible why the vast majority of Jews, beginning already with Jesus' own day, had not accorded him appropriate recognition—if indeed they had even known of him at all.[11]

---

[9] Mark 9:9: ". . . he ordered them to tell no one about what they had seen, until after the Son of Man had risen from the dead." Biblical quotations are from *The New Oxford Annotated Bible with the Apocryphal/Deuterocanonical Books*, New Revised Standard Version, edited by Bruce M. Metzger and Roland E. Murphy (New York: Oxford University Press, 1994).

[10] E.g., 1:28, 45; 2:13; 3:7f.; 4:1; 5:24; 7:36b; etc.

[11] We encounter a similar dynamic in 16:8, the original ending of Mark's Gospel: ". . . [the women] fled from the tomb . . . and they said nothing to anyone, for they were afraid" (16:8). The empty tomb story was unknown until it surfaced (was fashioned?) during Mark's day. Here, again, Mark availed himself of the motif of concealment—as if to say that the episode of the empty tomb was still unknown by Jews because the women had kept what they had seen secret!

PERIOD 2—FROM JESUS' DEATH
THROUGH 200 C.E.

Our second chronological period extends from Jesus' death (ca. 30 C.E.) until the end of the second century. Here also it is difficult to determine how Jews were viewing Jesus—if we limit ourselves to Jewish sources. The philosopher-historian Philo of Alexandria, who died around 40 C.E., extends into this period, but his writings say nothing about Jesus. While some Dead Sea Scrolls may derive from these years, none mentions Jesus.[12] Nor are books of the Apocrypha and Pseudepigrapha that arise from this period helpful.[13] As for Josephus, we have already noted why his testimony about Jesus is problematic.

Might Christian writings be of assistance? Since the Gospel authors framed some sections of their narratives as responses to Jewish opponents of their own day (70-100),[14] could we not comb such accounts for telltale clues to what (non-Christian) Jews—later than Jesus' ministry—were now saying about him?

- Some Jews, for instance, were now alleging that Elijah, herald of the Messiah, had himself not yet appeared (Mark 9:11)—how, then, could Jesus be the Messiah?[15]

- Others were insisting that the Messiah was not expected to come from Galilee—so how could Jesus of Nazareth (in Galilee) be the Messiah (see John 7:52)?[16]

- Some doubted whether Jesus had been descended from King David (John 7:40-42; cf. Mark 12:35-37)—this was commonly thought a necessity for the Messiah.

---

[12] That some believe the Scrolls refer to Jesus and John the Baptist under symbolic names "simply proves that learned fantasy knows no limits" (John P. Meier, *A Marginal Jew: Rethinking the Historical Jesus*, vol. 1 [New York: Doubleday, 1991], 94).

[13] Barring, of course, late Christian accretions—e.g., chaps. 1-2 and 15-16 of 2 (4) Esdras (in the Apocrypha).

[14] See Michael J. Cook, *Mark's Treatment of the Jewish Leaders* (Leiden: Brill, 1978), especially 15-28.

[15] This induced the evangelists to enlist John the Baptist as Elijah (Mark 9:13 and especially Matt. 17:13).

[16] In response, Matthew and Luke presented birth stories showing Jesus of Nazareth (in Galilee) born instead in Bethlehem (in Judea).

- Some thought that Jesus had rejected or at least had failed to reaffirm the Law of Moses[17]—either stance was presumed inconsistent with being the Messiah.

- Jesus had been crucified—but the Messiah was supposed to triumph over Rome.[18]

- Jesus had been resurrected, his followers insisted—but skeptics were denying this claim outright.[19]

A later Christian source, Justin Martyr's *Dialogue with Trypho*,[20] likewise suggests how Jews of this second period were viewing Jesus. Composed between 155 and 161, this purported debate was set in the city of Ephesus (in what today is Turkey). The participants were Justin, an early church father, and Trypho, a learned Jew said to have fled Palestine in the wake of the futile revolt of the Jews led by Bar Kokhba against Rome (132-135 C.E.). The exchange was but a contrivance of Justin's imagination—with "Trypho" an invented figure (named, perhaps, after Rabbi Tarphon, a noted second-century critic of Christianity). Contrivance aside, however, the arguments that Justin attributed to Trypho must have reflected then-current concerns. Because Justin was modeling how Christians should respond to Jewish skeptics, he had to assign "Trypho" assertions cohering with what second-century Christians were genuinely hearing.

Jews (personified through Trypho) were now alleging that "you Christians have all received an idle report and have formed a Christ for yourselves, for whose sake you inconsiderately throw away your lives" ("Introduction"); the Hebrew Scriptures "never acknowledge any other God than the One Creator of all things" (§55); the idea that God descended to be born in the form of a man is "incredible and almost impossible" (§68). Christian views of Jesus rely on an overly selective and arbitrary citation of proof texts from Jewish Scrip-

---

[17] Mark 1:22, 27; 2:24; 3:2; 7:19b; John 9:16; cf. Acts 6:13-14. While Matt. 5:17 could be cited to the contrary (". . . I have come not to abolish [the law or the prophets] but to fulfill [them]"), this construction likely stems from Matthew himself, not Jesus. Reacting against Mark (and Paul), Matthew portrayed Jesus as a law*giver* (not *breaker*).

[18] Responses include Mark 10:33f. (Jesus' expected execution); Matt. 26:53 (he chose not to prevent it); Matt. 26:54 (he died to fulfill Scripture).

[19] They were countered by the creation of empty tomb stories: Mark 16:1-8, embellished by Matt. 27:62-66; 28:4, 11-15; also Luke 24:1ff. and John 20:1ff.

[20] *Writings of Saint Justin Martyr*, Fathers of the Church 6 (New York: Christian Heritage, 1948), 139-366.

ture—passages drawn, moreover, only from the Greek translation rather than the Hebrew original (§§27, 68); the image of Jesus in Christianity heavily depends on borrowings from Greco-Roman mythology (§67); crucifixion, moreover, resembles hanging, a mode of execution specifically cursed in Deuteronomy 21:23 (§89); Jesus, meanwhile, had broken with the Law of Moses—could the true Messiah abandon the very essence of Judaism (cf. §67)?

Indeed, (the Jew) Trypho appears less opposed to the notion that the Messiah had already arrived than to identification of that Messiah with *Jesus* in particular! Trypho thus teaches us not so much who Jews were thinking Jesus *was* but who they thought he was *not*! Most likely, Jews of this era did believe Jesus to have been an actual personage from Galilee who had claimed divine status and broken with the Law. He had declared himself the Messiah but utterly without substantiation. Since many Jews were undoubtedly disillusioned over Bar Kokhba's failure and death, the fact (not to mention the mode) of Jesus' execution could have made messianic claims on his behalf appear utterly preposterous.

PERIOD 3—EARLY RABBINIC LITERATURE
(THIRD THROUGH SIXTH CENTURIES C.E.)

In early rabbinic literature (from Babylonia as well as Palestine), we encounter statements about Jesus from specifically Jewish sources. Even so, since the Talmud, Midrash, and related works are vast compendia of Hebrew law and lore, their allusions to Jesus must be adjudged strikingly sparse. These mentions are also so widely scattered that we must "hunt and peck" simply to assemble a viable portrait—combining views from different rabbis, generations, and academies. Compounding the problem is confusion over whether some passages that did not originally allude to Jesus later became misconstrued as indeed about him. Rabbinic texts dealing with other figures (e.g., ben ["son of"] Stada, Peloni ["a certain person"], [ben] Netzer) became subsequently misapplied to Jesus.[21] Supposed cam-

---

[21] E.g., in *Sanhedrin* 67a, a reference to ben Stada (*not* Jesus) attracted a later addition: "they hanged him on the eve of Passover" (cf. John 19:31), the clause used in conjunction with Jesus per se in *Sanhedrin* 43a. On ben Stada, see Tosefta *Shabbat* 11:15; Tosefta *Sanhedrin* 10:11; *Sanhedrin* 67a; *Shabbat* 104b; on Peloni, see Mishnah *Yebamot* 4:13; Tosefta *Yebamot* 3:3, 4; *Yebamot* 49ab; *Yoma* 66b; on (ben) Netzer, see *Sanhedrin* 43a; *Kethubot* 51b (also Isa. 11:1).

ouflaged references to Jesus (e.g., under the name of "Balaam"[22]) need not all have been framed with Jesus in mind. Once so processed, however, even mistaken allusions to Jesus entered into the mix of presumed rabbinic perceptions of him, thus complicating, even corrupting, an already perplexing enough mosaic.[23] In such a fashion did rabbinic understandings of Jesus both grow and yet go awry. What results is not only a crude kind of composite but virtually a caricature of sorts.

A proper analysis of this conglomeration of traditions would be daunting, requiring (to start with) the compartmentalization of texts according to their chronological and geographical origin. Granted, the findings from such an exercise might clarify somewhat how rabbinic traditions about Jesus had developed. But given the considerable impact of rabbinic traditions on later Jewish assessments of him, it is unclear, overall, whether these conclusions could be of much practical import.

In terms of the rabbis' cumulative understanding of Jesus, some had come to think that Jesus, while in Egypt, had become schooled in the art of sorcery along with the charms and formulae needed to perform feats of magic. Possibly this was how rabbis explained (or explained away) the miracles that the Gospels credited to Jesus—since "miracles," to believers, were easily dismissible by skeptics as trickery.[24] As for datings of Jesus, these are likewise puzzling. The rabbis mentioned Jesus in connection with various figures whose time frames, when combined, spanned at least two centuries.[25] Yet Gospel

---

[22] E.g., Mishnah *Abot* 5:19; Mishnah *Sanhedrin* 10:2; *Sanhedrin* 106ab. An apparent allusion to Jesus in P. *Taanit* 65b is based on Num. 23:19 (from the Balaam story).

[23] Scholars themselves differ on what passages originally referred to Jesus. See R. Travis Herford, *Christianity in Talmud and Midrash* (London: Williams & Norgate, 1903); Joseph Klausner, *Jesus of Nazareth*, trans. Herbert Danby (repr., New York: Macmillan, 1943), 17-54; Morris Goldstein, *Jesus in the Jewish Tradition* (New York: Macmillan, 1950), 17-139; Jacob Z. Lauterbach, "Jesus in the Talmud," in *Rabbinic Essays* (Cincinnati: Hebrew Union College Press, 1951), 471-570; David Catchpole, *The Trial of Jesus: A Study in the Gospels and Jewish Historiography from 1770* (Leiden: Brill, 1971), 1-71.

[24] *Shabbat* 104b; P. *Shabbat* 13d; xii,4; cf. Mark 3:22; Matt. 9:34; 12:24.

[25] For an early-first-century B.C.E. dating, see *Sanhedrin* 107b and *Sotah* 47a; for a second-century C.E. dating, see *Shabbat* 104b; see also *Gittin* 90a. The rabbis could also have been confused in dating the figures they mentioned in some connection with Jesus (e.g., Yehoshua ben Perahyah; Pappos ben Yehudah), and thus misdated Jesus himself, accordingly.

testimony assigned Jesus' ministry to the narrow period when Judea was ruled by Pontius Pilate (26-36 C.E.)—and when Jesus had been "about thirty" (Luke 3:23). (Of course, by their later day, the rabbis—especially in Babylonia—would have had few guidelines for dating Pilate's rule either.) On an even more basic matter, the Talmud allotted Jesus merely five disciples even though the Gospels consistently assigned him twelve.[26] Was it simply a rabbinic convention that often teachers had five disciples (five were accorded Johanan ben Zakkai, traditional founder of the Jamnia [Yavneh] academy; and Judah ben Baba ordained five disciples of Rabbi Akiba[27])? Alternatively, is it at least remotely conceivable that the rabbis deprived Jesus of having "twelve" disciples so as to obstruct claims that Christianity (symbolized by twelve disciples) had supplanted Judaism (symbolized by twelve tribes)?[28] Likewise puzzling is how the rabbis could confuse Jesus' mother, Mary, with Mary Magdalene (a lapse typical of some modern Jews as well)![29]

Elsewhere, however, the rabbis seemed not only fully aligned with Gospel traditions but even overly accepting of them. They naturally viewed anti-Jewish sentiments attributed to Jesus by the Gospels as originating with him personally—rather than as retrojections by the later church. They also took for granted that Jesus had proclaimed himself divine; accordingly, any Jew who worshiped him was compromising monotheism. Ironically, therefore, the same Jesus who had designated the *Shema* ("Hear, O Israel: The Lord our God, the Lord is one" [Mark 12:29, citing Deut. 6:4]) his preeminent directive could also be summarily accused of having denied Judaism's cardinal teaching![30] Mindful that some Jews had indeed been lured into Christian ranks, the rabbis denounced Jesus himself for having attempted to "entice and lead Israel astray," that is, into apostasy and

---

[26] *Sanhedrin* 43a; cf. Mark 14:10, 17, 43; Matt. 10:2; 26:20, 47; Luke 6:13; 22:14, 47; John 6:70f.; cf. 1 Cor. 15:5.

[27] See Mishnah *Abot* 2:8 for Yohanan ben Zakkai; *Sanhedrin* 14a and *Abodah Zarah* 8b for Akiba.

[28] Cf. Matt. 19:28: "you who have followed me will also sit on twelve thrones, judging the twelve tribes of Israel"; see also Luke 22:28ff.

[29] *Shabbat* 104b; cf. *Hagigah* 4b and accompanying medieval *Tosaphot* commentary. In the 1970s, a major Jewish organization objected that the play *Jesus Christ Superstar* portrayed Jesus in "incestuous" association with Mary Magdalene, "his own mother"! See Lauterbach, *Rabbinic Essays*, 529-32.

[30] Cf. Tosefta *Shabbat* 13:5; P. *Taanit* 65b; and late midrashic works: *Shemot Rabbah* 29.5 (to Exod. 20:2); *Debarim* Rabbah 2:33 (to Deut. 6:4).

idolatry.[31] All told, accordingly, the rabbis could deem fully credible Gospel renditions of Jesus' Sanhedrin trial. These formulations cast Jesus as condemned for "blasphemy" (Mark 14:64 and par.)[32] and held Jewish, not Roman, authorities responsible for his execution (both of these assumptions were to become vigorously challenged by Jews during period 5). Nonetheless, while accepting these premises, the rabbis denied that Jesus' trial had been in any way speedy or unfair, for a herald (so they fancied) had announced throughout Palestine for forty days: "He is going to be stoned, because he practiced sorcery and enticed and led Israel astray. Let anyone who knows anything in his favor come and plead in his behalf" (*Sanhedrin* 43a).[33] That no one stepped forward confirmed Jesus' guilt and validated his Sanhedrin conviction.

However we explain these and still other rabbinic traditions, the overall judgment remains warranted: the rabbis convey little if anything reliable about the historical Jesus.[34] Plausibly, Jewish views of Jesus in any one era could have influenced—even determined—those of succeeding years. If, as argued, Jesus had not been well known among Jews during the time of his own ministry, the Jewish tradition might not have gotten off to an accurate understanding of who he was. Such a circumstance could readily have given rise not only to misconceptions about Jesus emerging relatively early on, but to their retention and embellishment by Jews of later periods as well. Certainly during period 3, the ancient rabbis' portrayal of Jesus appears already far removed from the actual figure. Depictions we encounter during the Middle Ages may seem more distant still.

---

[31] See Deut. 13:7-12; Tosefta *Sanhedrin* 9:7; Tosefta *Hullin* 2:22-24; *Shabbat* 116ab; *Sanhedrin* 43a, 67a, 103a, 107b; *Sotah* 47a; *Abodah Zarah* 16b-17a. Cf. Herford, *Christianity in Talmud*, 60ff.; Goldstein, *Jesus*, 117ff.

[32] That the rabbis processed Christian theology of their *own* day as blasphemy strengthened their presumption that Jesus had been a blasphemer himself.

[33] Cf. Tosefta *Sanhedrin* 10:11; P. *Sanhedrin* vii.16.25cd; *Sanhedrin* 67a.

[34] Is there no value in studying the disparities between Talmudic capital jurisprudence and Gospel accounts of procedures at Jesus' Sanhedrin trial? Works such as Haim H. Cohn, *The Trial and Death of Jesus* (New York: Harper & Row, 1971), misapply rabbinic traditions, since, if Jesus underwent any trial at all (see Cook, "Death of Jesus," 76ff.), it was not likely in a rabbinic-type court; see Ellis Rivkin, "Beth Din, Boulé, Sanhedrin: A Tragedy of Errors," *Hebrew Union College Annual* 40-41 (1969-70): 205-49; idem, review of Cohn in *Saturday Review*, June 19, 1971, 22, 61-62. Given the late date of many rabbinic traditions, Talmudic procedures (if *ever* followed) reflect the post-70 C.E. era, irrelevant to Jesus' day.

PERIOD 4—THE MIDDLE AGES

Jewish assessments of Jesus were expressed in many medieval writings of an apologetic and polemical nature. We also have records of publicly staged debates pitting Jewish and Christian disputants against one another.[35] Nonetheless, these texts conceal as well as reveal. Their argumentation relies on subtleties of biblical and rabbinic interpretation, philosophy, theology, and mysticism. It seems unlikely, therefore, that these materials afford us any clear reading about how Jesus was generally perceived by the wider Jewish populace.[36]

Moreover, how seriously may we take the transcribed remarks of Jewish protagonists in publicly staged disputations?[37] Since "winning" a debate could well jeopardize the security of the Jewish community at large, political considerations certainly entered into what Jewish disputants publicly said or refrained from saying.[38] Evidently, Jewish characterizations of Jesus from earlier centuries now surfaced as potentially embarrassing for Jewish disputants, who frequently had to soften or explain away certain Talmudic mentions of Jesus—or even deny outright that the Jesus referred to in the rabbinic writings

---

[35] See Oliver S. Rankin, ed., *Jewish Religious Polemic* (Edinburgh: University Press, 1956); Frank E. Talmage, ed., *Disputation and Dialogue: Readings in the Jewish–Christian Encounter* (New York: Ktav, 1975); Daniel J. Lasker, *Jewish Philosophical Polemic against Christianity in the Middle Ages* (New York: Ktav, 1977); David Berger, *The Jewish–Christian Debate in the High Middle Ages* (Philadelphia: Jewish Publication Society, 1979); Hyam Maccoby, ed. and trans., *Judaism on Trial: Jewish–Christian Disputations in the Middle Ages* (East Brunswick, N.J.: Associated University Presses, 1982); Jeremy Cohen, *The Friars and the Jews* (Ithaca, N.Y.: Cornell University Press, 1982); Robert Chazan, *Daggers of Faith: Thirteenth Century Christian Missionizing and the Jewish Response* (Berkeley: University of California Press, 1989). On Jewish views of Jesus during the sixteenth through eighteenth centuries, see Goldstein's useful outline (*Jesus*, 216-21).

[36] On whether geographical distinctions should be drawn in this respect—comparing, for example, the general Jewish educational level in northern France with that in Germany—see Ephraim Kanarfogel, *Jewish Education and Society in the High Middle Ages* (Detroit: Wayne State University Press, 1991).

[37] The purpose of disputations was less to attack Jews than to win converts to Christianity and to confirm recent converts in their faith (particularly those who had become Christians under duress). Conquering "doubt" was more important than conquering Jews.

[38] See Martin A. Cohen, "Reflections on the Text and Context of the Disputation of Barcelona," *Hebrew Union College Annual* 35 (1964): 157-92; Goldstein, *Jesus*, 197ff.

was the Jesus of Christianity (it was someone else)! Official transcripts of these proceedings, moreover, may not duplicate what actually transpired; in some places what they record was not the live action, as it were, but Christian polemical revision composed after the fact. Thus, when filtered through all these broad and varying problems, the material we possess seems far more difficult to process than would appear at first glance.[39]

Furnishing us with a quite different kind of gauge is a medieval Jewish tract entitled *(Sefer) Toledot Yeshu* ("[The Book of] the History of Jesus"). Unfortunately, we know neither its author(s) nor any other details of its creation (date, place of origin, and so on). The earliest references to its existence stem from two French archbishops in the ninth century, but the tract likely circulated long before surfacing to their attention. The text warrants examination because it distinctly echoes and directly extends traditions we have earlier culled from rabbinic sources, now also interweaving with them Gospel motifs and, in places, even mimicking Gospel style. *Toledot Yeshu's* many versions and translations suggest that the attitudes and legends it perpetuated, embellished, or engendered had become widely disseminated on the popular level.

This parody's retelling of the life of Jesus (here severely abridged) began by introducing a chaste woman, Miriam (Mary), who lived in Bethlehem of Judea and was betrothed to a righteous man of the royal house of David. Residing nearby, however, was the disreputable Joseph Pandera (a Roman soldier?).[40] One night, pretending to be Miriam's betrothed husband, he forced himself upon her. In due course, she gave birth to Yehoshua, a name later shortened to Yeshu (Jesus).[41] When old enough, Yeshu began Jewish schooling. But as

---

[39] On a variety of these and related issues, see the insightful analysis by Susan Einbinder, *Trial by Fire: Burning Jewish Books*, Lectures on Medieval Judaism at Trinity University: Occasional Papers 3 (Kalamazoo, Mich.: Medieval Institute Publications, 2000), 1-35.

[40] For rabbinic mentions of a Pandera (Pandira, Pantera, Panthera, Pantiri, Panteri, Pantira, etc.), see Tosefta *Hullin* 2:22; *Shabbat* 104b; P. *Shabbat* end of X or 14d; *Abodah Zarah* 40d, 41a. See discussions in Goldstein, *Jesus*, 35ff.; Herford, *Christianity in Talmud*, 39ff.; Klausner, *Jesus*, 23; Lauterbach, *Rabbinic Essays*, 529-39. The church father Origen of Alexandria (about 248 C.E.) mentions (*Contra Celsum* 1.28, 32) a scurrilous tradition that a Roman soldier Panthera, stationed in Judea, was the extramarital father of Jesus. He quotes in this regard the pagan philosopher Celsus (ca. 178 C.E.), who claimed that he was told such by a Jew.

[41] The English name Joshua translates the Hebrew *Yehoshua*, or a later Hebrew/Aramaic form thereof, *Yeshua*—names that were fairly common in the first century

his antecedents became publicly known, he was forced to flee to Galilee.

Later, as an adult, he returned to Judea bent on entering the Jerusalem Temple—whose foundation stone bore the letters of God's Ineffable Name. Yeshu was determined to learn the letters because their possession would enable him to perform magic (miracles). Yet the knowledge of these letters was ordinarily impossible to retain because they were guarded by lions of brass. Upon roaring, the lions induced forgetfulness. Cleverly, Yeshu smuggled a small parchment into the Temple. Upon learning the letters, he inscribed them on the parchment which he then inserted into an open cut on his thigh.[42] As he was leaving, the lions roared—and he promptly forgot the letters. But he later regained access to them upon finding and removing the parchment from his thigh. Thereafter, he was able to perform astounding feats to silence his opponents!

The Jewish leaders, after numerous attempts, finally managed to arrest him. They charged him with practicing sorcery and attempting to beguile and lead the Jews astray. Shortly after his execution, however, his followers told Queen Helene[43] that they had found his tomb

---

C.E. *Yehoshua* can mean "the Lord is salvation" or "the Lord will save/saves/has saved." The English form, Jesus, goes back to the Latin (*Iesus*), which in turn transliterates the Greek form (*Iēsous*) of these Hebrew or Aramaic names. It is commonly asked: by what Hebrew/Aramaic name(s) was Jesus actually addressed? This cannot be definitively determined because the earliest (i.e., extant) sources we have that mentioned him were composed in Greek. Another commonly posed question concerns the regular noun *yeshua*, which can mean "salvation." Since the name *Yeshu*—as in *Toledot Yeshu*—appears to abbreviate the name *Yeshua*, was the shortening an attempt by Jewish tradition to evade or prevent any association of Jesus with "Savior" or "salvation"? More likely, *Yeshu* was simply a natural shortening of *Yeshua* (with no polemic intended), analogous to the way *Yosi* shortened *Yosef* ("Joseph").

[42] This seems predicated on rabbinic traditions of ben Stada's making "a cut upon his flesh" (Tosefta *Shabbat* 11:15; *Shabbat* 104b).

[43] It is unclear who "Queen Helene" is supposed to be. The most likely candidates are: (1) Salome Alexandra (wife of Alexander Jannaeus), who continued the Hasmonean dynasty by assuming rule over Palestine upon her husband's death. She reigned from 76 to 67 B.C.E. She was also the sister of Simeon ben Shetah, identified by rabbinic traditions (see, in the Mishnah, *Abot* 1:8 and *Hagigah* 1:2) as a leading sage (specifically, he belonged to the third of five sequential pairs [*zugot*] of leaders) and as succeeding in this capacity Yehoshua ben Perahyah—of whom Jesus was said once to have been a disciple (see *Sanhedrin* 107b). Could "Salome" (which was sometimes rendered "Saline") have been mistakable as "Helene" (see Goldstein, *Jesus*, 304 n. 95)? (2) Queen Helena, sister and wife of Monobaz I, king of Adiabene (in the upper Tigris region), and visitor to the holy land. Together with her son, she con-

empty—he had been resurrected! Jewish leaders were thrown into consternation, unable to imagine how this had transpired. One upset dignitary, Rabbi Tanhuma (actually, he lived centuries later than Jesus), chanced upon a certain gardener who professed that he could explain the tomb's emptiness because *he* was responsible for it! Fearful that Yeshu's disciples would steal his body and proclaim him resurrected, the gardener himself had removed the body and buried it in his garden. (Recall here Matt. 28:15 and John 20:15: Matthew informs us that Jews of his own day were discrediting the resurrection as a hoax. The disciples had taken Jesus' body, then declared him resurrected. In John, Mary Magdalene initially mistook the resurrected Jesus for a gardener who she assumed had removed the body; *Toledot Yeshu* accepted and then capitalized on Mary's original surmise!)

   Toledot Yeshu is outrageous, to some disgraceful. While hardly a historical source about the person it describes, it yet accurately reflects the climate of Christian Europe, where Jews, a persecuted minority, were often under relentless pressure to convert. A counternarrative impugning Gospel claims of Jesus' virgin birth, miracles, empty tomb, and resurrection was potentially helpful in warding off proselytizers. Unfortunately, this kind of formulation also appears to have markedly shaped and misdirected elements of the popular Jewish mind-set about Jesus for generations to come. Well into the twentieth century, European Jews were still recounting to their offspring Yiddish folkloristic tales about *Yoshke Pandre* (Yeshu [son of] Pandera)![44]

PERIOD 5—THE EARLY MODERN ERA

Quite obviously, Jewish views of Jesus before the modern period had become a gross distortion of the actual figure. The several centuries

---

verted to Judaism around 30 C.E. (see Josephus, *Antiquities* 20:17-96). In 45, amidst a famine in Palestine, she purchased food in Egypt and Cyprus for those starving. She made various gifts to the Temple and spent the latter part of her life in Jerusalem (where she built herself a palace; see Josephus, *Wars* 5:252; 6:355). After she died in Adiabene, her remains were transferred to Jerusalem. (3) Saint Helena (ca. 255-ca. 330), the mother of the Emperor Constantine the Great and legendary finder (ca. 326) of the cross. During her visit to the holy land, she founded basilicas on the Mount of Olives and in Bethlehem. Since we are not dealing in *Toledot Yeshu* with genuine history, identifying the queen may not warrant further investigation.

[44] Nearly a dozen versions of *Toledot Yeshu* are extant, most printed by Samuel Krauss. See idem,"Une nouvelle recension hébraique du Toldot Yesu," *Revue des Etudes Juives* n.s. 3 (1938): 65-88, and references therein to Krauss's earlier studies.

when many Jews were kept behind ghetto walls further delayed any enlightened change.[45] So isolated, Jews remained relatively stagnant on other fronts as well, generally unaware of, or oblivious to, the extraordinary formative developments that had been playing themselves out on the wider stage: the discovery of the New World, the Renaissance, the Protestant Reformation, and the commercial and industrial revolutions. When, however, ghetto walls were flung open in the early nineteenth century—largely as a consequence of Napoleonic conquests—Jews exiting into Christian Europe-at-large felt directly confronted by claims about Jesus. Some Jews now, at long last, began to put aside centuries of misconception about him. Aiding them was a sobering undertaking by Christian scholars referred to today as the "Old Quest for the Historical Jesus."

Scholars pressing this quest realized the importance of reconstructing Jesus' life in the light of his specifically Jewish context, and they thus anticipated the relevance of ancient Jewish literatures, including rabbinic, in revealing and detailing this milieu. What primarily interested them were not ancient Jewish understandings of Jesus per se but rather depictions of the institutions and thought patterns that had formed the backdrop for Jesus' ministry (the Temple, Sanhedrin, and synagogues; Jewish festivals and customs; theological and ethical teachings and Pharisaic parables; liturgical elements and refrains; and so on). Jewish scholars, in turn, now became encouraged to assist their Christian counterparts in understanding especially the Hebrew and Aramaic literature that most Christian scholars felt incapable of handling by themselves. As a by-product of this reciprocity, books and lectures by Jewish historians themselves[46] soon began to incorporate discussion about Jesus, Paul, and Christian origins in relation to the Jewish context of intertestamental times.

The collective results of such new Jewish assessments of Jesus can now be sketched out in terms of three broad contrasts:[47]

---

[45] The medieval period can thus be said to extend longer for Jews than for non-Jews, ending perhaps with the nineteenth-century opening of the ghetto walls. See also Goldstein, *Jesus*, 221: "The medieval period for the Jewish people ends in 1776 (or 1791) . . . with the declaration of human rights, with the respect accorded in a democracy for each man's religion."

[46] Beginning with Abraham Geiger, *Das Judenthum und seine Geschichte* (Breslau: Schletter, 1864), 118ff., and passim; also Heinrich Graetz, *Sinai et Golgotha, ou les origines du judaisme et du christianisme*, trans. Moses Hess (Paris: Lévy Frères, 1867); see idem, *History of the Jews*, vol. 2 (Philadelphia: Jewish Publication Society, 1893).

[47] Surveying early modern Jewish scholarship on Jesus are Herbert Danby, *The Jew*

1. During late antiquity and the Middle Ages, Jews had commonly caricatured Jesus as a sorcerer who had attempted to beguile the Jewish people and lead them astray. The modern Jewish reassessment stripped away such earlier misconceptions, restored respectability to Jesus' image, and then reclaimed him as a Jew who had established no new religion! The elements of Christianity that had produced its break from Judaism were now said to have arisen only after Jesus' death.

2. Having rehabilitated and restored Jesus to respectability within the contours of Judaism, Jewish scholars now had to reconsider why their rabbinic forebears had seemed so resolute, even precipitous, in their decision to execute him. There inevitably ensued a reevaluation of reasons for his arrest, eventuating in the judgment that Roman officialdom (not Pharisaic/rabbinic leadership) was primarily—if not solely—responsible for Jesus' death! Consistent with their new reconstruction, Jewish scholars also surmised the actual reason for Jesus' arrest to have been not blasphemy, apostasy, sorcery, or enticement (as per early rabbinic literature and *Toledot Yeshu*), but rather Roman officialdom's suspicion that Jesus was a subversive. Presumptions of Jesus' seditious aspirations and activities, whether justified or not, had occasioned his arrest and his crucifixion not by "the Jews" but rather by Pontius Pilate, operating in conjunction with his appointee/subordinate, the high priest Caiaphas.

The Gospel writers, it now became urged, must have been succumbing to pressures in their own day while shaping their narratives of Jesus' trial set decades earlier. It was their fear of Rome[48] that had

---

and Christianity: Some Phases, Ancient and Modern, of the Jewish Attitude toward Christianity (London: Sheldon Press, 1927); Claude Montefiore, "Jewish Conceptions of Christianity," *Hibbert Journal* 28 (1929-30): 246-60; Thomas Walker, *Jewish Views of Jesus: An Introduction and Appreciation* (New York: Macmillan, 1931); Samuel Sandmel, *We Jews and Jesus* (New York: Oxford, 1965); Walter Jacob, *Christianity through Jewish Eyes* (Cincinnati: Hebrew Union College, 1974); Shalom Ben-Chorin, "The Image of Jesus in Modern Judaism," *Journal of Ecumenical Studies* 11 (1974): 401-30; Jakob Jocz, *The Jewish People and Jesus Christ* (repr., Grand Rapids: Baker, 1981); Donald Hagner, *The Jewish Reclamation of Jesus* (Grand Rapids: Zondervan, 1984).

[48] In 64 C.E., the emperor Nero scapegoated Christians for a fire in Rome (Tacitus, *Annals* 15.44), inflicting upon them "grievous torments" (Suetonius, *Life of Nero* 16). The earliest Gospel, Mark (ca. 70), reflects wariness of Rome's anti-Christian offensive. Judea's revolt in 66 raised the ominous specter of Roman vengeance against not only Jews but Christians (for Rome confused the two). To deter continued

occasioned their portrait of Pilate's attempted exoneration of Jesus a generation or two before. Faced now with the urgency of establishing Jesus' loyalty to Rome (and thereby the allegiance of their own communities also), Christian writers could hardly have felt comfortable casting Rome as culpable in Jesus' execution! Thus was blame lifted from Rome and necessarily assigned to some other quarter. Tensions with Pharisees/rabbis in the evangelists' day encouraged this shift of responsibility for Jesus' condemnation onto the Pharisees, the "chief priests," and the Sanhedrin instead. This displacement was accomplished literarily through the fiction that Jesus had a hearing before the Roman prefect, where the normally ruthless Pilate, supposedly convinced of Jesus' innocence, was yet pressured by Jews to crucify him!

3. In earlier centuries, the radical cleavage between Judaism and Christianity had been routinely traced to apostasy by Jesus personally. But modern Jewish opinion now generally shifted the decisive role in that parting of the ways to Paul. This conclusion was prompted by the consideration that not only are Paul's epistles (ca. 48-62) our earliest Christian writings, but that Paul's thinking (whether or not it was interpreted correctly) may have vitally determined directions taken by various segments of later Christianity. The emphasis here was not so much on what Paul actually said or intended as on the influential role those who interpreted Paul (even in widely diverging fashions) played in how Jesus came to be portrayed by later Gospel traditions (ca. 70-100).

The conceptualization here was that the earliest images of the historical Jesus and his teachings in many cases passed through the filter of Paul's interpretation concerning the meaning of the Christ (and thus as well through the lenses of others' interpretations of Paul's interpretation). The consequence of this filtering process was that Jesus' image and teachings were not simply preserved but also embellished and in some cases significantly transformed. With respect to subsequent Christian–Jewish relations, at least three Gospel themes of decisive importance were presumed to have been generated through this process, each bearing the impress either of what Paul himself had preached, or of how others construed or misconstrued that preaching. These motifs were:

Roman persecution of Christians, Gospel writers had to distinguish Christians from (non-Christian) Jews, and in a fashion to suggest that Christians were allies of Rome.

- that Jesus had rejected the Law of Moses (see Gal. 2:16; 3:10-11, 23-26; Rom. 7:1-6);

- that Christian missionaries had turned the focus of their preaching away from Jews and toward Gentiles instead (see Gal. 1:15f.; 2:7; 3:11-14); and

- that Jews had been superseded by Gentiles as God's chosen people (see Gal. 4:22-30; Rom. 9:6-12, 25-26, 30-32).

While the Gospels portray Jesus himself as reflecting, or encouraging, these three viewpoints, Jewish scholarship now generally came to deny that Jesus ever categorically rejected the Law of Moses, or counseled a turning from Jews to Gentiles instead, or sanctioned any notion that Jews had been superseded by Gentiles. Rather, it was Pauline thought, years after Jesus' ministry, that first stimulated the raising of these three issues, and advocates of these themes began to press them in earnest—and belatedly to ascribe them to Jesus personally. Earlier on, Jesus' intimate followers had vigorously opposed Paul himself precisely because they perceived Paul as distancing himself from what they believed had been Jesus' own fidelity to the Law and to the Jewish people!

Notably, the three themes in question had originally contributed centrally to the stereotyping by ancient Jewish tradition of Jesus himself as an apostate (as well as to the supersessionist and triumphalist theology of some Christians past and present). The very suggestion that these motifs derived more from how Paul was interpreted than from what Jesus personally had advanced now constituted a revolutionary reorientation of traditional Jewish thinking. For it meant that only after Paul's break with the Law were Jesus-traditions—supportive of Paul's attitudes—fashioned in direct accommodation to the earlier Pauline views!

RAMIFICATIONS FOR TODAY

The confines of this presentation do not allow for either a critique or a defense of this new Jewish orientation toward Jesus.[49] The task here

---

[49] See Michael J. Cook, "The Jewish Scholar and New Testament Images of Judaism," *Lutheran Theological Seminary Bulletin* 77, no. 1 (1997): 21-41; idem, "Jewish Reflections on Jesus: Some Abiding Trends," in *The Historical Jesus Through Catholic and Jewish Eyes*, ed. Bryan F. LeBeau, Leonard Greenspoon, and Dennis Hamm, S.J. (Harrisburg: Trinity Press International, 2000), 95-112.

has been only to survey evolving Jewish views with a particular focus on five chronological periods.

When it comes to Jewish assessments of the historical Jesus today, it is unrealistic to expect an absolute consensus in all respects. Nonetheless, most—if not all—of the following conclusions typify many modern Jewish portrayals of him:

- Jesus was a Jew, and so were his followers. He did not found Christianity, which was a later movement tracing its origins back to him.

- Jesus behaved as a Jew. Christianity's fundamental break with the Law should be attributed to Paul, not to Jesus, though Jesus may have had disputes with fellow Jews on particular legal issues or on what should be the proper emphases of legal observance.

- Jesus was a great teacher of Jewish ethics (occasionally likened, by some Jews today, to the Hebrew Prophets of old).

- Jesus should be viewed against the Jewish context of his day, not in isolation. Unlike the impression forthcoming from the Gospels, Jesus was indeed influenced by his times; it was not simply the times that were influenced by him.

- Such an approach reveals that Jesus' uniqueness may have resided more with his personality than with his originality. Since most of his teachings seem analogous to those of ancient Jewish tradition, what may most have distinguished Jesus was his charisma as a teacher, possibly a belief on his part that he had a personal mission (even a messianic one), and certainly his conviction that the end of the world order was imminent—hence his fervor to alert others to the coming of God's kingdom. But Jesus could hardly have imagined himself *divine*, for this clearly would have carried him outside the bounds of his own Jewish affiliation.

- Jesus may have deemed himself the Messiah, but, if so, he was mistaken; he did not bring about what was expected of the Jewish Messiah—namely, independence for Palestine from the hand of Roman oppression, together with restoration of the Davidic golden age.

- The charges on which Jesus was arrested were political in orientation. Possibly his preaching of the coming of the kingdom of God was construed as predicting or urging the overthrow of the

Roman establishment along with its appointee, Caiaphas (together with other pro-Roman elements within the Jewish priestly hierarchy). Most likely, Jesus was routinely arrested, as were other figures similarly perceived, and executed in a process whose underlying authority derived ultimately from Rome.

CONCLUDING THOUGHT

A fanciful Jewish tale of uncertain origin relates that the Messiah one day did appear. At long last, Jews and Christians were able to arrange a greeting and celebrate the establishment of God's reign. But, as has too often been the case in relations with one another, rather than simply rejoicing together (in this case, over the Messiah's arrival), Jews and Christians began to argue over who had been right over the centuries. Accordingly, during a hastily arranged "press conference," the key question turned out to be: "Messiah, is this coming your first or second?" To their chagrin, the Messiah ventured only a terse "No comment!"

In view of our world's conditions, it seems that the Messianic Age is not yet here. Rather than debating who has been right or wrong all along, would it not be more productive to pool our energies so to live together that, by the spirit of joint endeavors, we might ourselves refashion the world so it more closely approximates the Messianic Age? Then perhaps would the Messiah be induced to appear—and we have more substantive questions to pose during that press conference!

2

Jesus as a Historical Jew

ARNOLD JACOB WOLF

THE JESUS OF HISTORY, the man who was born in *Erets Yisrael* and lived and died as a Jew, is, in Christian dogmatic theology, one with the God who is beyond all limitations of time or space. A problem is how to reconcile the historical Jesus with the Christ of faith. Some have separated them entirely. Some have denied the human (Marcion) or the divine (Unitarians). No one has completely united what is inherently incommensurate.

After the work of Albert Schweitzer at the turn of the century, bold attempts to discover the "real" Jesus of history were suspended, in the light of Schweitzer's proof that the Gospels, as church documents, could only reveal the later Christ of the church. But in the 1950s the search was renewed, and now again the last decade has released a powerful desire to find out just who Jesus was. Inevitably, this brings the founder of Christianity (if, indeed, he was its founder) back to his Jewish roots. The historical Jesus turns out, not unexpectedly, to be Jewish through and through.

But is it possible to know anything for certain about that Jew of Nazareth? Or are we inevitably to get only another mirror image of ourselves, as Schweitzer predicted? Liberals see in Jesus a peasant revolutionary. Mystics find an eschatological seer. Christians christianize their Jewish founder. We only get out what we put in. There seems to be no clear way back to the original Jesus of the first century in the Land of Israel.

A powerful example of the "peril of modernizing Jesus" (H. J. Cadbury) is to be found in a brilliant lecture delivered at the University of Arizona in 1995 by Susannah Heschel, "Transforming Jesus from Jew to Aryan: Protestant Theologians in Nazi Germany."

Heschel shows that some of the most important New Testament scholars in Germany tried to prove that Jesus was racially not "Semitic" and ideologically the bitter enemy of "late" Judaism in its decadent form of the first century. They manipulated texts, transformed parables, and reinterpreted the Gospels to make them fit the Nazi view of a parasitic and dangerous Jewish religion and folk. No example could be imagined that proves more firmly that the Jesus we want is the Jesus we will get.

And yet the Nazi Party did not buy the theologians' revisionary Jesus. They did not welcome the scholars into their hierarchy nor use the new image widely or cunningly. They simply did not, apparently, believe what these New Testament experts told them. They smelled a rat. They could not, or would not, believe that Jesus was a goy. That indicates that there are limits to misreading, that history will out, and that a fairly trustworthy image of Jesus can be unearthed by a scholarship that at least tries for objectivity, accuracy, and authenticity.

CONSENSUS AND CRITERIA

There is a consensus among the new searchers for the historical Jesus. They differ on many issues: How much of the Gospel records Jesus' own words and deeds? How much of Judaism did he know and practice? Which brand of the many varieties of Judaism did he prefer? But no one thinks of him as anything but a Jew, a "marginal Jew" as John Meier claims perhaps, but a Jew nonetheless. A "Mediterranean Jewish peasant" maybe if John Dominic Crossan is right; a charismatic, a magician according to Morton Smith; or God-knows-what-kind of Jew—but a Jew for sure. A Jew and nothing but a Jew. A Jew totally within his Jewish faith and his Jewish roots. A loyal, perhaps even a revolutionary Jew, but a Jew and not an Aryan, a Jew and not a Christian, a Jew and not a cipher or an enigma that can never be understood.

How, then, do we know which passages in the Gospels reflect the words of Jesus? There are several criteria for authenticity that most of the new scholarship employs:

1. The criterion of dissimilarity. If a passage reflects neither a contemporaneous Jewish view nor the practice of the early church, then it probably is authentic. The compilers of the Gospels would not invent something that reflected neither a Jewish nor a later Christian view.

2. In apparent contradiction, the criterion of compatibility with first-century Judaism(s). Nothing that a first-century Jew could not possibly have said or thought would Jesus have said or thought. How this fits in with the first criterion is difficult to say.

3. The criterion of multiple sources. If several evangelists (or Josephus) say the same thing, it is more likely to be the reflection of what Jesus did or said. Unfortunately, Josephus says very little about Jesus, and that little is contaminated by Christian interpolations.

4. The criterion of compatibility with what Jesus did. Jesus' actions may (or may not) authenticate what he said. Of course, we cannot be sure exactly what he did. Did he drive the money changers from the Temple? Did he die on the cross under Roman orders? Do these deeds justify the claim that he predicted the end of the Temple as he knew it, or the criminal's death that he would necessarily suffer?

5. The criterion of embarrassment. Nothing that would embarrass the writers is their own addition. If Jesus was said to be baptized by John, or said to have died an ignominious death, he probably did.

6. The criterion of translation. If the Greek text seems to be a translation from an original Aramaic (or Hebrew?) saying of Jesus, it is more likely to be accurate. If it is vivid, there is a presumption that it is no mere editorial addition to the text.

All of these criteria are relative, though none is useless. The historical Jesus can be recovered with a high degree of plausibility, but scholars will disagree on his nature.

THE QUESTION OF ANTI-JUDAISM

For us Jews, the Gospel narratives present a great many problems, not the least of which is a clear anti-Semitism, found especially in the stories of Jesus' trial and crucifixion, but also throughout the four Gospels—animus against the Pharisees (which is to say the rabbis) and sometimes against the priests, the elders, or even the entire community of Jews. Is it possible to imagine that this anti-Jewish hostility was the true sentiment of Jesus of Nazareth, who was in every way a Jew? A marginal Jew, perhaps, a revolutionary Jew, as we have suggested, a dissenting Jew—but there were lots of dissenting Jews and they never became anti-Semites. All of the Gospel narrators, the evangelists, were Jews, except perhaps for Luke. They were more or less committed Jews, Jews who knew the Hebrew Bible, and who knew the Jewish religion even when they held positions somewhat different from the version of that religion practiced by their co-religionists.

So the question of anti-Judaism remains, and it is impossible to resolve. Are the anti-Judaic, sometimes downright anti-Semitic, passages authentic to Jesus or not? We would tend to say "not." The New Testament is a document of the Gentile Roman Catholic Church of the second, third, and fourth centuries, and that church has clearly revised the teachings of Jesus and the early stories about Jesus in order to give the Romans the benefit of all doubts and to make the Jews who later "rejected" Jesus look bad.

On the Jewish side, there has been a great deal of simple avoidance. We didn't talk about Jesus. We didn't think much about Jesus. We had no official view of Jesus, except occasionally a perverted and negative one. I wonder whether this was prejudice or fear or revulsion, or, perhaps, even a kind of attraction. Jesus was saying the kind of things about the Jewish religion that a lot of Jews would like to say but can't get away with. So we don't think about Jesus, we don't talk about Jesus, but in our heart of hearts he seems to be our brother. Like many of us, he, too, is a dissenting Jew.

The conventional Jewish view is that Jesus was a fairly good Jew but Paul was an anti-Semite who created Christianity. The problem is that Paul was at least as Jewish as Jesus. He calls himself a Pharisee. E. P. Sanders and Krister Stendahl, among others, have proved that the letters of Paul are typical Jewish documents of a few later centuries. Paul certainly was not less Jewish than Jesus. One cannot any longer say that he was the founder of Christianity, unless one realizes that somehow Jesus gave him a lead, an entering wedge for a new religion. Religions are not invented out of nowhere. Paul did not create the Jesus of the New Testament.

JESUS AND THE ESSENES

Many have tried to place Jesus in the community of the Dead Sea Scrolls, which most people believe to have been an Essene community. The Essenes were in some ways very like Jesus, and in some ways very different. Let me list the similarities and the differences, following James H. Charlesworth.

God was the same for the Essenes and for Jesus. They shared the Hebrew Scriptures as their guiding source. A possible fondness for certain books is particularly interesting. Jesus and the Qumran Scrolls both quote the prophet Isaiah over and over again, and never quote the book of Esther. They seem to have had similar tastes; some pieces of the tradition and not others were important to both of them. They both read the Scriptures in an eschatological, messianic way. The Hebrew Bible was not just a book to be studied, or a law to be obeyed. It was a plan for the future, a plan written in code. Both Jesus and the Essenes were suspicious of the Temple cult. They both shared possessions, exemplified celibacy, and condemned divorce. They both reflect a mood of eschatological expectation, a new covenant for an old people. They breathed the same air of expectation, judgment, and hope.

These similarities were striking enough to lead some of the early students of the Scrolls sometimes to identify Jesus with the Teacher of Righteousness and the early Christians with the (putatively) Essene community. But their dissimilarities are at least as important to an impartial observer. Jesus moved in entirely open circles of devotees and opponents, while the Qumran community was almost hermetically sealed. They were committed to obey elaborate laws of purity; Jesus hardly credited even the common Jewish norms of purity. He was apparently a kind of missionary; his disciples clearly were, while the Essenes were uninterested in proselytes, since they believed the future lay with them in any case. He spoke in beautifully simple (though sometimes obscure) parables; they in a code, sealed with a thousand seals. They were hierarchical, authoritarian, reclusive. He was the founder of an open, welcoming community. They were predestinarian, basing themselves on an opaque, mystical interpretation of Scripture. He was attempting to open the Torah to existential relevance. Nor did the two agree on angelology, martyrdom, the Sabbath, the calendar, or the resurrection of the dead, so far as we can tell.

A PEASANT WITH A GENIUS FOR RELIGION

It is difficult to place Jesus in any of the conventional streams of first-century Judaisms. He is said to have debated with the Pharisees, but these proto-rabbis themselves are understood in vastly different ways by modern scholars. Thus, for example, the recent *Encyclopedia of Religion,* published by the University of Chicago, has two separate articles on the Pharisees, reflecting the different views of Jacob Neusner and Ellis Rivkin, and neither of these views has won wide support. Anyway, many have thought that Jesus himself was a kind of Pharisee, though it seems to me better to think of him as an *am ha-arets*, a peasant with a genius for religion.

In what way was Jesus unique, or, at least, unusual?

He practiced celibacy and had no family, nor did most of his apostles. He took a hard line on divorce, absolutely forbidding it, according to one source. He ignored the strictures on personal purity and went out to lepers and outcasts. He fraternized with sinners and apparently did not require repentance before admitting them to fellowship. He assumed a kind of personal authority that classical Judaism believed had given way to collegiality and debate among rabbinic authorities. Thus, for example, he revised Sabbath legislation according to his own interpretation of Scripture.

He was said to have healed the sick and (like Elijah and Elisha in earlier times) to have resurrected the dead and given hope to many. It is far from clear whether or not he believed himself to be the promised Messiah, but if he did, he would not be the first Jew (or the last) to claim the title. All of these add up to the image of a somewhat unusual first-century Jew, but clearly one within the bounds of the possible.

3

"Who Do You Say That I Am?" (Mark 8:29)

A New Jewish View of Jesus

Byron L. Sherwin

M OST CLASSICAL JEWISH theological teachings express a negative view of Jesus. Though the twentieth-century Jewish philosopher Martin Buber called Jesus his "brother,"[1] much of classical Jewish theological teaching considered Jesus an "other" (*otoh ha-ish*, literally, a derogatory term for "that man"), that is, an apostate who subverted the teachings of Judaism, a Jew whose teachings were utilized by his followers as a justification for the persecution of the Jewish people in many lands over many centuries, and as the paradigmatic false Messiah. Jews, in effect, excommunicated Jesus from the Jewish faith and from the Jewish people. What is proposed in this essay is a radical reassessment of the place of Jesus in Jewish theology.

The present endeavor is to formulate a new Jewish theology of Jesus grounded in the framework not of contemporary historical scholarship but of classical Jewish theological rubrics. Such a new Jewish theology of Jesus cannot be evaluated primarily in terms of its

---

[1] Martin Buber's description of Jesus as "my great brother" is found in the "Foreword" to his study of the relationship of Judaism and Christianity, *Two Types of Faith*, written in 1948. Probably the most positive view of Jesus and of Christianity among classical Jewish thinkers is found in the writings of the eighteenth-century German rabbi Jacob Emden. See, e.g., Harvey Falk, "Jacob Emden's Views of Christianity," *Journal of Ecumenical Studies* 19 (winter 1982): 105-11.

confluence with modern *Wissenschaft*, but rather with regard to these two criteria: (1) Is it defensible within the framework of Jewish theological teaching? Specifically, does it violate any belief fundamental to Judaism? Does it negate any established Jewish religious legal dictate (*halakhah*)? Is it inconsistent with any critical Jewish religious belief or practice? (2) Is the view offered inconsistent with contemporary Jewish theological self-understanding? Specifically, can it and would it be accepted, at least by some segment of the contemporary "faith community" of Jews?

To be sure, for reasons that will become apparent, some Jews will consider the view put forth below to be a viable theological option, though not necessarily one that they might be willing to accept. Others will dismiss it outright. Nonetheless, my position is that the Jewish theological view of Jesus offered below meets the criteria we set out above: it is not inconsistent with the rubrics of Jewish theological discourse; it offers a theological reformulation of Jewish views of Jesus that reciprocates the many recent courageous theological reformulations of Christian views of Jews and Judaism; and it provides a reduction of barriers for *theological* discourse between Jews and Christians regarding that which is most important for Christians, that is, the person of Jesus. Before offering my specific proposal, it is first necessary to delineate five premises upon which this Jewish theological view of Jesus is based.

FIVE PREMISES

1. The first premise is that Jewish theological teachings about any subject must be understood within the context of Jewish theological discourse. Consequently, it would be inappropriate for us to use here categories, assumptions, or theological topics and issues proper to Christian understandings of Jesus.[2] The Jewish theological question is, who can Jews believe Jesus is?

---

[2] On Christology and Judaism, see a fine summary of recent scholarship in John T. Pawlikowski, "New Trends in Catholic Religious Thought," in *Twenty Years of Jewish-Catholic Relations,* ed. Eugene J. Fisher, A. James Rudin, and Marc H. Tanenbaum (New York/Mahwah, N.J.: Paulist Press, 1986), 169-90. See also, e.g., Allan R. Brockway, "Learning Christology Through Dialogue with Jews," *Journal of Ecumenical Studies* 25 (summer 1988): 347-57.

2. The second premise is that, while Christian claims about Jesus do not constitute an issue on the Jewish theological agenda, they must be an issue on the social agenda of the Jewish people, because these claims have led to the mistreatment and persecution of Jews. The Jewish interest therefore relates to how claims affect Christians' attitudes and actions toward Jews. As Rabbi Eugene Borowitz put it,

> We have been so hurt by past Christian teaching and practice, we are so worried about the terms on which the world (still so strongly influenced by Christian opinion) will permit us to survive, that our first question to any Christian is likely to be: "What do you believe is your Christian obligation to the Jews and what will you be doing about it?"[3]

3. The third premise is the affirmation of and the commitment to religious pluralism, which assumes that no religion has a monopoly on truth, that theological diversity reflects the divine will, and that more than one faith plays a role in God's plan for human redemption. This is a stance developed by Jewish theologians in the Middle Ages, enhanced in the sixteenth century by Eliezer Ashkenazi's interpretation of the biblical story of the Tower of Babel—God divided the people into different faith-languages to prevent the absolutism that inevitably stifles free and creative thought and authentic religious expression[4]—and insisted upon in our own time by Rabbi Abraham Joshua Heschel, who held that the Torah is not the only way of serving God, and that "human faith is never final, never arrival, but rather an endless pilgrimage."[5]

---

[3] Eugene B. Borowitz, *Contemporary Christologies: A Jewish Response* (New York/ Ramsey, N.J.: Paulist Press, 1980), 23. The recovery of the Jewishness of Jesus may pose a problem for the formulation of contemporary Christologies by Christian theologians; see, e.g., Philip L. Culbertson, "What Is Left to Believe in Jesus after the Scholars Have Done with Him?" *Journal of Ecumenical Studies* 28 (winter 1991): 1-17.

[4] Eliezer Ashkenazi, *Sefer Ma'aseh ha-Shem* (Venice, 1583), sec. "*Ma'aseh Bereshit*," chap. 31 (my translations, as are all other translations throughout, from Hebrew, French, and German).

[5] See Abraham Joshua Heschel, "No Religion Is an Island," *Union Seminary Quarterly Review* 21, no. 2,1 (January 1966): 117-33. Reprinted in *No Religion Is an Island: Abraham Joshua Heschel and Interreligious Dialogue,* ed. Harold Kasimow and Byron L. Sherwin (Maryknoll, N.Y.: Orbis Books, 1991); page references are to *No Religion Is an Island* (pp. 14, 18-19, 16).

In this connection, I would like to draw special attention to an idea advanced by the fifteenth-century Italian Jewish scholar Rabbi Abraham Farissol. It is unique in Jewish literature and virtually unknown, but is particularly deserving of our consideration in the present context. Farissol made the creative—and the distinctly pluralistic—suggestion that, while Jesus did not meet the Jewish definition of the expected Messiah, there is a sense in which even Jews could say that Jesus has in fact functioned as a redeemer *for Christians*. He wrote:

Let us assume that their Christ is a Messiah for them, and we [Jews] shall neither deny nor affirm that which befell their Messiah. For to my mind it is distinctly feasible that they be justified in designating him as their rightful redeemer. For they have declared—and it is in fact true—that since he came and imparted his doctrines, they have been redeemed and cleansed of the pollution of idol-worship.[6]

4. The fourth premise is that with regard to Jewish theological teachings on Jesus, an innovative way should be found to incorporate a positive view of Jesus into Jewish theological teachings. The main reason for this, simply put, is that Jesus was a Jew. Despite attempts of Christian historians and theologians to deny that Jesus was a Jew— for example, the efforts of some German theologians to demonstrate that he was an Aryan—Jesus was indisputably a Jew. Indeed, almost every Christian nation has tried to expropriate Jesus from his own people—the Jews. It is time for Christians to accept Jesus as a Jew. It is also time for Jews to reclaim him as a legitimate and honored member of the Jewish people—as a brother.[7]

---

[6] Quoted from manuscripts of Abraham Farissol's *Magen Avraham* in Samuel Lowinger, "Recherches sur l'oeuvre apologétique d'Abraham Farissol," *Revue des Études Juives* n.s. 5 (1940): 38.

[7] For a succinct summary of positive views of Christianity and Jesus by Jewish scholars since the 1950s, see, e.g., John T. Pawlikowski, *What Are They Saying about Christian–Jewish Relations?* (New York: Paulist Press, 1980), chaps. 3, 4. The article on "Jesus" in the *Encyclopaedia Judaica* states that the Synoptic Gospels "present a reasonably faithful picture of Jesus as a Jew of his time . . . as a Jew who was faithful to the current practice of the law"(Cecil Roth, ed. [Jerusalem: Keter Publishing House; New York: Macmillan, 1971], vol. 10, cols. 10, 13). Even the earlier *Jewish Encyclopedia*, in its entry on "Jesus of Nazareth," stated, "in many ways his [Jesus'] attitude was specifically Jewish, even in directions which are usually regarded as signs

The sainted Rabbi Leo Baeck, who was the most important Jewish leader in Nazi Germany and who survived the horrors of the Holocaust, wrote that in beholding Jesus,

we behold a man who is Jewish in every feature and trait of his character, manifesting in every particular what is pure and good in Judaism. This man could have developed as he came to be only on the soil of Judaism; and only on this soil, too, could he find his disciples and followers as they were. Here alone, in this Jewish sphere, in this Jewish atmosphere . . . could this man live his life and meet his death—a Jew among Jews.[8]

And about the Gospels, Baeck wrote:

The tradition of the Gospel is, first of all, in every [respect], simply a part of the Jewish tradition of that time. . . . It is a Jewish book . . . because a Jewish spirit and none other lives in it; because Jewish faith and Jewish hope, Jewish suffering and Jewish distress, Jewish knowledge and Jewish expectations, and these alone, resound through it—a Jewish book in the midst of Jewish books. Judaism may not pass it by, nor mistake it, nor wish to give up all claims here. Here, too, Judaism should comprehend and take note of what is its own.[9]

Recent Jewish and Christian scholarship of the New Testament and of Judaism in the first century demonstrates that Jesus was much more a part of than apart from Jewish life and thought in his time and place than had previously been assumed. Jesus lived, taught, and died as a Jew. Indeed, one cannot fully understand the life and teachings of Jesus when separated from the Jewish context from which they derive. This realization has led some contemporary scholars to maintain that it is precisely because earlier Jews and Christians failed to

---

of Jewish narrowness" (Isadore Singer, gen. ed. [New York/London: Funk & Wagnalls, 1904], 7:162.) More recently, see, e.g., writings of Jewish scholars such as Geza Vermes, David Flusser, Ellis Rivkin, Alan Segal, and others. See also the essays in *Jesus' Jewishness*, ed. James H. Charlesworth (New York: Crossroad, 1991). Cf. G. David Schwartz, "Is There a Jewish Reclamation of Jesus?" *Journal of Ecumenical Studies* 24 (winter 1987): 104-9.

[8] Leo Baeck, *Judaism and Christianity*, translation and introduction by Walter Kaufman (Philadelphia: Jewish Publication Society, 1958), 101.

[9] Ibid., 63, 102.

appreciate Jesus' rootedness in the Judaism of his time and place that
led them to believe that Jesus' teachings are anti-Semitic or anti-
Jewish. For these scholars, an appreciation of the Jewish nature of
Jesus' life and teachings can serve as the basis for a more sympathetic
view of Judaism by Christians and for a more sympathetic view of
Jesus by Jews. For both Christians and Jews, understanding Jesus as
a Jew can serve as the basis for removing barriers between Christians
and Jews, and for establishing a foundation for fraternal dialogue. It
may be observed, however, that the recovery of Jesus' "Jewishness"
poses new problems for the formulation of contemporary Christologies. However, that concern is beyond the scope of this essay. The
concern here is with the meaning Jesus may have for Jews today. In
that regard, the recovery of the Jewishness of Jesus may offer more of
an opportunity for Jewish theologians than for Christian theologians.

5. The *fifth premise* is that Jewish theology cannot grant Jesus a
status greater than it might grant any of his contemporaries. Judaism
cannot consider him to be greater than, for example, Moses or the
prophets of Israel. Even the greatest rabbis of Jesus' time and place
are not considered prophets by Judaism. Nor can Jews consider Jesus
the final Messiah, Messiah son of David. For Jews, the final Messiah
is yet to come. For Judaism, neither Jesus nor anyone else is yet the
finally awaited Messiah. Though Jesus is called "rabbi" by his disciples, this designation of him is nowhere accepted in the rabbinic
canon. Just as Jews cannot accept Jesus as *the* Messiah, or as a
prophet, they cannot accept him as a rabbinic authority.

While classical Jewish sources consider Jesus as a *false* messiah, I
believe a Jew can affirm that Jesus was not a false messiah but a *failed*
messiah.[10] Let us consider the concept of failure and then the concept
of messiah.

A FAILED MESSIAH

Failure simply means not reaching one's ultimate goal. In this sense,
the Hebrew prophets were failures, because they did not achieve their
ultimate goals of convincing the people to repent and to obey God's

---

[10] The idea of Jesus as a failed rather than a false Jewish messiah has already been
suggested by Rabbi Irving Greenberg, "The Relationship of Judaism and Christianity: Toward a New Organic Model," in *Twenty Years*, ed. Fisher et al., 197-203.

will. Moses was a failure, because he did not enter the promised land, and he did not guide the people into the land. Even God failed, for according to Jewish tradition the reign of God was supposed to begin with the revelation of the Torah at Sinai, but the people built the golden calf and God's expectation was not realized. Indeed, God failed so badly in creating the human race that he had to erase it with a flood and start again, like an artist who makes a mistake and must erase it, accept failure, and begin again. Indeed, the greatest individuals are always failures, because their goals are so exalted. Not all failures are great people, but—in a sense—all great people are failures. Precisely because their goals exceed their abilities, they are not able to accomplish more than reasonably can be expected.

In his study of biblical leadership, Martin Buber observed:

The Bible knows nothing of the intrinsic value of success. On the contrary, when it announces a successful deed, it is duty-bound to announce in complete detail the failure involved in the success. When we consider the history of Moses, we see how much failure is mingled in the one great successful action. . . . True, Moses brought the people out of Egypt; but each stage in this leadership is a failure . . . and yet his work survives also in a hope which is beyond all these failures. . . . This glorification of failure culminates in the long line of prophets whose existence is failure through and through. They live in failure; it is for them to fight and not to conquer. This is the fundamental experience of biblical leadership.[11]

As a final and ultimate messiah, Jesus was a failure because he did not bring about the final and complete redemption of the world. If he had completely succeeded, a *parousia*—a second coming—would not be necessary. Summarizing earlier Jewish traditions regarding failed messiahs, Maimonides wrote, "If he does not meet with full success, or is slain, it is obvious that he is not the (final) Messiah promised in the Torah. He is to be regarded like all the other whole-hearted and worthy kings of the House of David who died and whom God raised up to test the multitudes."[12]

---

[11] Martin Buber, "Biblical Leadership," in his *Israel and the World: Essay in a Time of Crisis,* 2nd ed. (New York: Schocken Books, 1963), 125-26.

[12] Maimonides, *Mishnah Torah—Book of Judges,* "Laws of Kings and Wars," 11:4 in uncensored editions.

Having discussed failure, let us discuss the messianic idea. For
Christians, Jesus was *not* a failed messiah because he brought complete spiritual redemption. Jews do not accept this. But, even if Jews
would accept it, Jesus would still not have been a successful messiah.
According to Jewish theology, messianic redemption is not limited to
the spiritual realm. The dominant motif in Jewish messianism is that
messianic redemption occurs in time and space, in history, in the
sociopolitical realm. For messianic redemption to be complete, it
must take place in the physical as well as the spiritual realm. For
Judaism, the physical and the spiritual are interrelated, interlocked.
The Jews could not accept Jesus as the Jewish Messiah because he did
not bring the type of redemption anticipated by Jewish teachings
about the messianic age.[13] For example, Jewish messianism anticipated a messianic era that would fulfill the prophetic dream of a world
without war—a world at peace, a world where "nation shall not lift
up sword against nation, nor shall anyone experience war anymore"
(Isa. 2:4), a world ruled by justice and compassion, a world devoid of
prejudice and physical oppression. As Martin Buber wrote, shortly
after the Holocaust, "we [Jews] demonstrate with the bloody body of
our people the unredeemedness of the world."[14]

Until peace, justice, and compassion reign, Jews will continue to
view God's kingdom as *yet to come*. Jews will continue to view our
world as premessianic, as unredeemed. However, while our world
cannot be viewed by Jews as a redeemed world, and while Jesus cannot be viewed by Jews as *the* ultimate and final Jewish Messiah, my
radical suggestion is that he may be considered *a* Jewish messiah, a
failed rather than a *false* Jewish messiah, part of rather than apart
from the life of his people and their messianic hope.

THE MESSIAH SON OF JOSEPH

Classical Jewish theological literature speaks of a failed messiah. In
most texts, he is named Messiah son of Joseph (or Messiah son of
Ephraim). He is a preliminary messiah, coming in anticipation of and

---

[13] See, e.g., Joseph Klausner, "The Jewish and the Christian Messiah," in his *The
Messianic Idea in Israel: From Its Beginning to the Completion of the Mishnah*, trans.
W. F. Stinespring (from the 3rd Hebrew ed.) (New York: Macmillan, 1955), 519-31.

[14] Quoted in Ernst Simon, "Martin Buber: His Way Between Thought and
Deed," *Jewish Frontier* (February 1948): 26.

paving the way for the final Messiah, the Messiah son of David. He is a messiah who dies to prepare the way, to provide the opportunity for the final redemption to take place.[15] This idea of a suffering messiah is native to Jewish messianism. According to some Jewish historians, the idea of the Messiah son of Joseph was developed by the students of the greatest rabbi of the second century, Akiba, to justify their master's claim that Bar Kochba, who led a revolt of Jews against Romans, was the Messiah. When Bar Kochba was defeated and killed, it was clear that Akiba was wrong; he was not the final Messiah. Wars still occurred; political oppression continued. As was noted before, Jews could not accept as a final messiah anyone who did not bring an end to war and oppression. So Akiba's students concluded that their teacher could not be wrong, that is, Bar Kochba was a messiah, but not The final messiah. He was the Messiah son of Joseph, not the Messiah son of David.[16]

According to other Jewish historians, the idea of the Messiah son of Joseph was developed as an attempt to give Jesus a place within Jewish messianic theology. In this view, the idea of the Messiah son of Joseph was developed to try to convince those Jews in the first few centuries who believed in the messiahship of Jesus that he was indeed *a* Jewish messiah, though not *the* final Jewish Messiah. This attempt, it was hoped, would prevent a separation of such Jews from the Jew-

---

[15] For sources about Messiah son of Joseph, see the Talmud, *Sukkah* 52a. The classical text in midrashic literature is *Pesikta Rabbati,* chaps. 36, 37. In this text, one also finds the idea of the Messiah as a suffering messiah. This idea of a suffering messiah is, in my view, native to Jewish messianism. The idea of Messiah son of Joseph was developed in midrashim of the gaonic period (i.e., immediate post-Talmudic period, seventh to ninth centuries). See these collected by Yehudah Even Shmuel Kaufmann, *Midreshei Geulah* (Jerusalem: Masada, 1954), especially 90-112, 133-42, 318-23. See the discussion and sources collected in Klausner, "The Jewish and Christian Messiah," 483-502. An attempt to demonstrate the significance of the idea of Messiah son of Joseph for Christianity is found in Richard von der Alm in his *Die Urtheile heidnischer und jüdischer Schriftsteller der vier ersten christlichen Jahrhunderte über Jesus und die ersten Christen* (Leipzig: Wigand, 1864).

[16] For Bar Kochba as a messiah, see, e.g., Palestinian Talmud, *Ta'anit* 4:3; and *Lamentations Rabbah* II, 2, no. 4. Akiba's colleagues said, "Akiba, grass will grow on your cheeks if Bar Kochba is the Messiah." The idea that the Messiah son of Joseph was developed by Akiba's students was the theory of Joseph Klausner. It may also be noted that Rabbi Akiba died a martyr's death and that his father's name was Joseph. On Jewish and Christian perceptions of the alleged messiahship of Bar Kochba, see, e.g., Adele Reinhartz, "Rabbinic Perceptions of Simeon bar Kosiba," *Journal for the Study of Judaism* 20 (December 1989): 171-95.

ish community. Those who hold this view argue further that the claim
that Jesus descended from David and was the Davidic Messiah was
ascribed to Jesus by the Gospels long after his death, and without any
basis. In fact, they claim, Jesus was the son of Mary and Joseph;
hence, the name "Messiah son of Joseph."[17]

The idea of the Messiah son of Joseph developed throughout late
antiquity and the Middle Ages. Important Jewish leaders and
thinkers, such as the great sixteenth-century Jewish mystic Isaac
Luria, were considered to be the Messiah son of Joseph.[18] According
to one tradition, a Messiah son of Joseph comes in each generation to
prepare the way for the final redemption. If the generation is unworthy, he is not followed by the Messiah son of David. If the generation
is worthy, the Messiah son of David comes.[19] According to Jewish
tradition, the Messiah son of David has not yet come, but a number
of Messiahs son of Joseph may already have come.

JESUS AS A MESSIAH SON OF JOSEPH

What I would propose is that Jesus be considered *a* Jewish messiah,
that is, a Messiah son of Joseph. This would give Jesus a place within
Jewish theological discourse and would end the centuries-long tradition of his virtual excommunication from the faith community of
which he was a part. Further, it should provide him not only with *a*

---

[17] A good summary of the views of a number of scholars regarding the origin of
the idea of the Messiah son of Joseph may be found in Joseph Heinemann, "The Messiah of Ephraim and the Premature Exodus of the Tribe of Ephraim," *Harvard
Theological Review* 68 (January 1975): 1-15. See also Charles C. Torrey, "The Messiah Son of Ephraim," *Journal of Biblical Literature* 66, no. 3 (1947): 253-77.
Though most texts regarding the Messiah son of Joseph postdate (some substantially)
the rise of Christianity, Torrey claims that "the doctrine antedated the Christian era
by several centuries" (p. 255). I agree that the idea predated Christianity and is intrinsic to Jewish messianism rather than being an "aberration," as George Foot Moore
suggested in his *Judaism in the First Centuries of the Christian Era: The Age of
Tannaim*, vol. 2 (Cambridge, Mass: Harvard University Press, 1927), 370.

[18] On Isaac Luria as Messiah son of Joseph, see, e.g., Meir Benayahu, ed., *Sefer
Toledot ha-Ari* (Jerusalem: Hebrew University Press, 1967), 199; see also p. 258,
where Luria is described as dying for the sins of others.

[19] See, e.g., Hayyim Vital, *Sefer Pri Etz Hayyim* (Koretz, 1784), *"Sha'ar ha-Ami-
dah,"* chap. 19, p. 52b. Note also on that page the reference to Isaac Luria as the
Messiah son of Joseph.

role, but with a *messianic* role within Jewish theology. This role would acknowledge the life and teaching of Jesus as *preparatio messianica*, consistent with the tradition of the Messiah son of Joseph, thereby including him in the divine plan for human redemption.

While the church regarded ancient Judaism as *preparatio evangelica*, prominent medieval Jewish authorities such as Judah Halevi and Moses Maimonides acknowledged Christianity as *preparatio messianica*. While Christian doctrine often regarded Judaism as being an obsolete faith, this Jewish attitude acknowledges the presence of a divine plan for the role of Christianity within the history of human redemption.[20] Judah Halevi described Christianity as "the preparation and the preface to the final Messiah we expect."[21] Maimonides described Jesus as one who "served to clear the way for the King Messiah, to prepare the world to worship God with one accord."[22]

Already in the Middle Ages, Jewish theological texts mention Jesus in the context of discussions regarding the Messiah son of Joseph. While most of these texts do not accept Jesus as a Messiah son of Joseph—that is, as a Jewish messiah—this may be because they were reacting to Christian persecution of Jews at that time. Perhaps today, however, we can affirm an identification of Jesus with the Messiah son of Joseph. One may further assume that it would not have been necessary for medieval Jewish thinkers to reject this identification of Jesus with the Messiah son of Joseph unless such an idea already had been proposed within Jewish circles.

Identification between Jesus and the Messiah son of Joseph is already alluded to in the writings of the thirteenth-century Spanish Jewish mystic Abraham Abulafia.[23] It is explicitly stated in the writings of the sixteenth-century Jewish official and commentator don Isaac Abravanel. Abravanel considered the tradition about the Messiah son of Joseph to have been the source that influenced the formulation of the "historical Jesus." In Abravanel's view, the earliest Christians accepted the idea of the Messiah son of Joseph but

---

[20] See Heschel, "No Religion Is an Island."

[21] Judah Halevi, *Kuzari*, 4:23.

[22] Moses Maimonides, *Mishneh Torah—Book of Judges*, "Laws of Kings and Wars," 10:4 in uncensored editions.

[23] See, e.g., the discussion in Moshe Idel, "Abraham Abulafia on the Jewish Messiah and Jesus," in his *Studies in Ecstatic Kabbalah* (Albany, N.Y.: SUNY Press, 1988), 53-55, 59, 60, and sources noted there.

changed his name to Jesus.[24] Furthermore, as is well known, Christian tradition often identifies and compares Jesus with the prophet Jonah (e.g., Matt. 12:40; Luke 11:30). In Jewish mystical texts, including some of those composed in seventeenth-century Poland, Jonah is identified with and compared to the Messiah son of Joseph, with clear references to the further identification of Jesus with a particular portrayal of the Messiah son of Joseph.[25]

The final Messiah, Messiah son of David, is often compared by Jewish texts to the seventh day of the week, the Sabbath, because the messianic era is described as the sabbatical age that comes at the end of human history. The day before the Sabbath is "the sixth day," in Hebrew—*Yom ha-Shishi*. In Hebrew, each letter is also a number. The Jewish mystical tradition put great value in numerology, that is, in the numerical value of Hebrew words. The numerical value of *Yom ha-Shishi* is 671. The numerical value of *Yeshu ha-Notzri*—Jesus of Nazareth—is also 671.[26] Here is a numerological description of Jesus as *preparatio messianica*.

---

[24] See don Isaac Abravanel, *Mashmia Yeshuot* (Amsterdam, 1644), 13; *Ma'ayenei ha-Yeshua* (1607), pp. 45, 74. See discussion of this text in Idel, "Abraham Abulafia," 60, and Joseph Saracheck, *The Doctrine of the Messiah in Medieval Jewish Literature* (New York: Herman Press, 1968), 263. The death of the Messiah son of Joseph is already mentioned in the Talmud (see *Sukkah* 52a). Besides the identification of Jesus with the Messiah son of Joseph in Abulafia and Abravanel, we also find such an identification in Flavius Mithridates (a fifteenth-century Jewish convert to Christianity) and the Sabbatean Abraham Cardozo. See Flavius Mithridates, *Sermo de Passione Domini,* ed. Chaim Wirszubski (Jerusalem: Israel Academy of Sciences and Humanities, 1963), 121 n. 4. On Cardozo, see the manuscript published by Gershom Scholem in his Hebrew work, *Texts Concerning the History of Sabbateanism and Its Metamorphosis* (Jerusalem: Mosad Bialik, 1974), 289: "The first messiah . . . is Jesus of Nazareth who corresponds to the Messiah son of Ephraim." As noted above, Messiah son of Ephraim is another name for Messiah son of Joseph.

[25] See Yehudah Liebes's Hebrew essay, "Jonah as Messiah ben Joseph," in *Studies in Jewish Mysticism, Philosophy and Ethical Literature* [in Hebrew], ed. Joseph Dan and Joseph Hacker (Jerusalem: Hebrew University Press, 1986), 269-315. As might be expected, the particular portrait of Messiah ben Joseph with which Jesus is identified is not a very positive one, e.g., in the writings of the seventeenth-century Jewish mystic Samson Ostropoler, who died a martyr's death in 1648.

[26] This numerology is noted by Idel, "Abraham Abulafia," 59, referring to Abulafia. On Abulafia's identification of Jesus with the sixth day, see p. 51, quoting from manuscript New York, JTS, 843, fol. 80a. It is interesting that a number of medieval Jewish thinkers described Jesus and his disciples as Jewish mystics, that is, as kabbalists. See, e.g., the text of a fourteenth-century Spanish Jewish work quoted by Gershom Scholem in his essay "Zur Geschichte der Anfänge der christlichen Kabbala," in

A NEW VIEW FOR JEWISH THEOLOGY

Though the view of Jesus presented here may have been anticipated by classical Jewish theological literature, it is virtually unprecedented within Jewish theological discourse. It goes far beyond whatever has been suggested until now. It offers Jesus and Christianity not only a place but a messianic role within Jewish theology. Jews will undoubtedly find it much too bold. Christians may consider it not a great enough leap.

It was Martin Buber, the first Jewish thinker to refer to Jesus as "brother," who foresaw the time when

> the Jewish community, in the course of its renaissance, will recognize Jesus; and not merely as a great figure in its religious history, but also in the organic context of a Messianic development extending over millennia, whose final goal is the Redemption of Israel and of the world. But I believe equally firmly that we will never recognize Jesus as the Messiah Come, for this would contradict the deepest meaning of our Messianic passion.[27]

Having offered a Jewish theological view of Jesus, permit me to conclude with a personal view of Jesus. Jewish children do not spend much time thinking about Jesus, but as a child, I did. Growing up in the years after the Holocaust and knowing the fate of the Polish Jews, it is perhaps not surprising that I thought of Jesus as a Polish Jew. As a young child, I knew that Jesus died a terrible death, and I knew that millions of Polish Jews died horrible deaths. As a child, I even heard Hitler called the "anti-Christ," and he was compared to Pontius Pilate. Therefore, since I was a child I have pictured Jesus dressed like and living like a Polish Jew. Such a view of Jesus as a Polish Jew is also found in the artwork of two of the greatest Jewish artists to come from Poland: Marc Chagall and Maurycy Gottlieb.

I picture Jesus as a tortured, wandering, wounded Polish Jew crawling in pain into the doorway of a Polish Catholic home during

---

Essays Presented to Leo Baeck on the Occasion of His Eightieth Birthday (London: East and West Library, 1954), 177 n. 2. This idea was popular among the Christian kabbalists of the Renaissance period, e.g., Pico del Mirandola.

[27] See Buber quoted in Simon, "Martin Buber," 26. This citation is also quoted more accessibly in Maurice S. Friedman, *Martin Buber: The Life of Dialogue* (New York: Harper, 1955), 279.

the Nazi occupation and asking for refuge. A small child finds him and calls his parents: "Mommy, Daddy," says the child, "there is a wounded Jew at the door asking for help and he says his name is Jesus." The parents come to the door and ask: "Are you a Jew? Are you Jesus?" And the man replies, "Who do you think that I am?"

4

Talking Torah with Jesus

HERBERT BRONSTEIN

> Two who sit together, and between whom are words of
> Torah—the Divine Presence (*Sh'chinah*) suffuses them.
> —Hananiah ben Teradion (rabbi ca. 100 C.E.)

"**I**F JESUS WERE AMONG US TODAY, he would be most comfortable, not in a church, but in a Reform Jewish synagogue." This was the view, spoken half a century ago, of the then president of the Reform Jewish Union of American Hebrew Congregations, Rabbi Maurice Eisendrath. I remember thinking at the time that Jesus, a first-century Galilean Jew, on the contrary, might very well be most comfortable not in a Reform but in an Orthodox Jewish synagogue. He would at least understand the Hebrew language of prayer. But in any synagogue, given an understanding of the vernacular, Jesus would recognize various phraseologies of the prayers and would be at home with much of the content, metaphors, and ethos of synagogue prayer as it exists today. But because, at least according to some Jewish followers of Jesus, he believed in short simple prayers (Matt. 6:7), he might be taken aback by the length and repetitions of many of the services today. This would be true also, by the way, of many of the rabbinic founders of Judaism in Jesus' time and in the decades after (see *B. Berachot* 61a; *Sifre Num.* 105).

On what basis did Rabbi Eisendrath make his particular claim? As does everyone, he looked at Jesus through particular prisms or lenses —in his case, the biblical scholarship he knew in his time and his own understanding of Judaism. Eisendrath, an ardent exponent of Reform Judaism, construed the moral consciousness of the prophets and

45

sages of ancient Israel to be the essence of the Jewish faith and osten-
sibly believed that Jesus represented a similar approach.

LOOKING THROUGH PRISMS AND LENSES

We all have to look at the texts about Jesus through prisms, some of
which obscure, some of which clarify. This has been true from the
time well after Jesus' death when he and his teachings were first
depicted through the prisms of the Gospels themselves. The Gospel
of Matthew, for example, portrays the views of a passionate advocate
of a group of Jewish followers of Jesus who is attempting to convince
other Jews of the truth of a religious position centered on the person
of Jesus and on Jesus' reported teachings. In some places, the Gospel
of Matthew opposes Jesus to other Jews—in particular, to those
"scribes and Pharisees" who were founders of what has become, in
the long run, "mainline" Judaism. Because of this ancient conflict
between two Jewish groups at the time, various passages of the
Gospel of Matthew express a resentful and even vituperative tone,
accusing the Pharisees of hypocrisy (Matt. 23:13-36). This harsh
invective on the part of the author(s) and later editors of the Gospels,
including the charge of responsibility for the death of Jesus, has contributed greatly to the tragic suffering of the Jewish people and to the
Holocaust in Christian Europe.

For over the prism of Matthew's own description of Jesus is laid yet
another! Whatever Matthew wrote about Jesus, about his life, times,
and teachings, is now overlaid by the editing work of representatives
of the later institutionalized hierarchy of the Christian church. This
happened after Christianity became the official religion of the empire
—ironically the very empire, Rome, that had crucified Jesus along
with many other Jews, for threatening Roman imperial power over
Judea. This additional editorial stratum of the Gospel shifted responsibility for Jesus' crucifixion from imperial Rome onto a population of
various Jewish groups with disparate views now all heaped together as
one: "the Jews." Because of this overlay, "the Jews" are depicted as
demanding the death of Jesus and taking upon themselves and their
children forever the blood-guilt for his execution.

But scholars can now look at this editorial palimpsest through the
lens of critical historical methods that enable us to identify and see
through these and similar distortions. Through this lens we see a time
of torturous oppression of Judea and Galilee, both material and cul-

tural, under the heel of Roman occupation. Through modern scholarship we are also far better able to meet Jesus himself. We can see
how at such a time of oppression and grinding poverty for most of
the population, there arose not only many healers and charismatics,
some on the model of earlier prophets such as Elijah and Elisha, but
also chieftain-type leaders of groups of Jews who reasserted old popular views about the revival of a Jewish kingship that would replace
the rule of Rome. Some teachers and preachers of a prophetic type
were calling the Jews to repentance as a means of countering "the
Rule of Arrogance" (a Jewish term for Roman rule) and to prepare
for the kingdom of God. Rome very often responded to these groups
with summary crucifixions.

CULTURAL CHANGE AND VARIOUS
JEWISH RESPONSES

It was also a period of underlying cultural change. From the time of
Alexander the Great there had been a heavy infusion of Greek culture,
which evoked from Jewry various reaffirmative self-definitions. It was
as well a period of significant economic change, the intrusion into a
primarily agricultural area of new commercial sectors. This produced
new social groups within Judean society, and therefore new outlooks
about how to live according to God's teaching, the Torah, in these
new conditions.

At a time of great challenge to the people and its faith, all the
groups were struggling with the question of how to apply the
received literal text of the Torah to everyday life. The group we now
call the "Pharisees" and their rabbinic successors engaged in broad
reinterpretation of the applications of Torah to everyday life. They
assumed the authority to make these changes on the basis of a "two-
fold Torah," the oral interpretive Torah and the written Torah text.
They extended, with many new spiritual ideas and observances, the
practical, ethical, and spiritual teachings of the Torah and the
prophets of Israel. They must have had a deep conviction that the
radical economic, social, and cultural changes they were experiencing
demanded this.

Their main opponents, the Sadducees, were followers of those who
believed themselves to be physically and spiritually descended from
the biblical priesthood. Though some of these were assimilated to and
co-opted by Roman power, they knew that their own authority was at

stake if there were changes in the application of the literal text of the Torah. They were therefore ultimately opposed to the changes espoused by the Pharisees.

Other groups, dispirited by the social and spiritual vicissitudes of the time, and in despair over the corruption under Rome of the priesthood and therefore of the Jerusalem Temple cult, simply "dropped out," as we would say, to cultivate their own purity and to wait for God to overthrow Rome and its evil minions, Jewish and non-Jewish alike. Some hoped to accomplish this through the leadership of a "Teacher of Righteousness" or "True Teacher."

If we understand this pressure cooker of repression, change and spiritual turbulence, we can also understand, for the sake of imaginary converse with Jesus many centuries later, "where Jesus was coming from." I try also to keep myself aware of where I am coming from. I have to be aware of my lenses as a Jew committed to my faith, as a rabbi, and as a student of the history of religions. To top it off, I am aware that I am someone who wears the glasses of a liberal perspective, religiously, socially, and politically. I am aware also that recent modern academic scholarship on Jesus has taken one of two approaches. One approach maintains that we can never retrieve the original teachings and authentic life of the person of Jesus himself, and that the attempt to do so is finally chimerical. Instead, such documents as the Sermon on the Mount and Jesus' parables express beliefs of later faith communities, removed from Jesus himself by at least a generation, perhaps longer, but for whom the figure of Jesus was central. The Jesus of the Gospels was shaped, in other words, by later groups out of a need to define themselves, to teach a faith about Jesus, and to assert their views against competing contemporaries.

On the other hand, of late there has been a resurgence of the endeavor to extract from the Gospels the actual core teachings and aims of the person of the historical Jesus himself and the genius of his own particular spirituality. This project involves a group of careful, responsible, and trained Christian scholars associated with the work and name of the "Jesus Seminar."[1] They too assert that the Gospels are overlaid with the issues and dogmas of later times. On the basis of their collective knowledge and shared criteria such as earliest stratum and independent witness, they arrive at a consensus of their best judg-

---

[1] Robert W. Funk, Roy W. Hoover, and the Jesus Seminar, *The Five Gospels: The Search for the Authentic Words of Jesus* (San Francisco: HarperSanFrancisco, 1997).

ments as to which texts in the Gospels are authentically "Jesus." In a sense that is all the very best informed can do.

WOULD I SIDE WITH JESUS?

On this basis, I ask myself, if I could step back in time and speak with Jesus, would I feel closer to Jesus than to some other Jews of his own times? I believe I could "talk Torah" with Jesus almost as easily as I could with my own spiritual ancestors, the Pharisees. I would feel much closer to Jesus than to the Sadducean Jewish opponents of the Pharisees. The Sadducees could not conceive of a religion of Israel outside the Jerusalem Temple, outside the sacrificial cult and without the priesthood. Jesus, like the Pharisees, could. Like the Pharisees, Jesus engaged in "interpretive oral Torah." In Matthew (see 23:2-3) he is quoted as asserting that the Pharisees are the true heirs of Moses, the rightful interpreters of Torah and Prophets. Though I might agree today with the Sadducees that there is little if any justification in the text of the Torah or in the Prophets for such innovative Pharisaic doctrines as the resurrection of the dead or the world to come, Jesus himself apparently did believe in these teachings, which would become part of the ongoing Jewish outlook and heritage.

What is important also is that Jesus seems closer to the religious statesmanship of the Pharisees, who, even more than he, decentered Judaism away from the Jerusalem Temple and outside the holy land and created a way of worshiping in "gatherings of the people" (synagogues, in Greek), who made the table in the home a new altar of God, and who, after the destruction of the Temple in 70 C.E., replaced sacrifice and the need for a centralized priesthood with "study of Torah, worship, and good deeds" (*Pirkei Avot*). Further, many Sadducean supporters of the priesthood and the literal text of the Torah had been corrupted by the control of the alien Roman regime, many of them hellenized, romanized, and ignorant of the practice of their own religion, even indifferent to it. That could not be said, to the contrary, of the Pharisees, nor of Jesus.

There is another way that I would feel closer to Jesus than to many other Jews of his time. Jews differed on how to relate to Roman rule, ranging from corrupt collusion, to avoidance of conflict as long as Rome did not interfere with the core of Judaism itself, to nonviolent resistance, to outright violent military revolt. Jesus, like most of the Pharisees, as reported in the Gospels and contextualized in Josephus's histories, opposed those Jews who espoused the overthrow of Rome by insurgent military force. These were the groups who assassinated Roman soldiers and engaged in other acts which Roman authorities considered terroristic brigandage. The militants later took control of Jerusalem in the war against Rome, and even after the Roman assault on Jerusalem died at places like Masada in last-ditch revolts against Rome.

With respect to these militants, Jesus is reported to have taught: "Those who take up the sword will perish by the sword," a corollary of "Render unto Caesar what is Caesar's and to God what is God's" (Matt. 22:21). Some have interpreted this as: Pay the oppressive taxes to Rome, and submit to Roman law insofar as it does not break God's law. This is a position similar to that of leading Pharisees who believed in pacific relations with Rome as long as the core principles of Judaism were not violated. In all of this there is consonance with the approach of the so-called Peace Party led by Rabbi Yochanan ben Zackai, a Pharisaic leader who (if anyone could be so designated) was a rabbinic founder of what has become Judaism today. Yochanan ben Zackai opposed the violent military path to redemption. His focus after the destruction of the Temple was on building a Judaism for the future. Those who died at Masada, Yodevat, Gamla, and other places did not save the Jewish people or Judaism; the Pharisees did. In these respects, I would feel far more comfortable talking to Jesus than to the Jewish militants of his time.

NOT A NEW RELIGION

Would there be further common ground between us for a meaning-ful conversation about Torah? Or would Jesus think of himself as the founder of an entirely new religion, later to be called Christianity—so that we would not even be in the same Jewish ballpark? I think not. His teaching, as it is clearly repeated, was as a matter of fact intended for Jews and was about Torah and the goal of Torah, the kingdom of God.

What basis do I have for thinking this? What is reported about the ancient sages in rabbinic literature and what is reported about Jesus in the Gospels. To give an example, in the Talmud there are collec-tions of short prayers composed by ancient Jewish sages, perhaps for their students or circles of followers (see *B. Berachot* 16b-17a; *Bera-chot* 60b). If in this group we found a prayer (Matt. 6:9-13) composed by a certain Rabbi Joshua (Jesus), would it be so different from the others in the collection as to elicit shock, a sense of the strange, or even surprise? The answer is not at all.

Jesus' prayer in whatever versions we find it (longer in Matthew; shorter in Luke), is unexceptionally Judaic in substance and even in form. Jews today, even those not especially pious or learned, would recognize phrases entirely familiar, beginning with the address to God as "Father," or "Our Father in Heaven" (Hebrew: *Avinu She-bashamaim*). The affirmations "Hallowed be Thy Name, Thy Kingdom come, Thy will be done on earth as it is in heaven" are, for Jews, reminiscent of phrases in the well-known *Kaddish* prayer. The plea for forgiveness and the implied call to forgive others for transgressions against us is more than familiar to a great majority of Jews from a stay of any length in the synagogue on the Day of Atonement (Yom Kippur). The sentiments behind "Lead us not into temptation, but deliver us from evil" are found repeatedly in Jewish prayer.[2] Many Jews also have heard the brief ancient Jewish address to God: "You know our needs before we utter them and order all things to the best. What is good in your sight do. We praise you, O God, who hears prayer."

Had not Jesus' prayer become associated with the doctrine of Jesus as divine or a savior Christ, and with a religious approach in many ways different from Judaism, were it not for the history of Christian-sponsored persecution of Jews and Judaism in the name of "Christ," Jewish people would feel comfortable with that prayer both in substance and spirit. In other words, if it had come from a non-christianized Jewish source, it might have made its way to some part of established Jewish liturgy. In fact, that it is a typical Jewish prayer argues for its authenticity with respect to Jesus.

If we focus on the very writings that the average educated Western person associates with Jesus, the so-called Sermon on the Mount, which includes the Lord's Prayer and other core teachings of what was to become the early Christian community, again we find many commonalties. It is around these teachings that I would begin my conversation with Jesus. Perhaps I would begin the conversation by asking him right off which of the renditions of the Beatitudes, that in Matthew (longer) or that in Luke (shorter) is closer to his original

---

[2] In the Talmud we find "Lead me not into the power of sin, not into the power of transgression, not into the power of temptation, and not into the power of shame" (*B. Berachot* 60b).

teachings and words. I would tell him that when I encountered those lines I thought of familiar psalm verses which begin with the Hebrew word *Ashrei* and which are often translated "fortunate" or "happy" instead of "blessed."

An often repeated mainstay of Jewish liturgy is a collection of praise verses that begin: "Happy are those who dwell in your house, they are ever praising you; happy the people to whom such blessings fall; happy the people whose God is the Lord" (Ps. 84:5). Similarly: "Happy are those who do not walk in the counsel of the wicked, nor stand in the way of the sinners, nor sit in the seats of scoffers, but whose delight is in the way of the Torah of the Lord, and on whose Torah [Teaching] they meditate by day and by night" (Ps. 1-2). Or: "Happy those who keep to the path, who walk in the Torah of God; happy are those who observe his decrees, who seek him with a whole heart" (Ps. 119:1-2).

The openings of the Beatitudes are usually translated "Blessed" in English, but the Greek *makarios* ("fortunate") has the sense of the Hebrew *Ashrei*. As Hans Dieter Betz puts it succinctly in his monumental work on the Sermon on the Mount: "[The Beatitudes] certainly point to a literary environment related to Jewish wisdom, the environment within which the Sermon on the Mount and the Sermon on the Plain had their origins as well."[3] Further, "The Old Testament and post-biblical literature contain a large number of Beatitudes, presenting them in a wide variety of forms and functions." So if what we pray is an indication of commonalties, then Jesus and I would certainly have enough in common to have a good conversation directly about Torah.

"It is reported," I would tell him, "that you insisted: 'Do not think that I have come to abolish the Torah or the Prophets. I have come not to abolish (or void), but to fulfill. For truly I tell you that until heaven and earth pass away, not one letter, not one stroke of a letter shall pass away'" (Matt. 5:17-19). I would tell him that many Christians have interpreted that to mean that he was in himself, in his person, the fulfillment of the Torah and covenant which they claim are now superseded. In the history of Christian theology this was an aspect of the attempt to make Judaism the "Other," the opposite of the Christianity in which Jesus supersedes the Torah and in which "Torah" is translated as "Law" and characterized as "Old" Covenant,

---

[3] Hans Dieter Betz, *The Sermon on the Mount* (Minneapolis: Augsburg Fortress, 1995), 102, 104-5.

legalistic, formalistic, tribalistic, ritualistic—in short, negative and negated.

"But Jesus," I would say, "you always used the word 'Torah' only in a positive sense. You seemed devoted to the Torah, the Teachings in the books of Moses and the prophetic literature." Frankly, I think Jesus would be either shocked or saddened, probably both, that his words were misconstrued. Jesus uses the same locutions—to "fulfill," or "void," or "abolish"—as are used in classical rabbinic texts such as the *Pirkei Avot* (Sayings of the Elders), some parts of which date from very early rabbinic times. In those texts the locution to "fulfill" (*l'kayyem*) the commandments is opposed to "to void" or "annul" (*l'vatel*) the commandments. Among those texts there is also an emphasis on fulfilling the least or the lightest of the *mitzvot* (commandments) with the same care as the weightier. This is exactly parallel to Jesus' own emphases.

SO MANY PARALLELS

One of my teachers, the late Professor Samuel Sandmel, a scholar of Hellenistic and Christian scripture, as a wry comment on the extensive literature of comparison between Jesus' sayings and teachings in ancient Judaism, coined the word "parallelomania." But the fact is that there are so many parallels between sayings of Jesus and ancient rabbinic teaching that it has taken entire books to catalogue the similarities. For example, as a way of getting to the essence of Torah, the basic principles of Judaism, we learn that the ancient rabbis often discussed the question, What is the most important verse of the Torah? When Jesus was asked this question, he answered, "You shall love the LORD your God" from the twice-daily Jewish affirmation of faith, the *Shema* (Deut. 6:4-5), and "You shall love your neighbor as yourself" from what Jews call "the Holiness Portion" (Lev. 19:18). "This is the great principle of Torah," Akiba said only slightly later. Of the same principle of mutualism, Hillel, just before Jesus, had said of this same teaching, "This is the whole of Torah; go and learn." One also is reminded of Akiba's death by torture at the hands of Roman authorities. Wanting to teach to the end, Akiba said while dying: "I never understood how one could fulfill the commandment, 'You shall love the Lord your God with all your heart, with all your might, with all your being'; now I am able to understand it and to fulfill it."

While there is no teaching that I know of in ancient Jewish litera-

ture equivalent to Jesus' "Love your enemies" (Matt. 5:44), there is
a teaching in the Talmud that deals with the same moral/spiritual
issue by commenting on the teaching, "You shall not take vengeance
nor bear a grudge" (Lev. 19:18). The ancient rabbinic text used the
implied distinction between "vengeance" and "grudge bearing" in
the original passage to convey a spiritual course in life: One should
not take active material vengeance for any kind of material hurt, even
retaliation against someone who would not lend you a tool by refus-
ing such a loan to that person in return. Even pointing out the difference to another person between one's own generous behavior and
the other person's churlishly ungenerous behavior to you in the past
is grudge bearing. Do not do it.

In the case of a very deep personal hurt, however, it is understandable if one feels it, bears it within oneself and on one's heart
without taking any form of vengeance or even verbal retaliation. Still,
the text concludes: "They that are reviled, but do not revile in return;
they that hear themselves being put to shame but do not answer back;
they who act out of love and accept the hurt, concerning them scripture says: 'They that love God shall be as the sun when it goes forth
in its might'" (Judg. 5:31, quoted in *B. Yoma* 23a). In other words,
this is what it means truly to love God. I believe that in discussing a
teaching such as this one and many similar rabbinic teachings, there
would certainly be a common ground between Jesus and any contemporary rabbi, if Gospel reports are true to life.

Many other instances could be cited. The teaching that we cannot
serve both God and mammon (a word meaning "money" in Hebrew)
had a long history in the religion of Israel many centuries before
Jesus, based on the confrontation between the first of the Ten Commandments, on the one hand, and the worship of the golden calf, on
the other.

THE KINGDOM OF GOD

Above all, what is central to Jesus' entire message is the "kingdom of
God," or the "kingdom of heaven," a central Judaic metaphor for a
world in which people conduct their lives under the sovereignty of
God's teaching. In all three Synoptic Gospels, it is clear that Jesus has
come to call people to the kingdom of God. If Jesus was Jewish, this
must be so. From the Song at the Sea, which climaxes the exodus
from Egypt ("God will rule forever and ever" [Exod. 15:18]) to

Isaiah's proclamation of the sovereignty of God, to the daily recitation in Jewish liturgy of the "Sanctification," the sovereignty of one God is central. Consider the *Shema*: "Hear, O Israel, the Lord our God the Lord is one, and you shall love the Lord our God with all your heart, with all your soul, with all your being" (Deut. 6:4-5). Among ancient rabbis, this affirmation of the faith was an act of commitment through the practice of God's commandments to live in the consciousness of the sovereignty of God. "God will reign" rings out at every key place of Jewish liturgy, carrying with it the belief that someday, somehow, people will live in accordance with God's teaching and the earth will be full of the knowledge of God, lived out in deed. The religious name for the Jewish people, Israel (in the Hebrew *Yisra'El*), means "God will rule."[4] It is no wonder at all that in the Gospels the beginning, the core and the end of what both John the Baptist and Jesus were teaching was the kingdom of God.

But what was Jesus' understanding of the kingdom of God? I would really want most to talk with him about this. What did he mean by it? How does one live by it in terms of everyday practice? What about the related question of Jesus as the Messiah? For the Jewish people this meant the true "anointed king" under the sovereignty of God. Did he truly believe that he was the *mashiach* (the "Anointed"), destined to bring about the kingdom of God or to serve the kingdom of God?

How Jesus interpreted the construct *kingdom of God* is a matter of dispute. It seems to me that today there are still three views about this. (1) In the letters of Paul and in Christian theology the sovereignty of God's teaching on earth has been supplanted by a concept of the supernatural salvation of the individual soul through faith in Jesus as Christ as savior, but supplanting the Judaic idea of Messiah (identified minimally with the end of social evils). In my view, Jesus' own understanding of the kingdom of God was quite different from the doctrine of salvation that developed in Christianity. (2) New Christian historical scholarship takes the view that Jesus believed that "the kingdom" is potentially immanent, present, in a living spirituality revealed in the life of a community. In other words, Jesus was teaching personal and communal renewal of the essential teaching of Torah in the hearts and minds and actions of a Jewish community. (3) Another view goes back at least to the beginning of this century

---

[4] Construed by the biblical folk etymology to mean "he wrestled" or "has striven with God"; see Gen. 32:28-29.

and is associated popularly with Albert Schweitzer's pioneering work *The Quest of the Historical Jesus*. According to that view ("imminent eschatology"), Jesus' message was a call to Jews to prepare their inner selves to be fit to enter the kingdom of God, which God was going to bring soon. According to this view, it was in that light that many followers of Jesus saw him as the promised Messiah, whose rule would replace the repressive rule of Rome.

This is a logical explanation of Rome's execution of Jesus. According to Gospel reports, the *titulus*, a written note regularly placed on the crucifix (perhaps in mockery) by Romans indicates that he was executed as *Rex Judeorum*, "King of the Jews." In any case Jesus, followed by crowds, was a direct threat to Roman rule over Judea. In either of the latter two views, most closely related to Judaism, and not Christianity, Jesus' proclamation calls Jews to the performance of God's commandments, fulfilling the teaching of the Torah and prophets. In both these two cases, the Jews are called to *Teshuvah*, an inward turning (usually translated "repentance"), a spiritual renewal and transformation.

DIFFERENCES BETWEEN US

If I were to sit down and discuss Torah with Jesus, there would nevertheless be differences between us along with all the agreements. According to the Gospel of Matthew, Jesus differed sharply with some Jewish sages. Differences of opinion, of course, are not an issue in Judaism. Rabbis and sages differed among themselves and still do. One of the differences in the Gospels relates to the extreme stringency of Jesus' demand for a righteousness "greater than that of the Pharisees." Remember, of course, that many scholars consider these differences as reflecting a time later than Jesus. But even so, if we assume that Jesus and his followers believed that the kingdom was coming soon, we can well understand at least one basic difference. Perhaps it was for only a short time that Jews would be expected to live on an extremely high level of inner purity as well as outward behavior.

For example, Jesus taught that calling someone *rakah* ("empty-head" or "moron") or a public insult of any kind was equivalent to murder, punishable by hell fire. To be sure we find certain rabbinic equivalents. For instance Rabbi Eleazar Ha-Modai taught that among offenses for which someone will lose their portion in "the world to come," even if they are learned in Torah and otherwise do good deeds, is insulting one's fellow in public (*Pirkei Avot* 3.15). It was a common practice to use hyperbole, exaggeration, for inspiration and moral teaching to emphasize how important certain behavior is. Along these lines there is a well-known ancient rabbinic homily that explains how someone who publicly insults another person has perpetrated the equivalent of murder. It is based on the Hebrew locution for murder, "spilling blood," and for insult, "whitening the face." When you insult someone, their face turns pale or white. Thus, when you have spilled the blood from their face, "whitening the face" is equivalent to "spilling blood." Therefore, insult is equivalent to murder. But if Jesus was actually implying a moral equivalent between murder and insult, I would have to differ.

In like manner, Jesus teaches that lustful *thoughts* are equivalent to the act of adultery itself. I would agree that there is a danger in succumbing to a pattern of lustful thoughts and feelings. But what is central in Judaism is what you actually *do*. It is the deed that counts. As to divorce, some ancient rabbis did agree with Jesus that adultery is the only ground for divorce. But the rabbinic consensus was concerned with a long view of the well-being of the community, with the state of marriage over many generations. Among them, the well-being of families and persons included other grounds for divorce as well. But Jesus could have been concerned to protect women, who could be divorced for frivolous reasons.

If Schweitzer was right, these differences, then, could be easily explained. If we assume that Jesus and his followers believed that the kingdom was coming soon, Jews could be expected, according to some of Jesus' stringencies, to reach a level of inner purity required to enter the kingdom of God. But the Pharisees were building a synthesis of communal practices on the premise that the kingdom was a long way off. Some Jews of course believed that God was sending a military messiah to overthrow Roman rule soon. But most Jews would have agreed with the sage who told Rabbi Akiba, "The grass will be growing from your cheeks long long before the Messiah comes."

I would want especially to discuss with Jesus what reason and motives he would give for doing God's commandments, the *mitzvot* today. If God's commandments were given only to purify the individual so that she or he might be able to "fit into" the kingdom of God, I would differ. For me, as for Judaism over the centuries, there are other reasons: gradually to help bring about the kingdom of God in covenant partnership with God; to preserve the harmony of the world (*Tikkun Olam*) or improve it; to live a good life here on earth; gradually, morally, and spiritually to refine humankind through practice of the commandments until what we call spirituality at its best is gradually interiorized—a view taken by Rabban Gamaliel in ancient days.

We would also discuss the question—a knotty problem today, as it seems to have been at Jesus' time—of authority. The Pharisees believed that they had the authority to interpret Torah by virtue of the oral transmission of Torah from Sinai through the succession of prophets and sages from Sinai to their own time. The Pharisees also sought a consensus of the exegetical or interpretive community of spiritual learning. As depicted in the Gospels, Jesus arrogated to himself the authority to teach outside the framework of Pharisaic authority. The dispute over observance of the Sabbath is an example. Jesus allowed his circle of disciples, according to a Gospel, to pick grain on the Sabbath (Mark 2:27; Luke 6:5), which, aside from the need to protect or save life, was work and therefore forbidden on the Sabbath. If Jesus believed in the coming of the end of the "present" order of the world, and the test was only fitness to enter the kingdom of God, then this might make some sense. But the Pharisees were building a community for the long term and this implied a shared synthesis of religious practice that could be lived out in Jewish communities worldwide over the centuries.

In the time of Jesus when there was a crisis of continuity for Judaism, and especially in the decades thereafter when the Second Temple was destroyed and the center of Jewish life in the land of Israel was coming to an end, the very future of the Jewish people was at stake. Taking seriously the concept that all people of Israel were a kingdom of priests and holy people, the Pharisees deterritorialized Judaism and in the spirit of the prophets continued the universalization of Judaism. They shifted the locus of Judaism from the Temple to the home and wherever Jews gathered in community, and they replaced the hereditary priesthood with a people of learning and religious practice.

Still today all over the world Jews have the same structure of holidays and patterns of worship, of weekly scriptural readings, of Sabbath and holiday observances, and shared institutions such as the Passover ceremonial feast, the conduct of the wedding service, and life-cycle observances. These have survived centuries of exile, disper-

sal, and widely differing geographical, cultural, and political conditions. All of this is the work of that same consensus of teaching
authority begun by the Pharisees. To make Judaism the religion of the
long haul a consensus of authority was required. Jesus apparently set
himself up outside of this authority. He undertook to "go it alone."
How I would like to converse about this issue with him! If he did
decide to go it alone, there certainly would have arisen differences
between him and the Pharisaic community of scholars in that period.
The memory of these differences even by the time of the editing of
the Gospels would persist. Furthermore, this difference over authority obviously became even more heated between the Jewish followers
of Jesus, as represented in the Gospel of Matthew and the mainline
Pharisaic community.

JESUS A GREAT TEACHER
BUT NOT UNIQUE

With all of this, were it not for the fact that Jesus became the "Savior
God" and "unique Master" of a religion at odds with Judaism and
indeed the source of much suffering over many centuries for the Jewish people, many of the teachings of Jesus or "Joshua" could have
been cited as admirable spiritual expressions with which many Jews
would agree and with some of which many Jews would disagree. But
along with all Jews I cannot think of Jesus as any more a son of God,
or a child of God created in the image of God, than any other of
God's children, and I am so bold as to say that Jesus would have
agreed with this. I think of Jesus in the same way as I do of Hillel and
Akiba, of Jeremiah, Siddhartha Gautama (the Buddha), certain Con-
fucian, Taoist and Hindu sages—all of them teachers—whose message was identification in the spirit of love and service with an
Ultimate beyond oneself.

This approach of viewing Jesus as a religious teacher came up in a
debate I had with James Hamilton, one of the leading "Death of
God" (so-called) theologians. We were good friends in Rochester,
New York, during the very height of the "Death of God" movement.
Notwithstanding our theological differences, Jim Hamilton and I
were in solidarity with regard to social issues. We were both heavily
involved in the civil rights and the anti–Viet Nam War movements.
Together we raised our voices against the national program of fake

fallout shelters, which was being intensely ballyhooed by then Governor Nelson Rockefeller of New York. We were involved together in many community organizations and in interfaith dialogue.

In that debate, he maintained that since "God is dead"—in other words since belief in God was no longer possible, Judaism was "in trouble." But, he said, in Jesus Christians have a unique and ultimate expression of religious teaching. Jesus was and is, he claimed, the exemplar of spirituality par excellence, beyond any others, and therefore Christianity would remain valid even though "God is dead." My response was yes, Jesus was a great teacher, but not unique. What about Jeremiah? What about Socrates? What about Confucius? What about Buddha? Instead of answering this he said: "Herb, you make it your way, I'll make it my way!" We all had a good laugh; but, in my opinion this was not a valid answer.

If I could sit down and converse with Jesus, I would agree with him on many points because we are both Jews and many of our basic premises are still the same. Since the prophets of Israel are the background of both of our mentalities, his plea for spiritual renewal (*teshu-vah*) and the kingdom of God are shared aspects of our faith. He does find a place in the highest ranks of the teachers of many faiths whose spirituality approached the truth that threatened oppression and exploitation. Because of that he died. He does belong in the ranks of those who in life and death taught the emptiness of a life lived only in the service of one's own success. As does the Torah, he taught total devotion to God through service to others, and the redemption of the world from all kinds of hurt, from hate and evil through a life of loving-kindness, or what Jews call *G'milut Chasadim*.

PART TWO

APPRAISALS AND INTERPRETATIONS

5

That Troublesome Cousin

ANDREW VOGEL ETTIN

"WHO DO YOU SAY I AM?" To engage the question that Jesus addressed to Peter (Matt. 16:15; Mark 8:29) already presumes that one cares enough to answer it, and for many Jews—perhaps for most Jews at some time or other—that presumption grates on the nerves. Why should we be asked? Why should we care? Why should we have to care? Truly, for many, it is easier not to care. For them, as Jews in a culture dominated by the signs of Christianity, Jesus marks the separation "between *Yisrael* and *kol ha'amim*," between Jews and "all the [other] people," between us and those for whom Jesus is the defining presence in human history while also being a source of much woe—woe for us. Indeed, did not Jesus claim, at least according to Luke 13:51, that his purpose was not *eirēnē*, "peace," but rather *diamerismon*, "division"?

Yet Jesus is a fact with which some of us feel compelled to deal because his signs surround us and his modern messengers confront us. Sometimes they confront us with eager interest precisely because we are Jews and he—their "He"—was one of us. It is that original identity that makes him less easy to shunt aside than other religious founders, for Jesus, unlike Muhammad, stands in our face. Sometimes, however, those envoys come with more oppressively pointed interest because they deem his eagerly anticipated "return" to be dependent on our acceptance of him as *Him*. So it is the looping of that historical line back toward us that may induce some of us Jews to seek out versions of Jesus that can allow us to deal with him on our own terms, reclaiming him as our own but only on our own terms.

63

If, therefore, we do not absolutely avoid confronting Jesus, our engagements with him are likely to be marked by either anxious tension or a peculiar yet perfectly understandable rhythm of approach and recoil. His ethical teachings may draw our assent to their humane values. However, his controversies with all the varieties of Judaism in his own time may even more strongly repel us. Granted, we may speculate that the contentions over interpreting and applying biblical laws (like political and theological disagreements of our own time) have been exaggerated by the polemics of the era as well as by the politics of the Gospel writers within their own milieus. Surely even if we accept the implication that all of "the Sadducees" constituted a homogeneous bloc of literalists, it is impossible to believe that all of "the scribes and Pharisees" were nothing more than what the New Testament represents them to be, thorough hypocrites and jealous connivers each and every one of them. The sweeping condemnations in the New Testament of the only identified Jewish groups in Jesus' time (whether those condemnations come from the mouth of Jesus or from a follower) turn Jesus into more than just an antagonist of the Sadducees' interpretations and a critic of the Pharisees' behavior; they make him the adversary of Judaism itself, as they reduce those who practiced and taught Judaism into scorned, satirized stereotypes.

A FAMILY EMBARRASSMENT

Here, then, is the first of several Jewish views of Jesus: Jesus seems like a cousin whose behavior many years ago caused such distress in the family that he is seldom mentioned, and then never without tones of discomfort. Mentioning him means that one cannot help engaging in a conversation about what he said or did and what it has meant to the *mishpachah*, the family, over the course of time (or, more rarely, what it might mean to us today). He is *that* one, the world-famous one whom we deem notorious because he became a celebrity by saying insulting things in public about the family, the one who got in trouble with the law for his outrageous behavior. One catches here and there a hint of pride that, being talented, illustrious, and widely admired, he is (after all) *mishpachah*. One also senses with deep discomfort that liking him too much would insult our common past, as if ignoring the suffering his oft-quoted words and opinions had caused.

Therefore, one may try to avoid looking or listening too closely to him, for fear that one may find the persona too attractive in spite of that history. This Jesus begins as an engaging egotist who ends up fatally believing in his own presumptuous myth. Following him on his path means joining him on a walk to the cross, which for him meant death (or, his adherents say, life everlasting). For the Jew, following him means dying to the Jewish community, history, and culture so as to be "reborn" or "completed" in Christian life. For the religious Jew, it also means compromising what we have understood to be the purposes of life and death, the proper dimensions of monotheism, and the ultimate inaccessibility of the Ultimate Oneness that is beyond language, space, time, or knowing. We cannot listen long to this man Jesus before being confronted by the allegation that he was the unique incarnation of that Oneness and its primary link with humanity. Even when we begin inquiring "What do you say," our considerations of authenticity and authority ultimately halt at his own question, "Who do you say I am?"

VICTIM OF HIS OWN PRESS

Another view: the real character of our human cousin Jesus has been obscured by the publicity hype and media distortions of his most devoted followers. Beneath it all, we can perceive an insightful teacher and social critic (one out of many in his time), having a good feel for the useful *mashal* (parable) and a clever turn of phrase, as well as a high opinion of his own certitudes. However, his actual identity has been covered by so many layers of translation and transference that the original Yeshua cannot be cleanly uncovered. Instead of the man himself, we get a question turning the issue of identity back to us: "Who do you say I am?" A clever stratagem, that phrase, to flip the challenges of revelation inside out. Moses never asked that question. His was, "Who does *anochi Y-H-V-H* claim to be?" Elijah never asked it. His question to the Baalists was, "Who is God?" Notice that "Who do you say I am?" is very different from, "What do you think of me?" The question Jesus asked inquires about fundamental identity. It is an egotist's question, in so many ways totally irrelevent to anything definingly Jewish—What difference does it make to say *who* he is?— yet in some few but important ways, absolutely critical.

A DISORDERED PERSONALITY

Or perhaps it means something else, pointing to yet another Jewish view of Jesus. When he asks, "Who do you say I am?"—does he not know? Did he become so muddled by his own convictions and by others' desires for him to be something in particular that amid the conflicting viewpoints he no longer knew for sure who and what he was, except as his adherents defined an identity for him? Should we hear in his question a note of puzzlement or even urgency? Matthew and Mark record subtly but pointedly differing responses from Peter, as if Jesus or his disciples would get to choose the one they most liked. His reply in Matthew 16:15 grandly identifies Jesus as "the Messiah, the Son of the living God," while in Mark 8:29 Peter stops simply with "the Messiah," politically a dangerous enough claim but one that was safely this side of an accusation of blasphemy.

Had Jesus realized that by acquiring, in the eyes of his followers, so many diverse identities, reflections of him had replaced his own essence? Is this why he never seems to be truly alone yet always seems apart from the surrounding crowd? Might it also be why he avoids life's most obvious defining and entwining personal relationships? Unlike most of the leading figures of Jewish biblical and rabbinic history, he never married, never raised a child, had no discernible relationship with the paternal figure who raised him (Joseph) or with any male family member, but surrounded himself with a coterie of adherents (including his mother), a substitute family whose members believed that he was capable of doing anything—indeed, even more: of being everything.

While so often seeming to claim a transcendent reality for himself, was he actually perplexed by what he saw of himself reflected by the devotees as well as the detractors around him? If he was an egotist, does he reveal through his query the egotist's insecurity, desperately needing affirmation from the outside to compensate for what he fears about himself? Does his self-confidence cover the reluctance to look inside? Having supposedly been a precocious, bright child from an ordinary family whose story was perhaps tinged with a hint of mystery or scandal, what might he have thought about himself and his origins? What might he have wanted to think or not think about them? We pose such questions because it is so difficult to extract this cousin, this Yeshua, from the Christianity in which his life and words are embedded. So we may want to answer back his question with our own: Who did you think you were?

HIDDEN BY A LOST VOCABULARY

Through text and context we may strive to grasp the answer at least to that question, even as we try to discern what it was that he might have said, might have thought he was saying, might have been heard to say. We can sweep to the side Christianity's theological construction of the life and words. What we cannot get behind are the barriers of language, plain and profound. Somewhere behind the words recorded for us in Greek were conversations and statements in Aramaic and Hebrew. Within the lost original vocabulary, sometimes but not always deducible, lived nuances and precision that make all the difference in meaning. Jesus' words were reported years later by interested parties with their own audiences and purposes, shaping them to many narrative and propagandistic ends. Even more basically, we should remember that oral language, parables, similes, and *exempla* live in the moment as responses to particular needs or incitements, and the one who speaks does not necessarily intend the words to be solidified into eternal positions. Yet when made solid, constructed into a "testament," they harden into constructions absolute and lasting.

FIRST-CENTURY HALAKHIST

Jesus' words are thus like the potsherds that archaeologists uncover and ponder for what they tell and do not tell us. For instance, in the passage from Luke 13:51 quoted above, the seemingly odd antithesis between "peace" and "division" probably attests to an original Hebrew phrasing that plays on the cognitive link between "peace" and "wholeness" through the consonantal root *sh-l-m* (*shalom, shleimut*).

But the verbal record may also hide, not disclose. Thus, when Jesus is quoted as saying, "I am the way" (John 14:6), does the Greek *hodos* express what he actually stated, and how would that have been heard by a fellow first-century Palestinian Jew? Might he not have been saying to a compatriot the sort of statement we often find in the Talmud, though in that work it would be couched as a third person affirmation of authority, rather than in Jesus' first person: "The *halakhah* is according to me"? In other words, was he claiming only that his interpretation of applied religious law (*halakhah*, from the root *h-l-kh*, to go or walk) was the "right" one, the one closest to what God intended? Or was he claiming something far more absolutely authoritative than that?

And when he proclaims, "I am the light of the world," does that sentiment, so difficult to translate into a Judaic concept, really express Yeshua, or a Hellenistic John, or the heat of a hostile confrontation with some of his opponents? In this inquiry, questions lead not to answers but to questions even more essential. Are we seeing in the Gospel stories of Jesus the inevitable refractions caused by the perspectives and purposes of different authors? Or do they record the shifts and turns of a man in the process of discovering and refining his thoughts as well as his sense of himself, tacking and turning as corrections become necessary? Or do they reflect a dialectical and empirical approach to teaching and *halakhah* that would be characteristic of a late Second Temple Jew in the role of teacher? If the last, then they record the conversation of a Yeshua who is not propounding a systematic theology but interpreting case law, balancing free interpretation in one instance with stricter in another, in response to the circumstances and issues of the day, the place, the situation.

"Who do you say I am?" Looking at Jesus' social, ethical, and halakhic pronouncements from the perspective of the subsequent writings of early rabbinic Judaism, we can often hear a Jew whose positions we can recognize and harmonize within his contemporary Jewish culture, someone often critical of the Pharisees but rather akin to them in outlook, yet seemingly influenced also by asceticism and a theological dualism such as we can discern in the Dead Sea Scrolls. This Jesus is verbally talented and quick-witted, sometimes a perceptive critic of social mores, often self-congratulatory and smug, a man who gladly makes himself the central player in a drama that will destroy his life and make his legend, an interesting figure for a biography.

Our answer to the Christian question is likely to dissatisfy the Christian because it concedes too little, and our fellow Jew because it may concede too much. If Jesus is modestly termed a first-century C.E. Jewish teacher, why not include his teachings in our own religious study and prayers? Here we face the problem of *contaminatio,* the impossibility of disentangling either the sayings of our cousin Yeshua from the Christian texts in which they are embedded or his *persona* from the Christianity in which he is enrobed and crowned.[1]

A "NEW" TESTIMONY?

Yet the implicit *cherem* (ban) can be explained further, against the backdrop of earlier prophetic Judaism, or the early rabbinic Judaism of Hillel (for example) that apparently coexisted with him, and certainly the Judaism that emerges after him and following the destruction of the Second Temple. To echo a famous quip: what is Jewish in Jesus' teaching is not unique, and what is unique is not Jewish. If one asks, What can I as a Jew learn from him and him alone, how could his teachings uniquely illuminate or shape my Judaism, the answer seems to be that he offers nothing that now seems singular. Whether it did at the time, or whether his magnetism derived more from the energy of his personality than his actual ideas, we can only speculate, if we join in scholarly attempts to disentangle the actual sayings of Jesus from those ascribed to him by the Gospel writers or to distinguish between what he might have communicated to his followers and the theological elaborations years later by Paul and John.

As some Jewish writers and artists have sensed, we can find in part of Jesus' life story a Yeshua we recognize and at least sympathize with, maybe even a personality we like. Those from an eastern European Yiddish environment are most likely to catch the correspondences with their own cultural experience: the bright young student from a humble background, the social critic or iconoclast with egalitarian inclinations, the teacher of humane values who lived simply but not austerely, the victim of an unholy alliance between an oppressive political regime and a puppet but authoritarian religious structure, and at the end of it all a Jew pitilessly condemned and murdered by the brutal might of an unjust society. This Jesus we feel that we know, not as an extraordinary figure but quite to the contrary a paradigmatic one: not simply Jesus as a Jew but The Jew as Jesus.

---

[1] Susannah Heschel studies attempts to engage the Jewishness-of-Jesus writings by leaders of modern Jewish religious reform and historical scholarship in the nineteenth century (*Abraham Geiger and the Jewish Jesus* [Chicago: University of Chicago Press, 1998]).

A MAN OF SELF-CONTRADICTIONS

Still again, confronting the total record transmitted by those who first recorded versions of his life and sayings, the Gospel writers, we want to turn around his question to ask, "Who do you say you are?" Reading Jesus' putative self-definitions (along with the affirmations thereof by his disciples, the subsequent Gospel writers, and Paul), we encounter something profoundly disturbing. This Jesus is alternately pugnacious and defensive, confrontational while counseling "turning the other cheek," contemptuous of his adversaries even as he proclaims the commandment of loving one's enemies, overbearingly opinionated albeit praising the virtue of humility. He is also increasingly bold and radical in his claims about himself. Perhaps, we may think, his young mother and her much older husband treated this talented child too indulgently. Seen through Jewish eyes centuries later, or more to the point *heard* through Jewish ears, he often sounds grossly arrogant, a dislikable figure whose fantastic professions of a mystical and even divine identity are gratingly blasphemous.

Or do we sometimes miss the tone? One might imagine some of his remarks as a deliberate, comically outrageous assault on the sensibilities of the Sadducee petty aristocracy or Pharisee *bourgeoisie*. So, perhaps, we might suspect this regarding Luke 6:5, in which he periphrastically proclaims himself *kyrios . . . tou sabbatou*, lord of the Sabbath, fully aware that the "scribes and Pharisees" are observing him while he just as carefully eyes them, gauging how far he can go in flouting authority and tradition at this time and place. But of course we may also perceive the escape door that he leaves ajar, if we hear beneath his portentously arching phrase "Son of Man" (*huios tou anthropou*) the Hebrew *ben adam* used by the prophets (e.g. Isa. 51:12; Jer. 49:18; Ezek. 2:1) to mean simply, "human being," or the analogous Aramaic *bar einosh* similarly used in the Talmud.

Reading the Gospel accounts, one begins to feel sorry for the exasperated, repeatedly insulted elders, trying to have a sensible conversation about Torah law or to ascertain the factual truth of reported assertions with this elusive, facile fellow who insists that he alone understands how to interpret Jewish Scriptures correctly, or even that he is somehow a transcendent being, and that they are fools and villains for not recognizing it. True, there may be much of the Gospel writers' tendentious shaping at work in these narratives, in which Jesus always has the right answers, leaving his opponents nonplussed and looking foolish; but the voice of Yeshua, the haughty self-assured scorner of those in authority, seems to come through authentically. This one we have argued with, grumbled about, and sometimes applauded on street corners, in coffee houses, and in classrooms. Sassy, smart, disdainful, sometimes glib, he may be accurately insightful or spectacularly and unjustly hostile.

THE JESUS-CULTURE

"Who do you say Jesus is?" That question most often confronts the Jewish teacher and religious leader today from curious or concerned Christians, or from congregants wanting guidance in responding to neighbors or co-workers. No one can inhabit or visit a Western or Western-influenced society without confronting what can be called the Jesus-culture. One meets it in casual encounters through the cross dangling from the neck of the supermarket cashier, the gospel music pulsating from the boombox on the beach, the Christian religious programs encountered again and again while channel-surfing, even the graffiti on bridges and signal boxes urging, "Try Jesus," just as much as in the highest forms of music, art, and literature.

It is not merely present but inescapable: highly visible and multitudinous churches in their many denominations; publicly observed Christian religious holidays; and weeks of commercial publicity heralding the church's two main festivals celebrating the religious import of Jesus. Shoppers during November and December are assaulted willy-nilly with crude Christian theological indoctrination in the form of "holiday" songs pouring from the sound systems or radios of most stores small and large, announcing (for instance), "Born is the king of Israel." Public as well as private supposedly nonsectarian schools transmit and celebrate some manifestation of Christian holiday culture, while publicly supported radio and televison stations abundantly offer celebratory Christian programs for Christmas and Easter. These are virtually impossible to avoid. Not being literate in the Jesus-culture leaves one functionally illiterate in the culture at large; so Jews perforce also receive that education. (It is not the same as an education in Christianity, though some few will acquire that as well, albeit often in simple and inaccurate ways, seeing no point in trying to discern the nuances of Christian doctrinal differences that divide denominations.)

THE CHURCH'S JESUS: A STRANGER

No sooner do we get close enough to see that fellow Yeshua more clearly than another figure obtrudes his presence, wanting to substitute a capital "H" in the pronoun "his." This is the church's Greek god-hero Jesus, a different rendering of our remote, contentious, scandalous cousin Yeshua, who is now turned into Paul's *ho tou theou huios Christos Iesous*, "the Son of God Christ Jesus" (2 Cor. 1:19). This one seems to speak, as Emmanuel Levinas might say, "in Greek," in a non-Hebraic cultural milieu that the Jew enters only by stepping into a different and non-Jewish cultural environment, while yet hearing reverberations of a covenant daringly and shockingly redefined. So the Jew may (as it were) look into the church as a visitor, only to turn away baffled if not repelled by what is taught there about that famous cousin. "Who do you say he is?" is a question to which the Christian may offer replies citing Hebrew Scriptures, yet those responses seem tortuously wrought through *post hoc* reasoning, offering Jesus as the answer to a question we never need to ask, rather than to the ones we have asked for centuries before and after. Cousin? No—now a stranger.

A Jewish encounter with Jesus, if the Jewish reader is informed and intellectually curious, will never be simple. We alternately approach and withdraw. We may sense that it can be useful to close the gap between ourselves and our kinsman; in drawing closer, we may hear how often his words resemble those with which we are familiar from prophetic and early rabbinic engagements with the Torah's teachings and values. Yet we dare not disregard the discordant, alienating proclamations (either those ascribed to him or the ones expressed by his followers as recorded in the New Testament). Granted, some scholars or apologists doubt the historical authenticity of the more daring claims made by or for Jesus, and in that way they situate Jesus more or less plausibly within a familiar but broad spectrum of first-century Judaism. Nevertheless, while scholarship can engage the challenge of trying to reconstruct the authentic words of Jesus and thereby produce a *Jesus without Christianity*, there is no way to talk about Jesus from the standpoint of the Jewish community as if we were oblivious of his mythic persona.

Holding the memory of our closer yet still unsatisfactory encounters with his humanness, we are left puzzled at best by who they say he is, and for that matter by his purpose as much as his fame. In the place of the celebrated vision of a *mamlekhet kohanim v'goi kadosh* (Exod. 19:6), a "nation of priests, a holy people," we now find the singular figure of *Christos/moshiach/Anointed One/Messiah*. The Torah had acknowledged God the *yotzer or*, maker of light, and proclaimed Israel *or goyim* (Isa. 42:6), a light to the nations; Jesus' testament proclaimed, *ego eimi to phos tou kosmou* (John 8:12), "I am the light of the world."

To the Christian those new verbal formulae mark the meeting points of flesh and word, of lived reality and theological doctrine, of incarnation and transfiguration. To the Jew, in those reformulations of Jewish concepts we lose sight of Yeshua our cousin, and in a profound way we lose him. Transfigured he is indeed, but into something unrecognizable, ahistorical, as if the spinner of parables had himself been turned into one. We suspect he would not recognize his image in this construction "Jesus." In that likelihood rests perhaps the final, ironic twist of his question, which will take on a different tone and import: "Who do you say I am?"

6

Yeshua the Hasid

DANIEL MATT

W HY SHOULD JEWS WANT to have anything to do with Jesus? In his name, Jews have been persecuted and murdered. Christianity claimed to have supplanted Judaism.

Centuries of Christian anti-Semitism laid the groundwork for Hitler's extermination of one-third of the Jewish people, so why should any Jew be interested in the life of Jesus and what he taught? The history of Jewish–Christian relations has tainted Jesus' image and rendered him impure. Yet, for Jews and Christians to live together amicably, they must reevaluate each other's tradition. It is not enough that the Vatican has absolved the Jews of collective guilt for the death of Jesus. Christians should appreciate Torah, rabbinic Judaism, and the eternal renewal of the Jewish people. And Jews should reclaim Jesus.

A GALILEAN *HASID*

I am not talking about what Jesus became—Jesus Christ—but rather about *Yeshua,* the impassioned rabbi who died for his vision of Judaism. Jesus was a Galilean *hasid,* someone passionately in love with God, drunk on the divine, unconventional and extreme in his devotion to God and to fellow human beings.

There were other *hasidim* in first-century Palestine, one of whom was strikingly similar to Jesus: Hanina ben Dosa. Hanina lived in Galilee, about ten miles north of Jesus' home town of Nazareth. Like Jesus, he was praised for his religious devotion and healing talents. Once, "Hanina was praying when a scorpion bit him, but he did not interrupt his prayer. His pupils went and found the scorpion dead at the entrance to its hole. They said, 'Woe to the man bitten by a scorpion, but woe to the scorpion that bites [Hanina] ben Dosa'" (Tosefta *Berakhot* 3:20).[1] Similarly, Jesus said, "Those who believe may step on snakes . . . and nothing will harm them" (Mark 16:18). Hanina's prayers were widely regarded as being immediately accepted by God, so he was frequently asked to pray for the sick and those in trouble. According to the Talmud, Hanina cured the son of Gamaliel from a distance; according to the New Testament, Jesus cured the son of the Roman centurion from a distance. Hanina, like Jesus, was known for his poverty and lack of acquisitiveness. Both had no expertise in legal or ritual teachings, but were famous, rather, as miracle workers whose supernatural power derived from their intimacy with God.

Inevitably, tension arises between the *hasid* and the established religious order. The *hasid* is a nonconformist who demands much of himself and of his followers. His intimacy with God, his confidence in the power of his words, and his unrestrained personal authority conflict with the conservative power structure.

Jesus came from Galilee, which made him suspect to both Jewish and Roman authorities since the *Galil* was a hotbed of revolution. Here the Zealots began their agitation against Rome. The Roman prefect Pontius Pilate killed several Galilean revolutionaries. To the imperial occupiers, any Galilean was a potential troublemaker. Galilean Jews also had a reputation for a lack of religious observance. Many of their ancestors had been forcibly converted from paganism to Judaism by John Hyrcanus I in the second century B.C.E. In Jesus' time, many pagans still lived there. The rabbis were suspicious of Galileans, who spoke imperfect Aramaic with a coarse guttural accent. The Talmud sometimes refers to Galileans with the term *am ha-arets* (people of the earth), meaning ignorant, illiterate peasants. Jerusalem's intellectual elite felt superior to these unsophisticated provincials.

Exhibiting the chauvinism that was typical of Galilee, Jesus insisted that he was sent to the Jews alone (Matt. 10:5, 15-24). The twelve apostles were forbidden to proclaim the gospel to Gentiles or Samar-

---

[1] In the following pages, I am drawing on Geza Vermes, *Jesus the Jew: A Historian's Reading of the Gospels* (Philadelphia: Fortress, 1973); E. P. Sanders, *Jesus and Judaism* (Philadelphia: Fortress, 1985); and idem, "The Life of Jesus," in *Christianity and Judaism: A Parallel History of Their Origins and Development*, ed. Hershel Shanks (Washington, D.C.: Biblical Archaeology Society, 1992), 41-83.

itans: their mission was to Israel alone. In fact, Jesus' disciples later become suspicious of Paul, who sought to preach to the wider world, since Jesus had focused almost exclusively on Jewish affairs.

JESUS' APPROACH TO TORAH

Paul, who never met Jesus in the flesh, taught that Christ had replaced Torah, yet Jesus himself was basically committed to Torah and the *mitzvot*. According to Matthew, Jesus declared:

Think not that I have come to abolish the Torah and the prophets; I have come not to abolish them, but to fulfill them. For truly, I say to you, till heaven and earth pass away, not an iota, not a dot, will pass from the Torah until all is accomplished. Whoever relaxes one of the least of these commandments and teaches men so, shall be called least in the kingdom of heaven; but he who does them and teaches them shall be called great in the kingdom of heaven. (Matt. 5:17-19)

These words may not be authentic, but Jesus' teaching derives from the Torah. (Similarly, Paul says in the book of Acts, "I assert nothing beyond what was told by the prophets and by Moses" [26:22].) Jesus is one of those who are searching for the essence of Torah. When asked by a scribe, "What is the most important commandment?" he answered with two of the *mitzvot:* "Love *YHVH* your God with all your heart, with all your soul, and with all your might" and "Love your neighbor as yourself" (Mark 12:28-34). Here the Gospel of Mark preserves something that is missing from the other Synoptic Gospels. In Luke's and Matthew's accounts of this discussion, there is tension between the scribe and Jesus. In Mark's version, they have a friendly exchange; Jesus and the scribe agree that these are the key *mitzvot*.

Elsewhere, Jesus formulates the essence by paraphrasing "Love your neighbor": "Whatever you wish that people would do to you, do so to them. For this is the Torah and the prophets" (Matt. 7:12). In the generation preceding Jesus, Hillel had offered a similar principle, but in the negative: "What is hateful to you, do not do to your fellow." Hillel was typical of the rabbis of his day: more down-to-earth, more practical. Jesus was more demanding, more extreme, more hasidic.

It is very difficult to find clear instances of Jesus actually trans-gressing the Torah.[2] His disciples, not Jesus himself, are accused of disregarding the ritual washing of the hands (Mark 7:1-8). This was not a biblical requirement for the laity. It was a purity law spread by the Pharisees, which only in Jesus' time had become a common Jew-ish practice. Galileans were often lax about purity laws such as this.

Again, it is not Jesus but his disciples who pluck ears of corn on the Sabbath and pull out the kernels (Matt. 12:1-8). In two secondary sources, we are told that the disciples did not pluck the ears, but removed the kernels by rubbing the ears with their hands.[3] Galileans regarded this as permissible on the Sabbath, while others ruled that it was permissible only when using one's fingers, not the entire hand. Thus, the behavior of the disciples of Jesus the Galilean may have accorded with a Galilean tradition.

There is no indication that Jesus and his disciples ate nonkosher food. According to Mark, Jesus said, "Not what goes into a man defiles him, but the things that come out of a man [i.e., what he says] defile him" (Mark 7:15). Mark interpreted this to mean that Jesus "declared all foods clean," but it is very improbable that this repre-sents Jesus' view. The first generation of Christians did not know that Jesus had "canceled" the food laws, and there is no evidence that Jesus commanded his disciples to ignore them.[4]

Of course, numerous New Testament passages do portray Jesus as being in conflict with the Pharisees. These stories, however, reflect the situation in the generations following Jesus when the Gospels were compiled. By now, the early church had adopted Paul's notion that the laws of Torah had been superseded by Christ, so the dietary and Sabbath laws were openly rejected. Battle lines were clearly drawn between Christianity and rabbinic Judaism, represented respectively in the Gospels by Jesus and the Pharisees.

This is not to claim that everything Jesus said derived from the Torah. Telling one of his followers, "Let the dead bury their dead" (Matt. 8:22), ran counter to the Ten Commandments' "Honor your father and your mother"—and to Greco-Roman piety as well. The point seemed to be that following Jesus superseded the requirements of piety and Torah. On a number of occasions, Jesus implied that the

---

[2] See Sanders, *Jesus and Judaism,* 245-69; idem, "Life of Jesus," 70-73.

[3] See David Flusser, *Jewish Sources in Early Christianity* (New York: Adama Books, 1987), 22.

[4] See Sanders, "Life of Jesus," 72.

Mosaic dispensation is inadequate and not final. There is a new age at hand, an eschatological revolution.

At times, Jesus was *more* demanding than Torah. In prohibiting divorce, for example, he went beyond Deuteronomy, which explicitly allows for divorce. From the *mitzvah* "You shall not murder," he concluded that one should not be angry with others since anger can lead to killing. From the *mitzvah* "You shall not commit adultery," he concluded that just glancing lustfully at a married woman is tantamount to adultery. Like a true *hasid*, Jesus was extreme in his ethical demands.

THE THREAT POSED BY JESUS

If Jesus basically followed the Torah, then why were the civil and religious authorities so upset by him? He associated with sinners, but this in itself did not violate tradition, since God too yearns for those who have "missed the mark"[5] to *return*, to engage in *teshuvah*. Various biblical prophets transmitted this message. Joshua told the idolatrous Israelites, "Turn your hearts to *YHVH*" (Josh. 24:23); Ezekiel demanded, "Make yourselves a new heart, a new spirit" (Ezek. 18:31); and Malachi transmitted this message from God: "Return to Me, and I will return to you" (Mal. 3:7). Eventually, the Midrash portrays God as pleading: "My children, open for Me an opening of *teshuvah* the size of an eye of a needle, and I will open for you openings through which wagons and coaches can pass" (*Shir ha-Shirim Rabbah* 5:3).

If Jesus promised sinners that, by simply believing in him, they could gain entrance into the kingdom of heaven, even without repentance, this would have upset many of the normally pious. But still, that doesn't explain the crucifixion. Jesus was arrested, tried, and put to death because he politically threatened both the Roman authorities and the Jewish aristocracy. He had come to Jerusalem at Passover time, the most popular of the three pilgrimage festivals and the one commemorating the liberation from Egyptian bondage.[6] Passover

---

[5] The Hebrew root *ht'*, "to sin," means, in the *hiph'il* conjugation, "to miss the mark."

[6] The other two pilgrimage festivals are Shavu'ot (Pentecost, or the Festival of Firstfruits) and Sukkot (the Festival of Booths).

was charged with political significance, and many pilgrims bitterly resented the current pharaoh: the Roman emperor Tiberius or his local representative, the prefect Pontius Pilate. Trouble was more likely now than at any other season, and normally the Roman prefect came to Jerusalem from Caesarea with extra troops for the garrison.[7]

In Jerusalem, Jesus attacked the money changers in the precincts of the Temple, overturning seats and tables.[8] He looked forward to a new, perfect Temple, which he probably believed would be given by God from heaven. This "cleansing" of the Temple (Mark 11:15-17; John 2:14-17) challenged the priestly aristocracy's political and religious authority, and Jewish leaders concluded that this Galilean should not be allowed to create further trouble.

Jesus may not have said, "I will destroy the Temple" or "I am king of the Jews." He may never have claimed to be the Messiah or the son of God. But his threatening actions and his talk of an imminent kingdom undermined the status quo with Rome. According to Josephus, Herod had similar concerns about John the Baptist, "a good man, who exhorted the Jews to lead righteous lives": "Herod became alarmed. Eloquence that had so great an effect on humankind might lead to some form of sedition. Herod decided therefore that it would be better to strike first and be rid of him before his work led to an uprising" (*Antiquities* 18.117-18).[9]

The Gospel of John portrays the priests as fearful that Jesus' popularity would lead to Roman intervention and disaster: "If we leave him alone like this, the whole populace will believe in him. Then the Romans will come and sweep away our temple and our nation" (John 11:48). According to this account, the high priest Caiaphas convinced his colleagues to sacrifice Jesus for the benefit of the entire people: "It is more to your interest that one man should die for the people, than that the whole nation should be destroyed" (John 11:50). John's account should not be accepted as historical truth, but it does reflect political considerations that influenced the tragic outcome. Caiaphas's alleged reasoning resonates ironically with the Christian claim that Jesus died for all people. In any case, it is fairly certain that Jesus was interrogated by the high priest and then executed on the orders of Pontius Pilate. The charge was sedition or treason.

---

[7] Sanders, "Life of Jesus," 75.

[8] Though, as we have seen, Jesus condemned anger, he himself exhibits a fair amount of righteous anger.

[9] Discussed by Vermes, *Jesus the Jew,* 50-51.

THE BETRAYAL OF JESUS

Jesus was a charismatic teacher and healer. He did not seek death in Jerusalem, but he pursued with inflexible devotion a path that led to his death, from which he did not try to escape.

Jesus condemned hypocrisy and injustice among his own people and sought to prepare his followers for the coming redemption, for the kingdom of heaven (*malkhut shamayim*). For Jesus, the kingdom was not a pious theory or a far-off promise. It was an immediate reality that could not be denied or evaded. Jewish mysticism later identified the kingdom with Shekhinah, the presence of God. Jesus too identified kingdom with presence: the kingdom is here and now. Jesus was compelled to make his fellow Jews aware of this awesome, humbling fact. To enter the kingdom, Jesus said, you must be like a child. Innocence is a window to the infinite, unavailable to the skeptical mind until it pauses and reflects.

Like later hasidim, Jesus felt that it was not enough to follow the Torah: One must become Torah, living so intensely that one's everyday actions convey an awareness of God and evoke this awareness in others.

Unintentionally, Jesus the Jew founded a new religion. Along with persecuting the Jewish people, Christianity has also spread the Jewish message of monotheism and biblical ethics throughout the world. Jews and Christians need to look at each other anew. Christians should appreciate not only their Jewish roots but also the vitality of contemporary Judaism and the Jewish people—Jesus' people. Jews can accept Jesus, not the Jesus of the church or Jesus Christ the Messiah, but the Jewish Jesus, a long-lost cousin who, for nearly two millennia, has been misunderstood and perhaps lonely. By appreciating Jesus as a Jewish teacher, a Jew affirms that the wisdom of Torah manifests itself in countless, unforeseen ways.

Jesus was a flower of Judaism cut down in full bloom. Seen through Jewish eyes, he was not the one-and-only son of God. The myth of the son of God explodes into the truth that every human being, every creature, every thing is an incarnation of God. Jesus should not be idolized. From a Jewish perspective, to turn him into the only son of God is to betray him.

7

A Letter from
Rabbi Gamaliel ben Gamaliel

STANLEY NED ROSENBAUM, TRANSLATOR

[Translator's note: Even in scholarly circles, Rabbi Gamaliel ben Gamaliel is but little known. His approximate dates, 31 B.C.E.–42? C.E., make him contemporary with the second generation of Tannaim, but none of his opinions is cited in the Talmud. He is remembered mainly for misanthropic epigrams, such as "What is thought fearless is often fearfully thoughtless," and "The more principles, the more enemies." The text presented in the annotated translation below is by far the longest extant piece attributed to him. I have tried to retain the flavor of the original Hebrew by adding such glosses as are necessary to make the text more immediately accessible.

The RaGBaG, as he is called, is thought to be the last son of Rabbi Gamaliel the Elder, mentioned in Acts 22 and in many rabbinic sources. However, Jews don't name children after the living. If his father died while the boy was in utero, accounting for the unusual name, then RaGBaG's dates don't accord with Gamaliel's as far as we know them. Consequently, a considerable body of opinion holds that the RaGBaG did not in fact exist and that this piece is, necessarily, a fraud or at best a latter-day attempt at Pseudepigrapha. I leave it to the individual reader to decide.]

Esteemed Philo,

I TRUST THAT YOU ARE WELL, may you continue to be so, and that the community in Alexandria is thriving despite the recent unpleasantness of which we have but lately heard. Not all my news will be unknown to you, but I trust you will indulge me.

Reports from Rome tell that Pontius Pilate is dead and by no natural cause. You may think me vindictive, but I am happy that I have lived to see it; the murdering rogue deserved no better than the fate he so freely dealt to others. I understand that Pilate backed Sejanus[1] in his machinations to gain the imperium and when that one fell, he too was ruined. This is hardly to be wondered at. Pilate lacked the diplomatic skills the first Herod displayed following the battle at Actium—the year I was born, else I should scarcely know the year of my birth.

With Pilate gone, our King Agrippa finally felt free to complain of him to Rome, telling of his high-handedness, confiscation of property, and even murder of our people without trial.[2] I was initially grateful that Caligula prevailed, for had Sejanus become emperor, who knows what evil would here befall us. But one is as bad as the next and Caligula is rumored to be unstable. I know that he purposefully insulted your community by insisting that his statues be placed in your synagogues.

It is near a hundred years since the accursed Romans have been in the land, a scourge to rival the Babylonians, may their memory be forgotten, and I have had the misfortune of being alive nearly three score and ten of those years. "By reason of strength," I might have ten more if the Psalm [90:3] is right, but in all candor, dear friend, I do not wish them. Better to die out of this world and trust God's mercy on me in the world to come than further to endure the Roman tyranny as my remaining strength fades.

As you will surmise, things here are no better than ever they were. Herod Antipas has lately contrived to murder "*mikvah*[3] John," a man who urged all to immerse themselves in the living waters of the Jordan before the great and terrible day of the Lord. He maintained that this act could atone for sin. Our priests most emphatically deny this claim; to admit it would, of course, make them unnecessary! John's "crime" was that he had the temerity to speak against Herod's illicit marriage to his brother's divorced wife. Shortly thereafter Herod was soundly thrashed by his Nabatean former father-in-law. He had put away the man's daughter in order to conclude the illegal marriage.

---

[1] Prefect of Rome's Praetorian Guard, who may have seduced the wife of Tiberius's son Drusus and so enlisted her help in poisoning him. Sejanus was executed by order of the Senate in 35 C.E. Pilate's fate is unknown.

[2] "Legacy to Gaius," in *The Judaic Tradition*, ed. Nahum Glatzer (Northvale, N.J.: Aronson, 1987), 123ff.

[3] The *mikveh* is the ritual bath required of male and female Jews to remove "ritual" impurities and make the worshiper fit to reenter temple or synagogue. RaGBaG's unusual spelling is nonetheless correct; it reflects Isa. 22:11.

Better for Herod if we had not done away with the multiple wives our fathers had. Here in Jerusalem they say that Herod's defeat was God's retribution for John's murder. Needless to add, John died without even the pretense of a trial.

All of our embassies to Antioch or to Rome to protest Pilate's excesses were useless, really. Vitellius pretended to recall Pilate, but he was not recalled; he went back to help Sejanus secure the emperorship. . . . How the Romans could have continued in office for so many years a man of such monumental brutality, corruption, and insolence is unfathomable. Apparently, the vaunted Roman "law" is something they impose on others without feeling the need of following it themselves. I fear, though, that it is Pilate's murder of one Joshua ben Joseph of Nazareth, even though it is some years ago now,[4] shortly after Pilate came here if memory serves, that may prove the most troubling of all their foul deeds.

This Joshua was a Galilean, as were most of his followers, and Northerners have always been the most uncomfortable under Roman rule. Revolts against Rome invariably begin there so that we Judeans have a saying, "Can anything good come out of Galilee?"[5] The first Herod brought himself to the favorable attention of Rome by putting down a band of rebellious Galileans who had rallied around one Hezekiah, and that happened only shortly before I was born. My grandfather, who had the story from some who managed to flee, told me of it. There have been other revolts since, including that of Hezekiah's son, most beginning in the North and all coming to the same, predictably bloody, end.

This Joshua, however, was, like John, a preacher of the reign of God that many now wish for. He had no political ambitions that I can discern. Joshua's very lack of political purpose, however, may have proved his undoing. He had disciples among the Zealots who must have attached hidden meaning to his saying, "I bring not peace but a sword" [Matt. 10:34]. Deluded fools. Joshua counseled not to resist evil but to "turn the other cheek" [Matt. 5:39]. Rather a prudent

---

[4] RaGBaG may have his chronology a bit mixed up here, for he implies that Jesus was killed before John, a theory that was proposed and refuted in the twentieth century. On the other hand, being so close to the events themselves, perhaps his account of things warrants further investigation.

[5] John 1:46. No Gospels were written in RaGBaG's time, but except for this reference, two others to John and the Good Samaritan of Luke, all New Testament references come from Matthew, as we would expect. Matthew was a Jew writing for other Jews.

counsel, I should say. It is rumored that one of his Zealot followers betrayed him to the Romans either in rage that Joshua would not call for a popular uprising or in hopes that his death would provoke one.

Romans do not differentiate between political and religious movements here any more than they do among Jews, Samaritans, and Galileans. They have among them observers of our history who say of us, "Where their religions talk, their politics stalk." And in fairness, with so many people here confidently expecting that God will raise an anointed one from among us, a messiah to deliver us, the Romans' present fear is not without foundation.

They watch popular movements with great vigilance. On more than one occasion Pilate had soldiers dressed as Jews circulate among us and break up our legitimate demonstrations by laying about with clubs, wounding many and scattering the rest. The real reason for the death of Joshua was the fear that his movement would become political.

At Joshua's crucifixion they mocked him as "King of the Jews," to which we objected most strenuously. Joshua had said, "The kingdom of God is within you" [Luke 17:21], by which I am sure he meant to comment on the verse that tells us "the Law is not in Heaven, but very near us to do it" [Deut. 30:11-14]. Such subtleties would be better cast before swine than wasted on Roman ears.

Since the Romans came we have not had the power of capital punishment and would exercise it with enormous caution if we did have it. It is a saying amongst us that a Sanhedrin that decreed one death penalty in seven years we would call "bloody."[6] I cannot believe that any Jew would betray a fellow to the Romans for crucifixion, no matter what our differences. Crucifixion is the most painful and protracted death imaginable, far from our practices.[7]

Yet perhaps this thought of mine is but a pious wish. I know that some priests implored Joshua to have a care not to incite the Romans to violence against us. Others, however, such as the Herodians of Boethus's party[8] have done very well by accepting Roman rule—at a cost of their places in the world to come, or so it is to be hoped—and might sell anyone to preserve their positions. The high priest's father-

---

[6] The Sanhedrin was Israel's judicial body, made up of Sadducees and Pharisees, with competence in civil and some criminal matters. The remark concerning capital punishment is in Mishnah *Makkot* ("Punishments") 1:10. A later rabbi, Eleazar ben Azariah, said "one [death sentence] in seventy years we would call bloody."

[7] The four legitimate methods are stoning, strangling, burning, and drowning.

[8] Boethusians were adherents of Simon ben Boethus, appointed high priest by Herod the Great in 24 B.C.E. and hence loyal to the Herodians.

in-law has the monopoly on changing foreign coins at the Temple, six days a week. It would be seven if they could. He and his greedy brood sit in their stalls on the southern end of the Temple complex and cheat Jewish brethren from abroad by giving them grossly unfair rates of exchange.

The foreign Jews have no choice; they cannot use coins with images on them even to buy sacrificial animals, so they must submit to this outrageous gouging or go home without having performed their sacrifices. Since the time of Zechariah [14:21], no one had said anything in public until this Joshua had the courage to beard them in their foul den. When the "customers" heard it, they all left in disgust.

So the Boethusians had no choice but to depart themselves, if only for a day, and in no good humor I can tell you. Their greed might, God forbid, cause them to acquiesce even in murder, especially of Zealots or those whom they can convince the Romans are allied with them. And I have heard it said more than once that the only good Samaritan is a dead Samaritan, though I do not know who authored this intemperate remark.

Ten years on and the hoped-for revolt does not seem to be happening. But tensions remain high. I would not advise any Jew from the Diaspora to come here now. Who is to say when the Zealots will take up arms against Rome in a war we cannot win? Meanwhile, there seems to be no end to the claims advanced by this new sect.

Some of Joshua's followers, especially amongst our women, insist that he was resurrected after the manner of Isaac who, they say, was killed by our father Abraham, ascended to Heaven and there was given life again. You have no idea, my dear Philo, of the incredible variety of stories circulating here. But then, your Alexandrian brethren maintain the equally absurd proposition[9] that the Greek translation of Torah was the work of seventy-two scholars who produced identical texts while working independently! I suppose, then, that fables are no one's sole possession.

It is most disturbing in any case, this rendering of Scripture into Greek. Almost, I should say, were it not such a cliche, a sword of Damocles. Admittedly, most Jews in your community have not enough Hebrew to read Scripture—I have heard this said even of you, dear friend—but do we really wish to cast it into a language where it may be read by any Gentile? Left to themselves, what will these pagans make of it? And what not?

---

[9] The *Letter of Aristeas* purports to be an account of the writing of the Septuagint at the invitation of Ptolemy II Philadelphus (285–246 B.C.E.).

If I am not being too misanthropic, let me observe that a martyred leader has one advantage over a living one; he cannot be killed again. The question is: Can such a one still lead? His brother James, whom I see often at the Temple, is become head of their Jerusalem faction, but more than a few believe the tale of Joshua's resurrection.

Resurrection is a controversial notion, amongst us at least. You will know how seriously the Egyptians take this matter, preserving the bodies of all with money enough to pay for it, regardless of merit. Joshua said that it is easier for a rope to pass through the eye of a needle than for a rich man to enter the gates of heaven [Matt. 19:24]. Being a man of some means myself, I hope that wealth is not a disqualification and give generously to the poor without any of them knowing whence it comes. But we have long been divided over questions of the world to come on other grounds.

Sadducees and Boethusians say there is no resurrection, but we Pharisees hold that there must be: how else explain Elijah's ascending into heaven and Enoch's walking with God when he was no more? The question as to whether the body itself will be resurrected cannot be answered from Scripture without forcing upon the text words that it does not contain. I say nothing against the allegorical reading of which, I know, you are so fond; many amongst us have long since deviated from the path of *pshat*, the plain meaning of text, to look for other, deeper meanings, and this informs our rabbinic *drashim*.[10]

Nowhere is this new use of Scripture more eagerly undertaken than among Joshua's adherents. They comb the Torah and the Prophets as well as the lesser writings looking for verses that they can equate with his reported deeds, which are magnified as they are repeated, even if they mutilate texts in the process. He is said by some to have fed a multitude as Elijah did, and by others to have raised a man from the dead, as did both Elijah and Elisha. Some claim that he walked on water, which no prophet has done. Others trace his lineage to Abraham but maintain that he was sired by no human father. If I am not needlessly repeating myself, who knows where all this fable-making might lead?

In any event, this Joshua had no harm in him. But he was, for all that, a curious, even a strange person about whom very little is known. He is said to have been an *illui* [a child genius] holding his own with elders when he was twelve—that will have been about the

---

[10] *Drashim* are rabbinical explanations or comments on Scripture that aim to produce moral imperatives; they are often homiletic.

time of Quirinius's abominable census[11]—and I have spoken to no one who can confirm it. "Tales from the North," as we say here, and not to be taken seriously. Perhaps anything said in the vulgar accents of the North, be it ever so apparent, would not be believed in Jerusalem.

One thing I will not do—you may have my oath upon it—is to dismiss out-of-hand the words of a Northerner, no matter where from. To do aught else merely shows our predilection for prejudgment. Were not Elijah, Amos, and Hosea also Northerners? And Jeremiah's family was from the North, though he was born not twelve stadia from where I now write. I often visit his grave to pray. And I have at whiles been impressed by what I have heard attributed to Joshua.

For example, not three months ago I heard it told that on a Sabbath he healed a man with a withered hand. When he was criticized for it, he responded with an argument about rescuing sheep on the Sabbath. "Which of you," he said, "if he had a sheep and it fell into a pit would not rescue that sheep even on Sabbath? And is a man not more valuable than a sheep?" [Matt. 12:9-14]. This is a *qal v'homer* argument and as such well known to us Pharisees. The Romans, who learned it from our Sages, call it *a fortiori*, "how much the more."

Now there is a curious flaw in Joshua's reasoning that I am sure you can easily see. Sheep die if not watered every day, whereas a man with such a condition could wait one day more, or one less if it came to that! Surely, Joshua must have known this, so why argue as he did?

Healing by words is not against the Law, and the strictest rabbi would not complain if we broke Sabbath to sustain a life; I have heard it argued that throat medicine may be administered then because the extent of danger cannot be known. By extension, other treatments may also be applied, and this on the request of the afflicted person.

But shall we break Sabbath simply to alleviate suffering, to effect a release from pain even as the Sabbath is itself a release? Is doing the "good" of a "good work" sometimes more important than avoiding the "work" required to do it? So much suffering is beyond our power to help, especially in these days, that I hesitate to judge. Extending the idea of release must be the real reason for Joshua's argument.

From what I know of Joshua's words, it must be said that he stood in the prophets' mighty line. It is long since anyone in Israel was

---

[11] This census was ordered in 6 C.E. Christian tradition misremembers or misappropriates it to 6 B.C.E.

known as a prophet, but you must admit, dear Philo, that he is "con-victed out of his own mouth" of being a prophet. Like Elijah, he called his disciples to leave their families [1 Kings 19:20]. Like Amos [5:21-24], he had nothing but contempt for people who make a pub-lic show of piety. Like Micah [7:6], he said that sons would be set against their fathers and daughters against their mothers.

Like Amos, too, he was not without honor except in his own land, as he wryly observed [Matt. 13:57]. Many now say that the Almighty no longer speaks through prophets. It were fearful to think that pre-cisely in these evil times the Lord should fall silent, but the prudent, as Amos said [5:13], hold their tongues in evil times—though he did not do so, to his everlasting honor. Would Amos himself dare to speak now, and to whom would he address himself? Such a one would likely not be escorted into exile, as Amos was, but more likely summarily killed, as was John.

The argument as to whether the man Joshua was or was not a prophet is, in the end, sterile. It matters more what he said and in this, I feel sure, he is a student of Hillel "after the spirit." Hillel died shortly after this Joshua was born, but left many disciples, and one of them could have been Joshua's teacher. Hillel said, "What is hateful to you, do not do to others," and Joshua said, "Whatsoever you wish that men would do to you, do even so to them." So we have here a brother Pharisee, even if from the North, doing midrash on great Hil-lel. And Joshua's midrash is not without value.

His followers make much of it, too much I deem. I prefer Hillel's rule because it calls upon us to respect the Law that God has set for us, that is, to stay within mutually agreed upon boundaries, and not impetuously to impose our will upon others, for good or ill. You know my saying, "Without the Law we would do as desire dictates, not what reason recommends." Yet within the fences of the Law there are times and situations, are there not, that call for action, not just passive observance?

Consider Joshua's parable that they call "the good Samaritan." Briefly, it says that a man beaten by robbers lay wounded by the road-side and was noticed, but not assisted, first by a priest, then by a Levite. Finally, a Samaritan passed by, tended the man's wounds, brought him to an inn and gave money to the innkeeper to care for him until he was well enough to resume his journey.

It might be wished that he had called it "the good priest and the bad Levite," or some such thing and changed the protagonists accordingly. Samaritans above all other Northerners have had an evil name here in the South since they contested Ezra's leadership of those who returned from exile, my family among them.

I can, however, defend the parable told in just the way Joshua told it. The actors in this little drama represent what you Greek-speakers will call the "alpha and omega" of people in society, in other words, all of us from highest to lowest. Priests and Levites, most of whom are Sadducees, still hold to the notion that whatever happens to one is what one deserves, be it good or ill. One need not repair to the Ten Words [Commandments] and claim that the man was punished for evils done by his ancestors [Exod. 20:5], though this was long held to be true and I have heard it espoused even today. These days, most of us hold with Ezekiel [chap. 18] that no person dies for the sin of another, rather each for his own, but it might still be maintained that stopping to help a wounded man would be interfering with the will of God; if he is wounded, he must have deserved it!

I cannot fault the conclusion, but reject the premise. Despite what some say against learning from your Greek friends,[12] a bit of Greek logic here would show the fallacy of the priest's and the Levite's argument. An effect, what follows an act, may have many causes. And even if the priests and Levites were correct and those hurt are justly punished, could we not say that to help the injured of any sort among us is to honor Micah's injunction [6:8] to "love mercy" even as we "do justice"?

On Yom Kippur we must first seek forgiveness from our fellows whom we have wronged during the past year. Could it be that failure to do right is a wrong? If we are made in God's image, surely we may practice a bit of the mercy which we pray he will show us. Is not that what is meant by Micah's "walking humbly with your God"? But for the *hesed*[13] of God, we might be the wounded man and not the sound ones who passed him by.

Since the parable is to apply to all people, Joshua did properly in constructing it as he did.

Do not think that I have become a Joshua follower any more than I am a romanizer. I admire the Romans for their skill in war and even more so for their magnificent public works, vanities that they are, these things men build. Herod's Temple is a wonder of the world, but

---

[12] He seems to be referring to what became a rabbinic dictum proscribing the study of Greek language. See Saul Lieberman, *Greek in Jewish Palestine* (New York: Feldheim, 1965), 16.

[13] The word *hesed* means "unmerited or uncompelled reward."

he did not live to dwell in the palace he built by the Salt [Dead] Sea. I would not accept from them, as have some of us, citizenship in their evil empire if freely offered. No, dear Philo, one may admire what one does not like and there are things about Joshua that remain troubling.

For one thing, he was not married. Jeremiah, of course, never married, but this he says [Jer. 16:2] was a command from God. The first scriptural commandment is "be fruitful and multiply" [Gen. 1:28] and I hold that the way to end evil is not for all of us simply to forbear from bearing, as it were, and thus put an end to humanity root and branch. As I have said, "Even if all mankind succeeded in destroying ourselves, no one would learn anything from it." Not even all of the Essenes are unmarried and he was not one of them as, I think, John was.

Early in Joshua's life, his family thought him deranged [Mark 3:21], so perhaps no woman's family would have him, but I cannot believe that, since, as I earlier said, he had many female followers. He seems rather to have cultivated them as well as tax collectors, lepers, and, of all things, Roman soldiers. That aside, some of the things he said, if they have been accurately retold, are troubling and not just to me.

It is reported that right before he was arrested he identified the bread and wine of his meal with his own flesh and blood. This proved to be too much even for some of his disciples, many of whom left him at that point [John 6:52ff.]. Little wonder! We go to great lengths not to consume the blood of animals, how much more so would we abhor to consume the blood of fellow men? His metaphor, you see, is too close to the bone.

Joshua is also said to have counseled that we "love our enemies," and this, I think, is so contrary to human nature that it asks the impossible. I admire the Romans, but I do not love them and some, like Pilate, I always hated. In this, I recognize that I do no honor to our Law, which asks that we hate the deed, not the doer. "O you who love the Lord, hate evil," as the Psalm says [97:10]. It does not tell us to hate our enemies as Joshua is reported to have said of us [Matt. 5:43]. I think the words have been placed in his dead mouth by some overzealous follower eager to besmirch us. Many purport to speak in the name of the dead, those who cannot be approached for verification of their words.

I ought to reserve my hatred for those who know the Law and yet decline to follow its precepts and ordinances, wicked men of Israel, not those lesser folk without the Law,[14] even the Laws of Noah, from

---

[14] Critics have been quick to point out that this is an obvious pilferage of Kipling's

whom proper behavior can hardly be expected. Hating Pilate, then, is my weakness and I own it. I hope you will not think less of me for it. Let us, in any case, move on to other matters.

Joshua said that he who looks at his brother with anger in his heart is as one who murders his brother and, again, he who looks at a woman with lust in his heart is as one who commits adultery with her. I read the Ten Words in Deuteronomy, part of the Northern Torah that was deemed binding upon us in Josiah's time, as saying exactly this. So it is not to be wondered at that Joshua, a Northerner, should uphold this high standard. Politically, their rejection of the House of David was ill-conceived—witness all the assassinations and usurpations that marked their history—but their moral stance, it must be admitted, is often higher than what we practice here.

However, such a commandment asks of us that we be as pure of mind and heart as we are in deed and that is a standard few, if any of us, North or South, can reach. It is enough, I think, that we refrain from breaking the Law though, upon occasion, we inwardly gnash our teeth in self-restraint.

On the other hand, in positive matters we are called upon to do more than just what the Law commands, for example, in leaving corners of our fields unharvested so that the poor may with honor glean from them. The rabbis have established a standard for this, one part in sixty, but they say that he who does only this has not really done enough.[15] In all this it matters but little what our intention is, more that we do at least what the Law ordains, and so with the rest of the commandments as well. As the people said to Moses, "We will do and by doing understand" [Exod. 24:3], or so I understand the true meaning of the verse.

Feeling ourselves unable even to do the whole Law ineluctably leads to setting the Law aside as undoable. Already I hear that Joshua's chief disciple, a man called Cephas [Peter], has declared that Gentile converts need not maintain the food Laws that God so clearly gave us. These are eminently doable; some among us seem even to delight in the most detailed and complicated of observances. I do not tithe mint and cumin, but I understand those who do. You know, Joshua may also have said as much. "Unless your piety exceed that of the Pharisees you shall not enter into the kingdom of heaven" [Matt. 5:20].

"lesser breeds without the Law" and that the author exposes himself as no earlier than a late-nineteenth- or early-twentieth-century author.

[15] Mishnah *Peah* ("Gleanings") 1:2.

In saying this, Joshua did not intend for us to set the Law aside. He said, "Do not think that I have come to abolish the Law, but to fulfill it" [Matt. 5:17]. This I comprehend. Ever since Amos the prophets have exhorted us not to let ritual piety serve in the place of good deeds, but to be, as it were, the foundation and platform upon which the edifice of good deeds, grander than any Roman building, might be erected.

I know that nothing on this earth remains as it was forever, no matter how much some might wish it. Our own movement, the Pharisees, is barely two hundred years old and the Essenes but little older. When they left Jerusalem it had indeed become a den of vipers with priestly families going to Antioch to bribe the Syrians for preferment. And after the Syrians had been expelled, Simon Maccabee had himself proclaimed High Priest though his family was not eligible for the office. Here I must point out that the connection between politics and religion, of which the Romans are so chary, was highly visible.

Some changes are not for the better, but others are. Hillel had to change the Law dealing with the extension of credit as the Sabbatical year approached, else the rich would have declined to lend money to the poor, to the complete impoverishment and ruin of the latter.[16] But that is a small thing compared to what is now being suggested in the matter of accepting Gentile converts.

Though I remain unconvinced that our father Jacob proselytized among the Egyptians, who regarded our ancestors as particularly vile, converts we have had; Ruth comes easily to mind, and some among the Greeks, whose translations of Scripture you may know, have been moved to convert by their own work! Many in the Roman empire have converted to our faith; many more would likely have done so but for their aversion to circumcision.

Converts have been people who gladly accepted our ways; they did not ask that the ancient ways be changed so that they might more easily attach to themselves the proud name of Jew [Hebrew *yehudi*]. Others have joined themselves to our communities and practice as we do without the formality of conversion, and we welcome them, but a flood of Gentile "converts" who magically dispense with central pillars of the Law such as circumcision and *kashrut* [Jewish dietary laws] might wash us away. Most Jews know that even full adherence to the Law is not sufficient for salvation. "Our deeds build for us—noth-

---

[16] This is the legal fiction known as *prozbul* ("corridor"), by which debts are "sold" to a third party only for the duration of the Sabbatical year.

ing," as we say on Yom Kippur, but deeds are nonetheless necessary. These deeds, the *mitzvot,* are God-given, though most would commend themselves to any right-thinking person—do not murder, do not kidnap,[17] do not swear falsely.

Since Moses' time, ours has been a government of Law, not of men. Tradition tells us that before the monarchy was established there was a period during which "each man did what was right in his own eyes" [Judg. 21:25]. We call this *tohu v'vohu,* "chaos," but anarchy is closer to the mark here. If we were progressively to strip away sections of the Law, we should soon be left with nothing but what each person individually saw fit to do. Even King David could not set himself above the Law with impunity.

I do not think that Joshua intended to set himself above the Law, but where one man teaches in his own authority others will come to teach in theirs, and sooner or later each will do what is right in his own eyes. His chief disciples are Galilean fisherfolk, hardly the kind of people from whom sound interpretation can be expected.

Let me not, however, demean these people. They must be Jews, for they argue amongst themselves as much as we do! Joshua could not have intended this. The last thing we need now is another faction, especially one that the Romans could find dangerous. How then might we sift Joshua's wheat from the chaff of his followers and so prevent a breach between us? And, I might add, avoid Roman wrath cascading down upon the just and the unjust alike. Where is the leader with the wisdom of Solomon and the strength of Samson to pull the pillars of our own house back toward one another without the roof falling in upon us?

If the Almighty, blessed be He, does not smite these Romans with plagues such as He visited upon Pharaoh and thus cause them to loose their grip on us, then I fear we will continue to witness revolts. And as a raven may provoke an eagle until, at length, the eagle turns and tears the raven apart, we too shall be torn apart. I should like to be more optimistic, dear Philo, but even as the passing of many years has dimmed my eyesight, the sight of my mind is clearer and this is what it sees.

---

[17] Reading "Do not steal" in the Ten Commandments as "Do not kidnap" is suggested by the parallel verse Exod. 21:16 and the observation that simple theft would be out of place in the context of crimes with capital implications, such as murder, adultery, and false witness. What is intended here is "Do not abduct [in order to enslave]."

8

A Jewish Reflection
on Images of Jesus

DANIEL F. POLISH

FOR JEWS, THE DISCUSSION OF JESUS is theologically the opposite of necessary. Jesus talk is as organic a part of Jewish thought
as, for instance, the discussion of the Hindu god Krishna.

There is one qualification to that statement—and it is an important
one. Jesus bears on Jewish life in ways that Krishna or the Buddha or
a pantheon of beings in other traditions do not. Those ways are not
theological but historical.

It is a commonplace by now to note that Christianity emerged
from within the Jewish tradition. Christian Scriptures presuppose, in
ways self-evident and obscure, the teachings of the Hebrew Bible.
The forms of Christian practice were appropriated from or modeled
after Jewish practice. Elements of Christian faith were appropriated
intact from the mother tradition. Other elements arose in conscious
contradistinction to Jewish teaching.

Nor was Jewish tradition itself left unaffected by the derivation of
the newer teaching from itself. Scholars have indicated manifold ways
in which Jewish tradition modified itself to preserve, accentuate, or
underscore its distinctiveness from Christianity. And, of course, in still
later times, Jewish practice returned the flattery of imitation by
appropriating various Christian practices into its own repertoire.

Jewish life shares with Christianity what it does not, in the main,
share with the religious traditions of Japan, China, or India—an
ongoing history of interaction. The Christian faith impacted on the
Jews through the instrumentality of the behaviors of Christians. What
has been characterized as the lachrymose aspect of Jewish history was

94

ideologically driven by Christian teaching: Crusades, Inquisitions, disputations, and the burning of Jewish sacred texts, expulsions, and pogroms all took place in societies that were, in every sense, Christian. Thus the person of Jesus was imposed on the consciousness of the Jewish people in a way that Krishna or the Buddha was not. Jews have lived the last two millennia predominantly in a Christian environment.

Environmental circumstances thus made Jesus part of Jewish consciousness. But, to return to the original point, nothing intrinsic to Jewish faith would require Jews to reflect on Jesus at all. But living, as indeed we do, in a Christian milieu would arouse the curious attention of Jews. So the question of the Jewish conception of Jesus is not beyond the pale of Jewish discourse.

MESSIANIC AND OTHER IMAGES

What, then, do Jews make of Jesus? The very question was first posed by Jesus himself, who is reported to have asked, "Who do people say that I am?" (Mark 8:27). Jesus as Second Person of the Trinity is clearly an idea that the average Jew cannot even begin to comprehend. Even scholars who can define the concept are not Jewishly drawn to embrace it. It is, simply put, incompatible with the Jewish understanding of monotheism. There is nothing in an honest reading of Jewish tradition that would conduce toward it.

Jesus as Messiah is not quite as easy to parse. For there is in Jewish tradition a rich history of individuals who claimed to be—and often were accepted by many as being—the Messiah. Indeed, there are Jewish groups in our own time who flirt with—or cross the boundaries into—making messianic claims for their venerated leaders. From Bar Kochba in the time of the rabbis to Shabbtai Tzvi in seventeenth-century Turkey, with many other claimants in between and beyond, people have presented themselves to be the promised one. Some even won themselves enormous followings. The significant difference between Jewish teaching and Christianity, however, is that the normative community has dismissed all these claimants as "false messiahs."

Jewish tradition, indeed, inculcated a profound skepticism of anyone who claimed to be the Messiah. But with regard to Jesus in particular, an extensive literature exists devoted to elaborating the ways that (*pace* Jews for Jesus and other messianic Jewish groups) the New Testament account of the career of Jesus in no way "fulfills the prophecies" of the Hebrew Bible or the anticipations of the Jewish community of antiquity. More significantly, the very idea that the Messiah has already arrived is diametrically contrary to what Jewish tradition teaches about the Messiah and the world as it will be after the Messiah's arrival. The traditional promise of peace, wholeness, human perfection, and plenty as the hallmark of the coming of the Messiah seems, sadly, still unfulfilled in Jewish eyes and makes implausible the claim that the Messiah has already arrived.

Thus, stripped of theological or messianic implications to Jewish understanding, we are thrown back to what Protestant Christianity, at least, has characterized as the quest for the historical Jesus. The challenge itself is a daunting one. Various Christian writers have struggled to identify a historical Jesus only to yield an array of varying and contradictory depictions. One group of scholars has sought to identify the "authentic words" of a historical Jesus in the Gospels only to settle on a virtual handful of utterances from the abundant statements attributed to him. A historical Jesus is difficult enough for a faithful Christian to delineate. How much the harder for a Jew conditioned to be skeptical in this particular realm.

What would a historical Jesus add to the universe of Jewish life? Jesus as itinerant rabbi? Most of the ideas attributed to Jesus in the Gospels are of a piece with teachings we find attributed to other teachers of that time. The Beatitudes and the Lord's Prayer both have many parallels in the words of contemporary teachers. Even the famous pronouncement in Matthew 22:36 about "the great commandment" is of a piece with the familiar rabbinic rhetorical convention of seeking the one great "clal"—overarching principle of biblical teaching.

Jesus as miracle-working preacher? Even here there was already significant precedent in the Jewish community of Jesus' day. Jesus as rebel against the prevailing norms of his community or teacher of an idiosyncratic interpretation of his tradition? The Talmud is replete with accounts of numbers of such people in the Judea of Jesus' day. Jesus as a political agitator who couched his incendiary message in a religious idiom? Even here there are ample enough instances of other people at that time filling this role. If our understanding of the historical Jesus is to be modeled on such familiar historical types, he does not bring anything to the universe of Jewish experience that would not be present without him. There is nothing in any of the various renditions of the historical Jesus that adds to the sum total of Jewish experience or changes our sense of what is possible within it.

THE IMAGE OF THE INFANT

There is one Jesus, however, that does not have a precedent in Jewish life: baby Jesus. The Jesus who is the focus of Christmas rather
than Easter. The Jesus who is literally at the center of so much Christian art and the subject of so much music has no analogy in Jewish
tradition. The infant Moses does appear at the beginning of the book
of Exodus—but with remarkable brevity. He becomes the subject of
precious little rabbinic elaboration—and is nowhere adored. Baby
Jesus, on the other hand, is often central and consistently unavoidable
as a component of Christian religious life.

How are we to understand the power of Baby Jesus in the Christian tradition? Like most religious rites and symbols, there is more
going on with this phenomenon than meets the eye—or may be
accessible to the conscious mind of the religious practitioner. It is eas-
iest for me, as an outside observer, to make sense of this religious phenomenon on analogy with a specific aspect of the religious tradition
of India. In that religious universe, we encounter the concept of
bhavas: the various modes of loving God. The various modalities of
human love that we experience in our own lives can become understood as intimations or analogies of the emotions we can feel toward
God. The various Krishna-centered expressions of faith articulate a
number of such modes or *bhavas.* The love we feel for family and
friends can be a way we understand what it is to love God. The emotions servants feel for their master, the feelings of a friend, or of a
lover, all are transposed onto emotions we can feel for God. And
among the *bhavas* is the love of parents for their child.

Even the compassion, the overwhelming sense of tenderness or
protectiveness we feel for our children, offers a glimpse to the religious seeker of what it means to love God. In the Hindu tradition,
this religious posture is related to the experience of Nanda and
Yasoda, the parents of Krishna, the incarnation of the god Vishnu.
Their love for their child was transposed into the love of the deity
whose manifestation he was. And their way of loving became a model
for all the devotees of Krishna in their relation to their deity. It is
understood that the experience of the powerful tenderness of parental
love is a portal through which all of us can pass in our quest to experience the profound sense of connectedness to God to which we
attach the label "love."

Significantly, Jewish religious literature offers us the opportunity to experience emotions that parallel the *bhavas* of India. The emotion of slavery to God is evoked in the life journey of Moses, who, after raising the people above Egyptian servitude, was eulogized as the servant/slave of God. The image of God as parent, and the filial devotion we humans feel to God in that guise, are frequently evoked in the Jewish liturgy. The powerful tug of true friendship is epitomized in the love of Jonathan and David. Traditional Jewish commentators understood the Song of Songs, which is devoted to "the flames of passion" that join lovers, as a metaphor for the love that unites God and the people of Israel. But that other great love, the love of parent for child, finds no expression in the religious life of the Jewish people. There is in Judaism no means to transmute that powerful human experience into religious affirmation.

It is this religious-emotional experience, lacking in their own tradition, which Jews can recognize and appreciate in the Christian tradition. For surely that *bhava* of love for the newborn is what is at the root of the veneration of the infant Jesus. Devotion to Jesus as a baby is encountered with such regularity and radiates such intensity that, articulated or not, it reflects more than an incidental dimension of Christian life. More than a mere curiosity or historical allusion, the power of the infant Jesus motif serves as a vehicle for finding powerful emotions within our own experience which can be transmuted— "lifted up" to serve a higher religious purpose. The love parents feel for their own infant becomes transmuted, through the engagement with Baby Jesus, to the love they can feel for God. The infant—in Christianity, Baby Jesus—becomes a doorway for the intense expression of a greater love.

This vehicle for religious expression which we encounter in Christianity is, strikingly, without equivalent or parallel in the Jewish tradition. Seeing it as part of the religious tradition of our neighbors, Jews are left to appreciate and admire it from afar. Here is one instance where the figure of Jesus offers one form of spirituality available to Christians that has no analogy in Jewish tradition or in the lived religious experience of Jews.

What, then, can Jews do with this understanding? In seeing parental love as a doorway into the love of God, they can appreciate the love they feel for their own children from a new perspective. Understanding the love of one's child as reflected in the Baby Jesus *bhava* in Christianity, Jews can experience their own parental love as an opportunity to experience a new dimension of devotion to God that is as valid for Jews as it is for Christians or worshipers of Krishna.

9

Jesus, the Rabbis, and
the Image on a Coin

ARTHUR WASKOW

ONE OF THE BEST-KNOWN, and most puzzling, stories of Jesus' life is the tale of an encounter concerning the image on a coin. The story appears in Matthew 22:15-22, Mark 12:13-17, and Luke 20:19-26. It is almost the same in all three places.

According to the story, some of Jesus' opponents among the Pharisees sent people to trick Jesus into saying something that would provide a pretext for his arrest. (The Pharisees were the religious grouping who initiated the reforms and reinterpretations of Torah that became Rabbinic Judaism, and who in general sided with the poor against the Roman occupation and its allies in the Jewish "establishment." Some scholars today see Jesus as himself a Pharisee, among their "radical" wing. In that case, "the Pharisees" as a body were probably not his opponents, but some among them probably were.)

One of them asked him, "Rabbi, we know that what you speak and teach is sound; you pay deference to no one, but teach in all honesty the life path that God requires. Give us your ruling on this: Are we or are we not permitted to pay taxes to the Roman emperor?"

Jesus saw through their trick and said to them, "Show me a silver coin. Whose image is on this coin, and whose inscription?"

Let us pause for a moment. What was the "trick"? Since the coin had Caesar's image on it, with the inscription "*Divus*"—God—use of the coin might constitute idolatry in Jewish law and thus be forbidden. But by Roman law the taxes must be paid, so the "trick" was that by answering one way, Jesus would break Jewish law; by answering the other way, he would break Roman law. Either way, he would be subject to arrest.

But Jesus had not quite answered. Instead, he had answered the question with a question. (Says the folklore, this is an old Jewish habit. As it is taught, "Why does a Jew answer a question with a question?" Answer: "Why not?")

According to Matthew, Mark, and Luke, Jesus answered: "Whose image is on this coin?"

The man who had challenged him answered, "Caesar's!"

And then Jesus did respond: "So give to Caesar what is Caesar's, and to God what is God's."

This answer, say Matthew, Mark, and Luke, took his opponents by surprise, and they went away and left him alone.

But for two thousand years, Christians have argued over what this answer means. What is Caesar's, and what is God's? Does the answer suggest two different spheres of life, one ruled by Caesar and one by God? Does it mean to submit to Caesar's authority in the material world, while adhering to God in the spiritual world? How do we discern the boundary? Why did the questioners go away? Was it simply because Jesus had avoided the horns of the dilemma they had brought and so could not be arrested for his answer? Or was there a deeper meaning to the answer? Is the answer simply a koan, an answer that forces the questioner to seek a deeper question or break through into enlightenment?

Now let us introduce a passage from the Babylonian Talmud, that compilation of the wisdom, the debates and dialogues, the puns and the parables, the philosophic explorations and the practical decisions of thousands of rabbis living over a period from about the beginning of the Common Era to about 500 C.E., some in Babylonia and some in the Land of Israel.

Our passage from the Talmud appears in *Sanhedrin* 38a (Soncino trans., p. 240):

> Our Rabbis taught: Adam, the first human being, was created as a single person to show forth the greatness of the Ruler Who is beyond all Rulers, the Blessed Holy One. For if a human ruler [like the Roman Emperor] mints many coins from one mold, they all carry the same image, they all look the same. But the Blessed Holy One shaped all human beings in the Divine Image, as Adam was shaped in the Divine Image [Gen. 1:27], "*b'tzelem*

elohim," "in the Image of God." And yet not one of them resembles another.

Let us absorb this. The rabbis drew an analogy between the image a human ruler puts on the coins of the realm and the image the Infinite Ruler puts on the many "coins" of humankind. The very diversity of human faces shows forth the unity and infinity of God, whereas the uniformity of imperial coins makes clear the limitations on the power of an emperor.

Now reread the story of Jesus with a single line and gesture added: "Whose image is on this coin?" asks Jesus.

His questioner answers, "Caesar's!"

Then Jesus puts his arm on the troublemaker's shoulder and asks, "And Whose Image is on this *coin?"*

Perhaps the troublemaker mutters an answer; perhaps he does not need to. Not till after this exchange does Jesus say, "Give to Caesar what is Caesar's and to God what is God's."

Now there is a deeper meaning to the response and to the troublemaker's exit. Jesus has not just avoided the question and evaded the dilemma: He has answered, in a way that is much more radical than if he had said either "Pay the tax" or "Don't pay the tax," a way that is profoundly radical but gives no obvious reason for arrest.

Jesus has not proposed dividing up the turf between the material and the spiritual. He has redefined the issue:

"Give your whole self to the One Who has imprinted divinity upon you!—You, you who are one of the rabbis, my brother rabbi—you know that is the point of this story! All I have done is to remind you!"

The coin of the realm will matter very little, if the troublemaker listens.

So the questioner walks away, suddenly profoundly troubled by the life question that he faces.

We might ask, why does the line I have inserted not appear in the three versions of the story that we have? It is possible that the line was censored out, as Christian tradition faced both the threats of an empire to shatter this religion and the invitation of an empire to become the established church. Or it is possible that Jesus never needed to say the words, because his Pharisee questioners understood the point perfectly well? After all, on the basis of the passage in the Talmud, we can easily imagine that the teaching comparing God's image on Adam to the emperor's image on the coinage was already well known among the rabbis.

For me, this reading of the two passages—one from the Talmud, one from the New Testament—brings with it two levels of greater wholeness, deeper meaning. The first level is that each of the two passages enriches the meaning of the other. Read together, they fuse the spiritual and the political, instead of splitting the world into two domains. In this reading, the claim of the divine Ruler to rule over an emperor includes the political realm. God can create infinite diversity and eternal renewal, and so is far richer than the imperial treasury—which can create only uniformity and repetition. But this is not just a philosophical or biological point. *Because* God rules over all rulers, *because* God calls forth from every human being a unique face of God, each human being must follow God, not Caesar.

Without the passage from the rabbis of the Talmud, this meaning of Jesus' response remains unclear. Without the tale of Jesus, the Talmud passage seems "merely theological" without a thrust into everyday life. To become whole and create wholeness in the world, the passages need each other. Yet the editors and framers of the Talmud and the New Testament took care that both passages appear in neither text. They were walled out against each other. So the second level of wholeness that this reading teaches me is the importance of mending the fringes of the Jewish and Christian traditions.

In Jewish tradition, what makes a garment holy is the careful, conscious tying of *tzitzit*—a certain kind of fringe on the corners of a piece of clothing. Just as a landholder must let the poor and the landless harvest what grows in the corners of his field, so these corners of a garment remind us that it is not that good fences make good neighbors; good fringes make good neighbors.

What makes a fringe a fringe is that it is a mixture of my own cloth and the universe's air. What makes *tzitzit* is that they are tied according to a conscious, holy pattern—not left as helter-skelter fringes. They are fringes that celebrate their fringiness.

That is what we need between traditions. Not the dissolution of all boundaries nor the sharpness of a wall, a fence, but conscious, holy fringes.

I think these two passages are *tzitzit* of both traditions, reaching out as threads of connection that also honor the two different garments on which they are tied. If we fail to tie such sacred fringes or let them become invisible, the garments lose their holiness. So let us turn with newly open eyes to see what Rabbi Jesus and the rabbis of the Talmud shared, as well as where they differed.

10

What Manner of Man?

HOWARD AVRUHM ADDISON

WHAT MANNER OF MAN IS THIS? Crowds gather around him wherever he goes. Some seek his healing powers; others just hope to touch his cloak. Who is he? I've heard tell that he has performed miracles like Elisha of old did at Baal Shalisha, taking but a few loaves and providing food for the hungry throngs (2 Kings 4:42-44). It is said that his is the soul of John the Baptist come back to life so that the call to repentance might again be heard in our land. His closest disciples swear that they saw him standing next to Moses and Elijah, holding converse with them. Do they really believe that he is the rightful successor to our holy liberator and to the fiery prophet from Tishbe? Or do they want us to believe that those two respond to their master's call? What manner of man is this and who do they really think he might be?

What kind of teacher is this? They say that he speaks with a spiritual authority far beyond that shown by masters of the law. His example and message bring God's love to the downtrodden. But this sounds much like the teachings of our recent patriarch, the gentle, caring Hillel. I heard that Hillel invited his disciples to bathe with him to teach that God cherishes not only our souls but our bodies as well. His rulings encourage working people to sing God's praises at dawn from scaffold and tree, rather than endanger their livelihood by charging them to stop and descend for formal prayer. Legend holds that he once secured a horse and groom to save an impoverished gentleman from shame and then ran three miles himself playing the groom when the appointed servant didn't appear. His invitation to

those wishing to enter the world of Torah—never treat others in a
way that you consider personally distasteful—now let's study.[1]

In the face of callous opposition, their master showed bravery and
compassion by transcending the strictures of Shabbat to heal the sick
in synagogue on that holy day. Yet those who tried to shout him
down knew little of our traditions. Did they not remember the principle that saving lives pushes aside Sabbath prohibition? Was it not
Mattathias, priest of Modein and his Maccabee sons who taught us
this in their battle against the Hellenist Syrians almost two hundred
years ago? (1 Macc. 2:41). Perhaps he needed to remind them and us
of God's healing love, that God's own Torah tells us the *mitzvot* were
given that we should choose life (Deut. 30:19).

Speaking of preserving life, I've heard tell that at times his disciples
have plucked ears of corn on Shabbat or eaten without ritually washing their hands. When asked, he responded, "King David's men illic-
itly ate the consecrated shew bread when they fled the wrath of King
Saul. . . . Nothing that goes into a person's mouth brings defilement,
only that which comes out of one's mouth can defile" (Mark 2:23-
27; 7:15).

His words are compelling. Surely lies and hurtful words and mean
acts defile. But if God truly cares about how we act, can't God's concern also extend to how we eat? To wash before a meal is to conse-
crate our hands to divine service so that all might achieve the level of
priests preparing for the offering. To bless our food is to acknowledge
the presence and goodness of the Creator before and after we take a
bite. In an emergency David's men did eat of the shew bread rather
than expose themselves to death. However, responses to emergencies
can differ from the rules that we might need to sanctify our daily lives.

He condemns scribes who offer long prayers and then plunder the
weak, who provide loopholes so that children can exempt their earn-
ing from their parents, in effect demeaning rather than honoring
father and mother. He is right to expose those whose legal casuistry
subverts the spirit of Torah. He is a lot like Jeremiah, who attacked
those who would use the Temple as a robber's hideout, seeking in it
ritual sanctuary from the consequences of their immorality (Jer.
7:11). He condemns the Pharisees, often equating these scholastics
with hypocrites. Israel's real sages share that view, telling us to be on
guard against those whose ostentatious piety is but a mask for the

---

[1] For the tales of Hillel, see *Leviticus Rabbah* 24:3 and the Babylonian Talmud
Ketubot 67b and *Shabbat* 31a.

meanness that lies within (*B. Sotah* 22b; Mishnah *Sotah* 3:4). Centuries ago Ezekiel wrote of a vision in which God tells the angels of desolation to begin the destruction of Jerusalem, not merely at the sanctuary but with those who bemoan abomination, but do nothing to protect the sanctity of God's name (Ezek. 9).

He tells us that the Torah sanctioned divorce only as a concession to our hardness of heart, that remarriage is tantamount to adultery. Must couples, after mightily trying to reconcile, be condemned to a life of misery? He's right. There will always be those who will cast off their spouses at the slightest provocation. The prophet Malachi had pictured the Temple altar itself weeping over the proliferation of groundless divorce (Mal. 2:14-16). However, the greatest of the early Pharisees, Shimon ben Shetach, offered another solution. He made dissolving marriage difficult and recognized its ongoing obligations by enjoining a minimum of support that a wife must be paid following divorce (*B. Ketuvot* 82b).

He speaks to us about losing our lives as they are, that we might gain our souls. If we have been living falsely, chasing after vanities, then he's right; mendacity and vanity should die away. But is the choice always so stark? Can we not also find God in the mundane activities of daily life? Surely the hundred blessings our sages enjoin us to recite daily call us to such awareness. And cannot even our own self-interest play a role in bringing forth new life and knowledge and progress? (*Genesis Rabbah* 9:7).

What sort of leader is this? I hate the way some elders try to trap him with malicious inquiries. They asked him if Judeans should pay Caesar's tax. Answer yes and he betrays his fellow countrymen in this oppressed, occupied land. Answer no and he can be accused of sedition to the prefect. I would have loved to see those elders' faces when he replied, "Render unto Caesar that which is Caesar's and to God that which is God's." But does he really have to eat with publicans, those who acquire concessions from Rome to collect taxes and then, for profit, squeeze their fellow Judeans far beyond the rates Rome requires? I admire how he extends himself to society's pariahs. True, it is the sick, not the morally healthy, that require healing. But has his companionship cured many publicans of their greed? Or does he give their plunder validation just by his presence?

No one can doubt that the Temple is not the sacred institution it should be. Some high priests do not survive the intrigue that goes on there for even one year. One such priest was so unqualified that he couldn't even understand Hebrew. Imagine, they had to prepare him for the Yom Kippur rites in our current spoken tongue, Aramaic (*B. Yoma* 116).[2] Yet worshipers come from many lands and need supervised currency exchanges so that they are not cheated when they purchase sacrificial animals or need to convert money to buy goods. In theory, he was right. God's Temple should be a place of prayer, not commerce. But what was accomplished by overthrowing the money changers' tables? Did the vulnerable, whose cause he advocates, gain more protection on that day?

One thing is for sure. He has the ability to reach out and touch people from all walks and stations of life. He brings comfort to the discomfited and has a compelling way of discomfiting the comfortable. Is it just coincidence that four other of his male associates share the name of his chief disciple, Simon? That a bereaved woman he consoled and a woman from society's margins are both called Mary, the same as his mother? Or, through association, is he teaching us that first rank in his retinue can be open to all, that it is the bereaved and bereft who truly give birth to what he is? Now that he is in prison I hear that his cellmate is a criminal named Barabbas. How fitting that even there, among the inmates, he can recognize a Barabbas, "son of the Father."

What manner of man was this? When his intimates returned to his tomb, his body was nowhere to be found. Some would proclaim him the Messiah risen from the dead. Personally, I am not sure what can be believed. I look around and have yet to glimpse a lion lying down with a lamb. There still seem to be more swords than plowshares, more spears than pruning hooks. But our sages speak often of *techiyat ha metim*, resurrection of the dead (Mishnah *Sanhedrin* 10:1), so why shouldn't his devotees believe that he has been the first to rise? They say that he will return to establish God's kingdom visibly on earth. Many others think the anointed One, son of David, has yet to come. Who's right? I guess we'll just have to wait and see.

---

[2] Daniel is the only book written in Aramaic.

PART THREE

PERSONAL VIEWS

11

The "J" Word

ALLEN SECHER

THE PHONE RINGS IN MY STUDY.

"Rabbi. This is Sherri Bernstein, Marcia Bernstein's mother. You're marrying Sean McCarthy and her at the Drake Hotel on Sunday. I just thought that we might get to know each other a bit beforehand so that we're not strangers at the wedding."

"That's a great idea, Sherri. Tell me something. Do you like Sean? And, will he make a good husband for Marcia?"

The answers are very much in the affirmative. We follow this with ten minutes of inconsequential banter about photographers, processional, and microphones. And then there's a deep breath. A pause. I'm ready.

"Tell me, Rabbi. I'm not quite sure how to ask this. But, will the priest? You know! Will he? You know!"

"Will he use the 'J' word, Sherri? No. It's a non-trinitarian service, cognizant of Jewish sensitivities."

There it is. The reason Sherri called in the first place. The banner headline. The "J" word. Sherri is not concerned about theology, philosophy, or ritual and by now has even reluctantly accepted the fact that Marcia is marrying a Catholic. But she knows full well that if she and her parents hear the word "Jesus" they will be both mortified and embarrassed. Why? Because the "J" word is the rallying cry of *The Enemy*.

I'm of Sherri's generation. I grew up in a heavily anti-Semitic small town in western Pennsylvania. Frequently I was on the receiving end of rocks aimed at my head and many of them connected. From the thrower came the shout "Jew bastard" or "Christ killer." On another occasion, I was refused emergency service in a Catholic hospital with the claim that there were no doctors present. And for me the heaviest blow came when I was not permitted to play on the high school golf team because the country club was restricted. The song I heard constantly and thus memorized as a kid was "Onward Christian Soldiers":

> Onward, Christian Soldiers,
> Marching as to war, with the cross of Jesus going on
>   before.
> Christ, the royal Master, leads against the foe;
> Forward into battle see his banners go!

The Enemy: Responsible for the Crusades, the Inquisition, and the pogroms. The Enemy who stood silently by while the Holocaust happened.

By marrying a "goy," daughter Marcia has gone over to the other side. She's consorting with *The Enemy*.

Never mind that Sean wasn't born during any of these events. He probably doesn't even know much about what they were. But we Jews have built-in memory sensors. Forget? Never. Forgive? That's something the rabbis talk about on Yom Kippur. Let the Goyim apologize. And apologize. And apologize.

Sherri Bernstein does have quite a legitimate, deeply emotional, though unexpressed concern. Sitting Shiva—cutting off her daughter as if she were dead—was never considered an option. Sherri favors the marriage. But she's embarrassed by it. Her memory of our history and her present desire to see her daughter happily married cause strongly conflicting emotions. The intermarriage has pressed powerful Jewish buttons that in her previous marginality, Sherri didn't even know she possessed.

INTERMARRIAGE IS A FACT OF LIFE

Sherri's daughter's marriage represents an ever-growing trend in the Jewish community. The 1990 National Jewish Population Study reported that 53 percent of the Jews who marry choose non-Jewish partners. Clearly that number has increased in the last ten years. Egon Mayer writes in *Love and Tradition*: "The greatest explosion of

Jewish intermarriage has occurred in America, precisely at a time of permissive parenting, sexual liberation and great Jewish self-assuredness. It has also occurred primarily among second, third and later generations of American-born Jews."[1] But putting your head in the sand, pontificating, and all the sermons in the world are not going to diminish reality. Intermarriage is a fact of life.

The "J" word will be a constant in Marcia McCarthy's life. With the proper support and encouragement, Marcia has a good chance of furthering her Judaism, even if it wasn't very solidly based to start with. If Bernstein marries Shapiro quite often there is no direct challenge to Jewish identity. More often than not, however, Rosh Hashana and Yom Kippur are remembered because of familiar tunes and the sound of the Shofar. And, questions 5 and 6 at Seder are "When do we sing Dayeynu?" and "When do we eat?"

Mayer continues:

Why is it that Jewishness seems to matter (*for the parents and grandparents*) most in intermarriages? All recollections of one's heritage are fragmentary. How frequently, how accurately, and with what degree of commitment one recalls his or her traditions, depends on a mixture of ingredients, the culture of the group, the history of the group and the biography of the individual.[2]

What the Jewish Population Study does not tell us is what the results were with couples and their children when the Jewish partner in an intermarriage had clergy support. Challenged by Sean's family, Marcia will be forced to explore her own roots. Those things she once took for granted and barely understood will now play a major role, and she will have to deal on an entirely different level with the dreaded "J" word.

My experience with couples who have struggled with their belief systems is that the Jewish partner often discovers a way to meet Jesus as a fellow Jew without coloring him with a Christian theology that would make him divine in some unique sense, the "Son of God" in a way that no one else can be.

---

[1] Egon Mayer, *Love and Tradition: Marriage Between Jew and Christian* (New York: Plenum, 1985), 102.

[2] Ibid., emphasis added.

Understanding first-century Jews helps. Those who told the early stories of Jesus were clearly drawing from their own Jewish roots. It was by looking at their own sacred heritage that they could recognize God's presence in this powerful man. And their way of responding to him was thoroughly Jewish. In the first century, and for centuries before, Jews had customarily called someone a "Son of God" if he was thought to be commissioned by God for some task or highly favored by God in some way. But this did not imply any overtones of divinity.[3] Jews then and now believe that all human beings are "children of God," made in God's "image and likeness." But when God is perceived as specially active through a particular person, then the divine presence is recognized in the singular: "son of God."[4]

So, in an intermarriage, if the Jewish partner can see Jesus in the light of first-century thinking rather than as the divinity he has become, the bridge to understanding in the marriage is less fraught with roadblocks. When Jesus is seen in his own appropriate Jewishness instead of as an enemy of the Jewish people—which, no matter what history has made of him, he himself would have denied—then not only does the intermarriage thrive, but the Jewish family's identity also benefits. When Sherri gave birth to Marcia, she never considered that her child would be marrying anyone but a fellow worshiper. But now, in this new confrontation, she and her family are awakening to a more thoughtful and reasoned Jewish consciousness. They are forced to deal with their heritage and, even more importantly, to appreciate it.

JESUS AT HOME

To begin to see Jesus in his own original context, one must know what it was like in the early decades of the first century. For centuries, the world for the Jew had not been what God had promised, and was now still further from being the longed-for perfect "kingdom." The Jews suffered under severe Roman domination. Their world was one of bitter desolation. One percent of the population—the rulers and aristocracy—controlled most of the property. Some of the land was in the hands of the small upper class, the priests and merchants. After all

---

[3] Much of this material is based on the work of John Dominic Crossan, primarily *Who Killed Jesus?* (San Francisco: HarperSanFrancisco, 1995).

[4] Psalm 2:7 and 2 Samuel 7:14 both use the term referring initially to David and Solomon.

this, whatever little remained was overly taxed by Rome and local despots in addition to the traditional tithes required to support the Temple. People saw their ancestral lands pass into the possession of foreigners through the debts they contracted to satisfy that taxation. Their world was characterized by poverty, oppression, and injustice. Where was God? Why did he not come to rescue them? No wonder Jesus was inspired to compose a prayer that asked for bread and cancellation of debts.

Into this scene of devastation and despair comes this articulate artisan, Jesus of Nazareth, who had heard of the prophets' dreams of a better world. In the teachings of his forefathers-in-Torah, he sees the instructions for creating such a world. Standing on a mountaintop, he cries out that the kingdom of God draws near; the time of deliverance has come: that the depressed will know better days; that those who mourn will find comfort; the hungry can look forward to full bellies; the rich will get their comeuppance; and peacemakers will prevail. Therefore he urges: Do not give up hope, for we shall all participate in this better world just as God has been promising. But there are things we must do to bring this about, he says, and he begins to outline them. Some recent commentators have called him "a peasant with an attitude." I prefer to view him as a tradition-inspired peasant revolutionary.

Jesus' *hasidim*, his disciples, thus begin what scholars now call the "Jesus movement" or the "kingdom-of-God movement," the nascent predecessor to Christianity. John Dominic Crossan says that the kingdom-of-God movement was "Jesus' program of empowerment" for dealing with the injustice, oppression, and poverty. This gross injustice was not just individual or personal. It was rather systemic and structural. Jesus, says Crossan, offered an alternative to the misery. Echoing in his passionate psyche was the familiar injunction of Torah, "Love your neighbor as yourself." He models an altruistic lifestyle of free healing—helping others without requiring anything in return, and a shared table with a place of social acceptance for all people without question, without regard to social classes, and with a generous sharing of one's riches with those in need. This "kingdom" would be a community based on love.

Love of neighbor was to Jesus "the second greatest commandment." The first, he said, was "to love God with all your heart, your soul (your essence, your life) and your might (your resources)." Jesus himself, says Crossan, lived "an alternative open to all who would accept it: a life of open healing and shared eating." It is in dialogue

with God that we create "the kingdom" and not in obeisance to
Caesar. Jesus' extended vision of this kingdom, according to Crossan,
was based on "fundamental egalitarianism, of human contact without
discrimination and divine contact without hierarchy."[5] On this basis
he strove to develop a "companionship of empowerment," in broad-
based communities that would live by these principles and, in their
mutual support of one another, would gradually escape the injustice,
oppression, and abject poverty from which they were suffering.

As individuals and communities found themselves empowered,
they were to empower others. This social reformer was determined to
bring on "the kingdom."

Is it any wonder, then, that in this inappropriate society, Jesus the
revolutionary would need to be eliminated? If you mess with our
standards of government, be prepared to suffer the consequences.

CAN WE RELATE TO THIS JESUS?

Is there a way for Sherri Bernstein to understand all of this? Perhaps.
For Sherri we need to create some more recent and relevant images.

In our contemporary history, we have seen the crucifixion of
countless populist preachers who reflect God's presence and who passionately want or wanted to change the world. Martin Luther King,
Mohandas Gandhi, Janus Korczak, Nelson Mandela, Hannah Senesh,
Cesar Chavez, Raul Wallenberg, Eleanor Roosevelt, Andrew Good-
man, James Chaney and Michael Schwerner, Paul Robeson, all of
whom suffered because they asked us to be "the chosen" and to enter
into the "kingdom of God." All of them were opposed, belittled, and
denied.

Perhaps I could say to Sherri, Let me tell you a personal story. I
was once jailed with a man in Albany, Georgia. While passively
demonstrating his dream for empowering the downtrodden and dis-
enfranchised, he was reviled, spat upon, jeered, pelted with rocks and
vegetables, set upon by dogs, man-handled by the local authorities,
and even denied basic needs. Yet his eye was constantly on the prize.
During our incarceration he never lost his sense of dignity, his pride,
his sense of self. His charisma lit our cell with rainbow hues. I sat mes-
merized as he spoke, hanging on his every word, willing to follow him
to the ends of the earth.

---

[5] Crossan, *Who Killed Jesus?* 211.

Was Martin Luther King one of "God's elect"? I don't doubt it for one moment. Could he walk on water? I thought he could. Crucified by an assassin's bullet, King remains one of the definitive martyrs of our time.

He stood on his own Mount in Washington, D.C., on that hot August day in 1963 and echoed the Beatitudes. Jesus had said in his Sermon, "Blessed are those who hunger and thirst for righteousness. . . . Blessed are the peacemakers. . . . Blessed are those who are persecuted for righteousness' sake: for theirs is the kingdom of heaven. . . . Blessed are you when people revile you and persecute you and utter all kinds of evil against you . . ." (Matt. 5:6, 9, 10, 11). In short, Jesus promises salvation for the dispossessed. And King pictures a situation no different from that which Jesus described to his audience:[6]

> The Emancipation Proclamation came as a great beacon light of hope to millions of Negro slaves who had been seared in the flames of withering injustice. . . . One hundred years later, the Negro still lives on a lonely island of poverty in the midst of a vast ocean of material prosperity. He is still languishing in the corners of American society and finds himself an exile in his own land. . . . We refuse to believe that the bank of justice is bankrupt . . . and we shall continue to work with the faith that unearned suffering is redemptive.

Salvation is preceded by the dream:

> I say to you, my friends, that in spite of the difficulties and frustrations of the moment, I still have a dream. . . . I have a dream that my four children will one day live in a nation where they will not be judged by the color of their skin but by the content of their character.
>
> I have a dream that one day every valley will be exalted, every hill and mountain shall be made low, the rough places will be made plain, and the crooked places will be made straight, and the glory of the Lord shall be revealed and all flesh shall see it together. . . . We will be able to speed up the time when all God's children, black men and white men, Jews and Gentiles, Protestants and Catholics, will be able to join hands and sing in

---

[6] Martin Luther King, "I Have a Dream," Washington, D.C., August 28, 1963.

the words of the old Negro spiritual, "Free at last! Free at last! Thank God Almighty, we are free at last!"

King is well versed in his traditions and leans on them for his eloquence. His standards of righteousness are fostered by biblical tradition. Like Jesus, he quotes the Torah, the Prophets, the Psalms.

Will the world build a religion around Martin Luther King? No. Respect? Yes. Love? Yes. Admiration? Absolutely. A role model for our children? For sure. A mentor and teacher? Without a doubt. This is the twenty-first not the first century. But, if she can see Jesus in King's light, or in the light of others like him, then Sherri's feelings may take on a different glow. Those heroic lives were value driven. That's what they stood for, what they preached, what they put into practice, and what they died for. In this world of Torah-centered dreamers, can Sherri find room for one more with utopian visions? Why can't Jesus have a place there too?

AFTER THE WEDDING

Can Sherri Bernstein live with this image and not cringe every time she hears the "J" word? I think so.

And what of Sean? Is it not possible that Marcia and her mother's new understanding and appreciation of this Jew they share in common might encourage his own devotion after the wedding?

Marcia and Sean are the vanguard of the new peacemakers. And "blessed are the peacemakers."

Jesus was "the son of God" and so are we all, Sherri. So are we all.

12

My Friend, Jesus

JOSEPH GELBERMAN

S OME JEWS BELIEVE that Jesus never existed. Others admit that he existed, but claim he was nothing more than a firebrand rabbi—certainly not the son of God as Christians believe.

My feeling is that both these arguments are irrelevant. What really matters is that millions of people believe that Jesus did exist and performed miracles. As for myself, I believe that Jesus did, indeed, exist and was a miracle worker.

In some ways I identify myself with Jesus. Jesus came from a very orthodox Jewish family, as I did. And, like myself, he one day decided that there was something not right with the Temple and its priesthood. He was not really attacking the priesthood and the religious customs of those days, but was opposed to those Temple priests who were turning their holy mission into a business. He was upset that the Temple often became a place for conducting business instead of worshiping God.

And let me tell you, I've seen that happen even today. People go to synagogue and, instead of being focused on prayer, can often be heard talking about business. That's not right!

I almost became part of that crowd. When I first came to this country from Hungary during the rise of Nazism, I served two or three congregations that were poor ones. They were located in storefronts and in basements, and there were no businessmen holding conversations about Wall Street in the back row. We were focused on our worship of the Almighty.

Then a few rich people came in and they were impressed by the way I led the service. They said, "You need a temple." The minute I

117

agreed to go upscale, I found myself spending more time discussing temple finances than the Torah with my wealthy benefactors.

And this is exactly what Jesus objected to. It's one of the reasons why I left a lucrative job as a rabbi in New Jersey to establish a very different kind of synagogue here in New York City—one without membership. I didn't want to worship or worry about money. I wanted to expend all my energies as a rabbi on the worship of God. Even today, my income comes from my counseling practice and not from my synagogue.

Jesus was a rebel, as I am. Even though I am very Hasidic (on the inside) in my religious thinking and certainly Jewish, my interest in studying other religions and the interfaith ministry I organized and continue to lead has incurred the wrath of a lot of my orthodox colleagues. I'm an outcast in orthodox circles, as Jesus was when he reached out beyond the mainstream of religious life.

But his rebellious spirit was in the tradition of Judaism—as is mine! After all, doesn't the Bible describe us as a "stiff-necked people"? He didn't like what he saw and he preached against it. Jesus was a rebel with a cause—perhaps even a member of the very ascetic Essene sect, who left Jerusalem for the mountains because of all the corruption they witnessed in the city. Unfortunately, the values which Jesus originally represented and what has become of Christianity since then are separated by many degrees. The following true story, I believe, sums it all up.

I was performing an interfaith marriage in Florida with a priest. Normally we shared the service, but this priest was traditional, and he said: "Let me do my thing and then you do your thing. In the meantime why don't you sit there in the front row until I finish?"

So I sat down, and usually when I sit down I always close my eyes and meditate. And this priest droned on and on. After a while I opened my eyes and in front of me I noticed a big crucifix on the wall. I'd never seen such a huge crucifix. I also noticed that Jesus was crying.

All of a sudden I heard a voice. Jesus was speaking to me. "Rabbi," he said, "what are you doing here?"

And I replied, "Rabbi Jesus, what are you doing here? And why are you crying?" Then we looked at each other for long moments. Jesus finally replied,

> Isn't it terrible that in my name they've killed millions of people? And I hear the cry of all their souls, all my brothers and sisters. Whenever you have a chance, tell them to stop killing in my name.

13

My Lunch with Jesus

LAWRENCE KUSHNER

WHAT LITTLE I KNOW ABOUT JESUS I learned from one man. R. was the one who first helped me, over a quarter century ago, understand about how God might really become a person. He and I were then young clergymen; he was the Episcopal priest and I was the rabbi in a small New England town. We were cautiously fascinated by each other's faith.

We visited each other's place of prayer; we visited each other's home. At a Sabbath service, I even invited R. to help me with the reading of the Torah scroll. That Christmas Eve, as our family was about to order out for Chinese food (they were the only place open), the kitchen doorbell rang. Through the window, I could see a car, with its headlights on, idling in the driveway. I opened the door; it was R. He was wearing his collar—a priest ready for the holy night—facing a rabbi in a sweatshirt about to pick up an order of take-out food.

"R., my God, what are you doing here? It's Christmas Eve. Aren't you supposed to be in church?"

"Oh, yes," he said, "We're just on our way over there now." (The man is making a social call on Yom Kippur!) He was holding a wrapped gift. "This was under our tree and it had your name on it. But I figured that since you might not have known to look, I'd drop it off in person."

Our friendship led us to a standing monthly lunch date. We decided to write each other a one-page essay on the same topic. We figured it might be a personal way to learn of another religion in greater depth. The topics were predictable: God, Bible, Israel, salvation. The only rule we set for ourselves was that we had to be completely candid and honest. By the sixth or seventh topic, we agreed we were ready to write about Jesus. This is what I wrote to R. twenty-five years ago and shared with him over our lunch.

> I am wary of Jesus. Not because of anything he taught or even because of anything his disciples taught about him. (Although some of the things John said about me and my people ought to be forever banned from public reading by any person who thinks loving people is important.) Whether they were mistaken or merely premature, the idea that God should at last take the form of a human being, that the yearning God and humanity share for one another should be focused in the mythos of one person is a very compelling vision: Word become flesh.
>
> For millennia we Jews had tried to make it work in the other direction, from the bottom up. Raising ourselves to the ideal of Torah's teaching. Judaism seeks to raise ordinary people to the realization of holiness, transforming flesh into word. Then came Christianity, teaching that Jesus represented an attempt to understand the yearning from the other direction. Truth be told: Neither tradition has yet succeeded.
>
> I am wary of Jesus because of history and what so many of those who said they believed in him have done to my people. Christianity, you could say, has ruined Jesus for me. Somehow through the ages the suffering of Jesus has become confused with the suffering of the Jewish people, my people. That is the key to my problem with him. His death has even become causally linked with some denial on *my* part. And this in turn has been used as a justification for my suffering.
>
> In this way Jesus means for me not the one who suffered for the world's sins but the one on account of whom I must suffer. (Is there anyone who could deny the intimate relationship of Christian Europe and the Holocaust?) Most of my early learning came from Jews who were unable to conceal this hurt-become-anger and who unconsciously portrayed him as enemy.
>
> Nevertheless, I still believe in the coming of an anointed one. A redeemer whose living example will initiate the ultimate humanism and compel even the angriest cynic into confessing that here indeed is a person in whom the eternal yearning for consciousness to behold itself had at last succeeded. The great Sinai teaching at last realized.

That's what I wrote and that's what I handed R. as we sat down to eat.

But then something surprising and transforming happened. R. finished the page, slowly set it down on his plate and looked up at me. His face was ashen. I winced, fearing that I had crossed some line, that with my smug bluntness I had injured my new friend. But to my surprise R. only whispered, "Please forgive me, forgive us. It could not have been Jesus *those* Christians served." His eyes were moist with tears.

What was more, this empathy he could not conceal seemed to grow directly from the core of his faith. "Your religion," I said, "it wants you to care about me *that* much?"

"Oh yes," he said. "Don't you see, I must continuously seek to find God in every person. Jesus is only the beginning. You, Larry, are easy, but the ultimate goal is to find my Lord within everyone, even people I like a lot less than you, even people I dislike, even ones I despise."

And then it dawned on me: So that's what it means to say that God can take the form of a human being. That event in the past, for him, imposes an obligation for what might happen in the future. And each human meeting is another potential opportunity to attain that ultimate goal. Right here across the table from me, was a truly holy man, one in whom the spirit had become flesh.

14

Jesus and Me

LANCE FLITTER

JESUS. I never really thought about Jesus much when I was younger. In my liberal Jewish home the subject of Jesus just didn't come up much. He was some Anglo-Saxon, bearded, beatific-looking guy I would see on TV occasionally around the end of December. Being influenced by Jewish culture I also had some vague, uncomfortable feelings about Jesus that were hard to define. I knew that Jews had been killed and tortured in Jesus' name throughout history. As I got older I knew "Jesus!" was a swear word. Even when I got interested in studying religion in my late teens and early twenties I never really studied much about Jesus or Christianity. I studied some Judaism and I became interested in Eastern religions such as Buddhism and Taoism. Most of my friends in college seemed to have similar interests, so when religious discussions came up Jesus was rarely if ever mentioned.

I grew up in Philadelphia and later moved to Maryland near Washington, D.C. Neither area is what you would call a bastion of fundamentalist or evangelical Christianity, and I never had Christianity "in my face" that much, so studying Christianity or Jesus wasn't something I really thought about. I knew that Jesus had been a Jew, I knew he was central to Christianity, and I knew I had some vague, uncomfortable feeling regarding him; but, in general, Jesus just wasn't important to me. Other than occasional, rather bland, intrusions of popular religious culture, Jesus just wasn't a part of my life or in my thoughts at all. Based on my experiences with other Jews, I think that this is still a fairly typical Jewish attitude toward Jesus, although, as I comment later, that may be changing.

So, for much of my life Jesus was essentially a nonissue, almost a complete stranger. That all changed about nine years ago when I started dating a Christian woman. I have never been what I would call a religious person. Religion's primary role in my life had been one of intellectual stimulation. That and some holiday celebrations. However, my girlfriend, who is now my wife, while not a fundamentalist by any stretch of the imagination, was religious and was involved in her church. In addition to getting me more interested in studying Judaism, for the first time I also became interested in learning something about Christianity.

As our relationship got more serious and we began discussing marriage and children, my desire to know more about Jesus and the religion of which he was the focus became more intense. Now I am married and have two children. My wife and I have decided to expose our children to both of the religious traditions from which we come. So Jesus is no longer a stranger. Through intimate association Jesus is now a part of my life. Jesus isn't "out there"; Jesus is in my home.

Apathy toward and disassociation from Jesus are no longer an option for me. Jesus is a part of my wife's life and will be a part of my children's lives. The question I have had to answer for myself is, How do I relate to Jesus? What do I think of him and about him? I'm neither a Jewish scholar nor a religious scholar. My perspectives are not meant to be scholarly and I don't claim any particular expertise beyond my own experience and that of others in similar circumstances. I just happen to be a fairly typical, mostly secular, American Jew who has had Jesus thrust into his life due to circumstance and has had to deal with it. Based on my experience with interfaith families nationwide, and being a member and leader of the Interfaith Families Project of Greater Washington, and considering the increasing number of Jews married to Christians, I realize that many Jews are or will be experiencing this phenomenon. I hope that an account of my explorations in this area will be of benefit to this community. What follows is a brief description of my continuing journey in trying to figure out what I think about Jesus.

WHICH JESUS?

I began by doing what Jews have done for millennia when they had a question, I turned to books. There is a wealth of books about Jesus, coming from a variety of perspectives. One of the first things I discovered in trying to figure out what I thought about Jesus was that I first had to answer the question, Which Jesus? There are probably as many Jesus theories and perspectives out there as there are people who have thought about Jesus, but I would say that there are two primary categories of Jesus perspectives, namely, the theological Jesus and the increasingly popular historical Jesus. There is some overlap between the two, but I think they are distinct enough to consider separately.

The theological Jesus represents the traditional religious perspective of Jesus. This Jesus essentially comes from a fairly straight reading of Christian Scripture and from the theological and religious interpretations of that Scripture by Christian clergy and thinkers through history. This is Jesus as God. Jesus the supernatural miracle worker. Jesus who rose from the dead. Jesus who provides salvation. This is also the Jesus that inspires much of Christian religious practice and thought.

By contrast, the historical Jesus is essentially a demythologized Jesus. It is an attempt to find the Jesus behind the stories; an attempt to understand who the "real" Jesus was. Jesus the man rather than Jesus the god. The historical Jesus perspective comes not just from Christian Scripture but also from historical documents and an understanding of the cultures in which Scripture was written. While the historical Jesus perspective does not necessarily deny any supernatural character of Jesus, the focus is on who Jesus was as a person.

As you would imagine, what one thinks about Jesus could vary considerably depending on which Jesus one is talking about. The situation is further confused because there are varying views within each of these major categories. My view also varies somewhat depending on what personal perspective I am using. I am both a humanist and a Jew and both perspectives color my views. So the question of what I think about Jesus is not a simple question. However, given these complications, I can still dive into the subject and share a few perspectives.

THE THEOLOGICAL JESUS

First, I'll consider the theological Jesus. There are a lot of stories about Jesus found in Christian Scripture. From my perspective, the stories that contain supernatural elements generally belong in this category. In the next section, under the "historical Jesus" heading, I will consider stories that are essentially "preaching" or nonsupernatural. In some ways this is a fairly artificial distinction, but I need to organize my thoughts in some fashion and this is what makes sense to me.

For what I would think are obvious reasons I don't accept the theological perspectives on Jesus. Despite the claims of some recent groups such as Jews for Jesus, the fact is that the primary theological Jesus concepts, most notably that of Jesus being God, lie firmly outside the Jewish perspective. In addition, as a humanist I am highly skeptical of all supernaturalism. I would need good evidence and reasons for believing such stories and I have yet to find any—and not for want of looking. Since the popularization of the internet I've had more than my share of discussions and debates with fundamentalist Christians. Taken literally the supernatural stories don't do anything for me.

There is a long-standing religious tradition that religious stories can be looked at metaphorically, not just literally. Many stories are treated in this manner within Jewish tradition. The interesting and sometimes frustrating thing about metaphor is that, if you try hard enough, you can pull almost any concept from almost any story. Even if we try to stay reasonable I think it is possible to pull meaningful things from the stories about Jesus involving supernatural events. However, I think the more important and fruitful topic is that of the historical Jesus. This is the Jesus that is potentially accessible to the Jew, and for that matter to anyone. I'll leave the theology to those more qualified to address it.

THE HISTORICAL JESUS

Trying to figure out what the historical Jesus was actually like is no simple matter. If one is going to be thorough, then the first question one should ask when researching a supposedly historical character is, Did such a character actually exist? The very notion of asking such a question might shock some people, but I think it is a reasonable question. The majority of scholars tend to agree that there was some historical person on whom the Jesus character is based, and I think that is significant. I was surprised to find, however, that there are some who disagree and think that Jesus is essentially a fictional character. I was also surprised at how little reliable evidence there is for a historical Jesus.

Outside of Christian Scripture, which for obvious reasons must be considered at least somewhat biased, there are remarkably few references to any such person: a couple of suspect references in the work of Josephus, a mention or two in some other works that seem to speak of Christian views of Jesus as opposed to direct experience with Jesus the person, a couple of references in the Talmud that may or may not refer to Jesus and that are questionable because of Christian influences on the Talmud.

None of these references appears to have been written at the time that Jesus lived, although some were within decades of his supposed lifetime. For someone who has had such a profound impact on human society, and who supposedly had a profound impact on the people of his time, there is remarkably little that objectively supports his existence. Personally, when I consider the evidence I find it more plausible to believe that some person did exist on whom the Jesus character is based than to believe that all the stories about him were simply made up or borrowed from other sources. I think some of that most likely occurred but, overall, I think it more likely that there was some historical person at the root of many of the stories. This is based more on a feel for the evidence than a clear, logical conclusion.

In any case, when searching for the historical Jesus, the main reference documents are Christian Scripture. Trying to figure out who Jesus really was entails examining Christian Scripture in light of what is known about the culture and environment in which Jesus lived. One can examine the stories about Jesus in light of this background and make some determination as to what seems most likely to be true.

So, given this, what was the real Jesus like? In my readings I've come across Jesus the theologian, Jesus the political revolutionary, Jesus the reformer, Jesus the socialist, Jesus the cynic philosopher, and more. Will the real Jesus please stand up! I think many of these views have something to offer. There is one foundation, however, that underlies all of these others and which I think is fundamental to understanding Jesus, namely, Jesus the Jew.

JESUS THE JEW

How do we know that Jesus was Jewish? He went into his father's business, lived at home until he was thirty, and had a mother who thought he was God! All kidding aside, while I am not a Jewish scholar or an expert on the history of the period, I know enough that when I read stories about Jesus his Jewish background is clear to see. In some ways it seems that Jesus may have rejected aspects of the Judaism of his time. However, even this fact seems relevant since he was a Jew and was responding to a system in which he grew up. I think that any understanding of the historical Jesus is impossible without considering the Jewish context in which he existed.

One of the central ideas in traditional Christianity is that Jesus is viewed as the one who does away with the Old Law. Jesus is frequently viewed as being very negative toward Jewish Law, and Judaism is frequently portrayed as an excessively legalistic system that somehow misses the point of what God wants. Judaism is certainly a legalistic religion. Whether one considers it excessively so is a matter of opinion. There is a long Jewish history of the Jewish people abandoning the Law in some manner or another, with the prophets usually showing up to whip the people back into shape. So, if Jesus did reject part or all of the Law, that would certainly not be unique in Jewish history.

There is another aspect of Jewish Law and tradition, however, that I think is important. Judaism has always been a religion with priorities. In the Jewish view, not all laws are created equal. Consider a story about Hillel, a Jewish leader and respected scholar who died when Jesus was supposedly around sixteen years old. It is even possible that Jesus could have met him. There is a story that one day Hillel was approached by a Gentile and asked to summarize Judaism while the questioner "stood on one foot." Hillel responded, "What is hateful to you don't do to your neighbor. The rest is commentary. Now go and study."

The rest is commentary? Does this sound like an excessive legalist? Yet Hillel is one of the most revered sages in Judaism. Hillel's pronouncement on the essence of Judaism might also sound somewhat familiar to Christians, since it is the negative version of the "golden rule" so often attributed to Jesus. The fact is that the golden rule existed within Judaism (and other cultures as well) long before the time of Jesus. It is simply an expression of the biblical commandment to "love your neighbor as yourself" (Lev. 19:18), which Jesus said is the second greatest commandment in the Law (Mark 12:31).

It is surprising that Jesus is so often portrayed as wanting to abolish the Law, since he himself supposedly said the opposite. According to Matthew, he stated that he came not to abolish the Law but to fulfill it and that not one letter of the Law should be changed until heaven and earth pass away (Matt. 5:17). There is some question as to the authenticity of this saying, but there are many instances in the Gospels of Jesus referring to Jewish Scripture or Jewish ideas. It seems reasonable, therefore, to suppose that Jesus did not intend a wholesale abolishment of the Law or Jewish tradition even if he didn't like parts of it.

JESUS THE RELIGIOUS REFORMER

I think another possible perspective, perhaps more likely, is that Jesus, like Judaism, had a set of priorities. While it is true that traditional Judaism has a copious amount of laws, there has always been a set of priorities as to what is most important. Consider the words of Amos regarding the sacrifices of the Hebrews at a time when the Hebrews were supposedly acting in an immoral manner. Speaking for God, the prophet says: "I hate, I despise your festivals and I take no delight in your solemn assemblies. Even though you offer me your burnt offerings and grain offerings I will not accept them. . . . But let justice roll down like waters and righteousness like an ever-flowing stream" (Amos 5:21, 22, 24).

Amos was not condemning sacrifice per se but rather making clear what God's priorities were. At least, this is clearly the perspective of the Jews of his time and later. Amos lived sometime around the eighth century B.C.E., and ritual sacrifices continued to be a central part of Judaism until the destruction of the Second Temple in the year 70 C.E. Such examples of priorities can be found throughout Judaism and its writings. For example, Judaism places a high value on life. Not only is one permitted to violate almost all of the commandments (of which Judaism generally recognizes 613) to save a life; one is obliged to do so.

Given the history of Judaism's setting of priorities on justice, mercy, kindness, and human life, and given Jesus' references to Jewish Law and, possibly, his own words that he did not want to abolish the Law, it seems more likely that Jesus, like many Jews before and after him, had a set of religious priorities. When he felt that people were not recognizing those priorities, he rebuked them. I think that some of the sayings attributed to Jesus, where he criticized the Law or legalistic Jews, make sense when viewed in this manner. It seems to me that the evidence supports the idea of Jesus as a religious reformer.

JESUS THE BREAKER OF SOCIAL BARRIERS

Jesus' primary objections to the Law seem to be focused on certain areas, particularly laws relating to ritual purity. Judaism contains many such laws. There are laws related to food (the laws of *kashrut,* or kosher food) that specify which food is acceptable and which is "unclean." There are laws of ritual purity related to our bodies. A person can become ritually "unclean" under certain circumstances.

Such laws tend to have a divisive impact. They certainly separated the Jews from the people around them, and they also had a divisive impact among Jews. Certain people were considered "unclean" or ritually impure, such as lepers or women during menstruation. In addition to ritual purity laws, there are also laws that establish what is essentially a class system, with the priests in many ways at the top.

A common thread I see running throughout the Jesus stories is of Jesus as breaker of social barriers. He seemed to preach equality among people and is portrayed as mingling with and even favoring in some instances those whose status in the Jewish culture of the time would have been low: people such as women, tax collectors, lepers, and so on. I think it likely that these ideas actually come from a historical Jesus, since they are distinct from the common cultural perspective of the time. This would make them stand out to the populace, make an impression and be more likely to be remembered and recorded. I think that the evidence on how the earliest Christians lived also lends support to this idea. According to my readings, they apparently lived in very egalitarian communities with common ownership of property, respect for women, and an openness that seems consonant with these ideas.

Thus, it seems to me that Jesus was very much a Jew; however, he was also following in a long Jewish tradition of setting priorities. As with many Jewish prophets and sages that lived before him, he seems to have placed a high priority on the ideal of loving your neighbor and on concerns related to people rather than ritual. This is a tradition that existed within Judaism before Jesus and that continues to exist to this day. There are movements or denominations of Judaism today, such as Reform Judaism, that stress the moral and ethical aspects of Judaism over ritual concerns. The idea of Jesus as a Jewish reformer is one I can relate to and one that I think is supported by the evidence. This Jesus broke traditional social boundaries and stressed Jewish laws and ideals related to love, kindness, and respect over, or even to the exclusion of, laws related to ritual.

JESUS AND THE GENTILES

While Jesus was certainly a Jew and his thoughts were formed in a Jewish context, it isn't quite clear how he related to non-Jews. There is more than one instance of Jesus maligning non-Jews in some manner. A clear example of this is found in Matthew 15:21-26. Jesus ignores a Gentile woman's pleas for help, referring to her people obliquely as "dogs." And he explicitly says, "I was sent only to the lost sheep of Israel." This seems at odds with the idea of Jesus as a breaker of social barriers. Jewish culture was, and in some ways still is, very separatist in nature, and Jesus certainly would have experienced that. But it seems that he would have rejected such attitudes if he professed the openness toward all people that he seemed to profess.

The parable of the Good Samaritan (Luke 10:29-37) sounds more like the authentic Jesus to me. In this parable he demonstrates that not only non-Jews but even the hated enemies of the Jews, the Samaritans, can be good people. What's more, the parable is a comment on the effect of Jewish laws of ritual purity, since the two people who passed by before the Samaritan came were a priest and a Levite. Priests and Levites are proscribed from touching dead people, so if they thought the man by the road could be dead they would not have gone near him to prevent becoming ritually impure. So the parable demonstrates both a social openness and a condemnation of ideas of ritual purity. These are concepts that I see appearing repeatedly with regard to Jesus, so I tend to think they are more likely to be authentic.

It seems likely to me that Jesus would have welcomed anyone who shared his egalitarian and humanitarian philosophy. I think it evident that he did cross social boundaries, including occasionally even those between Jews and Gentiles, which may have made him unpopular with some Jews, particularly with Jews associated with the traditional power structure, such as the Sadducees (the priests who controlled the Temple) and the leaders of the Pharisees (the precursors to the rabbis). It would be a mistake, however, to suggest that he was moving away from Judaism in any sense. He may have been open to all people, but I see him as welcoming them into Judaism, as I think that is what he professed, his own vision of Judaism. I do not think for one second that he was trying to start a new religion. In fact, I think he probably would have been appalled at the idea.

JESUS MESSIAH?

Another central question, one that relates to basic assumptions of Christianity, is whether Jesus thought he was the Messiah. I'm not really sure. I doubt that he was the first to think so, and certainly will not be the last. In fact, there was a Jewish Messiah wanna-be, who lived in the century following Jesus by the name of Simon bar Kosiba. He acquired a following including the notable Rabbi Akiba, who sur-named him "Bar Kochba," "Son of the Star," a messianic title (Num. 24:17). Bar Kochba led a revolt against the Romans that actually suc-ceeded for a couple of years but ended in enormous disaster for the Jewish people. So, it's not as if a Jew claiming to be the Messiah is that extraordinary.

It is important to note, however, that the Jewish idea of messiah is radically different from the Christian view. "Messiah" is the anglicized version of the Hebrew word *moshiach*, which literally means "the anointed one." ("Christ" comes from the Greek translation of the same word, *christos*.) In Jewish tradition the Jewish king is anointed with oil as a symbol of his kingship. There were some variations among Jewish conceptions of messiah, but the traditional Jewish view of *moshiach*, or messiah, is that he will be a fully human king who will lift the Jewish people out of their bondage or troubles and usher in a "messianic age," an idealized society in which "nation will not take up sword against nation, nor will they train for war anymore," and the "wolf will live with the lamb and the leopard will lie down with the goat." It will be the kingdom of God *on earth*. In other words, this human Messiah will usher in a "new age," and this new age will occur *immediately*, within his lifetime, as opposed to in a "second coming," and will occur here, on earth.

This is radically different from the Christian conception of messiah as savior in the sense of remover of sins, the Son of God who comes down from heaven in the humility of a human body to offer himself as the atoning sacrifice and will come again in glory to gather his faithful and establish his kingdom. (It is unclear whether this king-dom would be earthly or heavenly.) It is certain that Jesus would be familiar with the Jewish conceptions of messiah and, since he was speaking to a Jewish audience, if he did claim any sort of messiahship it would have been of the Jewish variety.

There is a significant amount of Christian Scripture that tries to justify Jesus as a messianic figure. There are frequent references to Jewish Scripture and to Jesus performing certain acts or saying certain things that could be interpreted as fulfilling Jewish "prophecies" about the Messiah. However, the prophetic portrayals of Jesus generally ring hollow to me, since they frequently seem contrived and generally do not represent a Jewish understanding of the prophecies in question. Sometimes the misrepresentation is actually rather humorous, such as when Jesus is reported to have ridden into Jerusalem on both a donkey and a colt (Matt. 21). I can imagine poor Jesus trying to straddle both of these animals. This is a mistranslation or misinterpretation of Jewish scripture (Zech. 9), where one animal is referred to as both a donkey and a colt.

When I read such descriptions, it seems that the authors are trying very hard to fit their Jesus into what they perceive as the Jewish concept of messiah; however, they don't seem to have a very good understanding of Jewish Scripture. Another common misinterpretation (one that seems to be losing favor in most modern Christian circles) is from the book of Isaiah: the reference to the "suffering servant," which Jews and most scholars understand to mean Israel.

So, in general I find little to suggest that Jesus thought of himself as a messiah figure. The openness of Jesus, which seems authentic, doesn't seem to fit with the fairly militant kingship that I think was the dominant conception of the Jewish Messiah at the time and the one that Jesus probably would have been most familiar with. Therefore I doubt that Jesus presented himself as a messianic figure.

There is a great deal more that could be said about what best represents the authentic Jesus, and numerous books have been written on the subject. But not as much work has been done on examining Jesus through Jewish eyes. I think that to understand Jesus you must place him in the context in which he lived, which means understanding Jesus as a Jew. I've tried to touch on two main subjects concerning Jesus, what I think his basic character and mission were and whether he thought of himself as the Messiah. I find nothing convincing to indicate that he thought of himself as the Messiah. As to his basic character, Jesus as a religious reformer resonates most with me. I find that consistent with his being a Jew and consistent with the overall feel of the stories about him. Jesus, like Jews before and after him, tried to emphasize the human and moral aspects of Judaism rather than the ritualistic aspects. I can certainly empathize with that, as I feel the same way and I think many modern Jews do as well. However, I also think his was a vision of a reformed Judaism, not an abandoned, rejected, or superseded Judaism.

JESUS, ONE OF OURS

In the beginning of this article I noted how for much of my life Jesus was a nonissue to me. Historically, Jesus was a subject shunned by Jews. Although this is still the case for many Jews, I think that is changing. As history has progressed and much of the animosity toward Jews has lessened (unfortunately not completely), more Jews are taking an interest, I think, in coming to some understanding of who this person so central to Christianity was in a way that is meaningful to Jews. After all, he was a Jew. To understand Jesus is to understand one of our own. I'm reminded of a joke . . .

An elderly Jewish woman ends up in a Catholic hospital. Facing her bed is a big picture of Jesus. A considerate nun, knowing the woman is Jewish, asked if she would like the picture taken down. "Oh no," replies the old woman, "such a success by one of our boys. Leave it up!"

I know that I will continue to work at understanding who Jesus was and what Jesus looks like through this pair of Jewish eyes. I suspect that as time goes by more Jews will be doing the same. My understanding of Jesus is certainly radically different from the traditional Christian understanding of Jesus. However, when my Jewish eyes look at what appears to me to be the "authentic" Jesus, I see another set of Jewish eyes and I can respect the person who looks back at me with those eyes.

PART FOUR

THE CONVERSATION CONTINUES

15

"How Do You Read?"

Jesus in Conversation with His Colleagues

LAURENCE EDWARDS

E VERY ACT OF HISTORICAL RECONSTRUCTION is partly an act of imagination. It therefore depends in large measure on the desire of the one doing the imagining to "read" the evidence in a particular way. In the case of Jesus, for instance, does one want to find reasons for further separation, for drawing hard lines between Judaism and Christianity? Does one wish to blur the boundaries into something vaguely referred to as "the Judeo-Christian tradition"? How shall we read the history of Jesus' time and place so as to hear him once again within it, as part of a Jewish conversation?

THE JEWISH MATRIX

The first century of the Common Era was a time of enormous complexity, so confusing, so full of danger, so full of potential. Consider the place of the Jewish people in the Roman empire. Judaism was a legally recognized religion (*religio licita*), but also suspect. (Some accused Jews of atheism, since no one could see their God.) There was also a large Jewish community in Babylonia, in the Parthian empire (Rome's main rival). Jerusalem was the religious center of the

The author wishes to thank Sr. Mary Ellen Coombe, N.D.S., with whom he prepared a study session for Catholic and Jewish educators that was the seed of this essay.

Jewish people, with its newly refurbished and expanded Temple and throngs of pilgrims on the major festivals, but synagogues were the local meeting places for most Jewish communities. Far more Jews lived outside the Land of Israel than in it, most of them speaking Greek.

There was Torah, and there were prophetic books and various other sacred writings, but the Bible as we know it was not yet canonized. Greek and Aramaic translations of the Jewish Scriptures were more accessible than was the original Hebrew. There was no prayer book, no Talmud, no Passover *seder* that would be familiar to us.

What was the attitude of Jews toward non-Jews, most of whom (in those days) were pagan idolators? How much assimilation was there? How much worrying, in a time of great cultural mixing, about how to preserve Jewish identity and maintain communal boundaries?

The Babylonian Exile and the destruction of the First Temple had set in motion a new era in Jewish history. Some have suggested that it was at that time that Judaism first became not just a national identity but a religion that began to attract converts. We see evidence of this in the later chapters of Isaiah (Deutero-Isaiah), and elsewhere. There are references to those who were drawn to Judaism (see Isa. 56:3): "Godfearers" they were sometimes called, individuals who attached themselves to the synagogue and to the Jewish community without necessarily undergoing formal conversion. When some of the Jews returned to the Land of Israel, at the time of Ezra and Nehemiah, they had to face immense issues of how to reconstitute the community. One of the biggest questions was that of identity—Who is in and who is out?

Five centuries later, arguments were still going on. There were many different views. In the first century, under Roman occupation, there were those who favored collaboration and those who were for violent resistance. There were those for whom the Temple was the center of everything and others who looked to the synagogue as a way of developing new Jewish practices. Some immersed themselves in the messiness of everyday life, and some went into the wilderness in search of purity.

Of the many Jewish parties and schools of thought from that time, the one we think we know the most about is the Pharisees. But in fact, we mostly know about them through later sources—rabbinic traditions and Christian Scripture. In fact, the only first-hand writings we have from individuals who say that they were members of this group are the works of Josephus and the letters of Paul.

The Pharisees seem to have been a fairly small group, devoted to the study and interpretation of Torah. They respected the rituals of the Temple, but mostly carried on their work outside of it. They adapted some of the laws of Temple purity in ways that could be observed by average Jews. They viewed the Torah as the constitution of Israel and took every letter seriously. They were not, however, literalists or fundamentalists. Rather, they embraced the idea of an oral tradition of teaching and interpretation stretching all the way back to Moses. The sources of their authority were their learning and their piety, and their main concern was to teach Jews ways of maintaining a sense of holiness by means of everyday practice. It may or may not have been their intention, but they are the ones who re-created and extended Jewish practice in ways that made it possible for Judaism to survive and flourish after the destruction of the Temple.

JESUS IN HIS SETTING

Into this reading of history, let us now place the figure of Jesus. Geza Vermes, who sees Jesus as a "charismatic healer-teacher-prophet," says that the picture of Jesus in the Synoptic Gospels "fits perfectly into the first-century Galilee known directly from Josephus, and indirectly from rabbinic literature."[1] Harvey Falk argues that Jesus is best understood as a member of the Pharisaic School of Hillel.[2] Whether a wonder-working teacher or a Hillelite Pharisee, it is certainly true that Jesus was a Jew of his time. It is easy to imagine Jesus taking part in many of the conversations and debates that helped shape what Judaism would become.

Or perhaps one should say "re-imagine," since most of the descriptions we find in the Gospels of Christian Scripture seem to show Jesus as being in conflict with the Pharisees and other Jewish teachers. Can we begin to recover the conversation that was going on back then? Part of the effort is one of reconstructing the hints and fragments that remain, peering out from existing sources, covered over by many layers of interpretation, so much of which is rooted in bitterness and separation. But why should we Jews dismiss his teaching just because of the way it was taken over and applied against us? Surely that was

---

[1] Geza Vermes, *The Religion of Jesus the Jew* (Minneapolis: Fortress, 1993), 4.
[2] Harvey Falk, *Jesus the Pharisee: A New Look at the Jewishness of Jesus* (New York: Paulist Press, 1985).

not Jesus' intention! Jesus, after all, was one of the great religious geniuses produced by Judaism. My goal here is to renew the conversation, based on a more complex understanding of what may have been going on back in the first century, and taking Jesus seriously as a Jewish teacher of that time.

Among the Pharisees and among their rabbinic successors there were significant differences of interpretation. This comes down to us most clearly through the often conflicting teachings of the School of Shammai and the School of Hillel. There are strong indications that one of the differences between these two Pharisaic/rabbinic groups had to do with the question of "outreach." Some of the best-known stories in the Talmud suggest that Shammai was usually more strict in his interpretations. Perhaps he was especially concerned about maintaining clear boundaries between Jews and non-Jews. Hillel, on the other hand, is portrayed as being quite open and interested in teaching Torah to Gentiles as well as to Jews. Consider this famous story from the Talmud:

> There was another incident when a particular idolator came to Shammai and said to him, "Convert me, on condition that you teach me the entire Torah while I am standing on one foot." He drove him away with the builder's rod which was in his hand. Then he went to Hillel, who converted him and said, "Whatever is hateful to you, do not do to your neighbor. That is the whole Torah, the rest is the commentary on it; go and study." (*B. Shabbat* 31a, my translation)

Jesus engages in a similar exchange, reported in several versions. In the Gospel of Mark (12:29-34), Jesus is asked which commandment is most important. He begins his response with the *Shema*:

> "The first is, 'Hear, O Israel: The Lord our God, the Lord is One; you shall love the Lord your God with all your heart, and with all your soul, and with all your mind, and with all your strength' [Deut. 6:4-5]. The second is this, 'You shall love your neighbor as yourself' [Lev. 19:18]. There is no other commandment greater than these." Then the scribe said to him, "You are right, Teacher; you have truly said that 'he is one, and besides him there is no other'; and 'to love him with all the heart and with all the understanding, and with all the strength,' and 'to love one's neighbor as oneself,'—this is much more

important than all whole burnt offerings and sacrifices." When Jesus saw that he answered wisely, he said to him, "You are not far from the kingdom of God." After that no one dared to ask him any question.

In Matthew's version (22:34-40) Jesus also quotes from the same passages of the Torah (more briefly, without "Hear O Israel, the Lord our God, the Lord is one"). In this version too the discussion is ended abruptly with his declaration, "On these two commandments depend all the law and the prophets."

"BUT HOW DO YOU READ 'NEIGHBOR'?"

It is Luke's version (10:25-37) that offers the longest discussion of the matter and seems to me most teacher-like in the way it engages and extends the conversation. First, the question is posed differently: "Teacher, what shall I do to inherit eternal life?" And Jesus responds not with the answer, but very Jewishly, with a question: "What is written in the law? How do you read?" And note here that it is not just "What do you *think*?" but "How do you *read*?" In other words, look at the text and tell me what strikes you as most important. His interlocutor comes up with what Jesus considers to be the right answer: "You shall love the Lord your God with all your heart, and with all your soul, and with all your mind; and your neighbor as yourself." And he said to him, "You have answered right; do this, and you will live."

This time the discussion is extended, in good rabbinic style, with a request for further clarification: "And who is my neighbor?" To this Jesus responds with his famous parable of the Good Samaritan:

"A man was going down from Jerusalem to Jericho, and fell into the hands of robbers, who stripped him, beat him, and went away, leaving him half dead. Now by chance a priest was going down that road; and when he saw him, he passed by on the other side. So likewise a Levite, when he came to the place and saw him, passed by on the other side. But a Samaritan while traveling came near him; and when he saw him, he was moved with pity. He went to him and bandaged his wounds, having poured oil and wine on them. Then he put him on his own animal, brought him to an inn, and took care of him. The next day he took out two denarii, gave them to the innkeeper, and said, 'Take care of him; and when I come back I will repay you whatever more you spend.' Which of these three, do you think, was a neighbor to the man who fell into the hands of robbers?" He said, "The one who showed him mercy." Jesus said to him, "Go and do likewise." (Luke 10:30-37)

A most interesting inversion: the question was "Who is my neighbor?"; in other words, "Whom am I obligated to love?" A traditional and reasonable interpretation of "Love your neighbor as yourself" understood it as applying only to a fellow Jew (one who is similar to yourself). The answer suggested by Jesus' parable is that the "neighbor" is "the one who showed mercy on him." It is not the one who is to be helped, but the one who helps. In other words, Jesus seems to be saying, "You have asked the wrong question. The point is not to figure out *to whom* I am obligated, but to *act* in a neighborly way." This is a beautiful example of engaging in a discussion of Torah, and of reading it in a way that extends the circle of obligation.

If Jesus' parable can be understood as expanding the category of "neighbor," there is another passage in rabbinic literature that wrestles with the same question. It begins with that same verse from Leviticus, and records a difference of opinion between Rabbi Akiba and Ben Azzai:

> *You shall love your neighbor as yourself* [Lev. 19:18]. Rabbi Akiba said: This is a great principle of the Torah. Ben Azzai said: *This is the book of the descendants of Adam: When God created human beings, God made them in the likeness of God. Male and female God created them* [Gen. 5:1-2] states a principle even greater. You must not say, "Since I have been humiliated, let my fellow also be humiliated; since I have been cursed, let my neighbor also be cursed." For, as R. Tanhuma pointed out, if you act thus, realize who it is that you are willing to have humiliated—one whom God made in the divine likeness.[3]

Rabbi Akiba (who is generally aligned with the School of Hillel) is clearly citing a long-standing tradition that views "Love your neighbor as yourself" as a central teaching of the Torah. Jesus, a century

---

[3] Variously recorded in Jerusalem Talmud *Nedarim* 9:4; *Genesis Rabbah* 24:7; *Sifra Kedoshim* IV, 12 (my adaptation).

or so earlier, was standing in the same tradition. Akiba seems to understand "neighbor" as referring to fellow Jews. Jesus (in the Luke version) extends the meaning of the term "neighbor." Akiba's contemporary, Ben Azzai, finds a Torah verse that reminds us that *all* human beings are created in the divine image, and that therefore the circle of obligation extends to all.

Each of these Jewish sages—Hillel, Jesus, Akiba, Ben Azzai—is wrestling with questions that go to the heart of the Torah's value system. Jesus attempts to summarize the essential teaching of the Torah by actually quoting two verses, as do Akiba and Ben Azzai. Now look again at the first story: Hillel offers a teaching similar to "Love your neighbor as yourself," but not by quoting from Scripture. Hillel, whom we usually consider to be firmly within the boundaries of Judaism, here does not quote Torah. (David Flusser does point out, though, that it is close to an early Aramaic translation/paraphrase of the verse.[4]) On the other hand, Jesus, often thought of as having moved beyond the boundaries of traditional teaching, quotes from the Torah. What is the context of these teachings? Where are they being directed?

A JEWISH CONVERSATION

In the Gospel narratives, Jesus is speaking to Jews. It is an internal, Jewish conversation. It is Torah study among Jews, all of whom are quite familiar with the verses cited. Hillel, on the other hand, is speaking in the Talmud passage to a Gentile, a potential convert. Hillel is doing "outreach," speaking in a way that will be more immediately accessible to one who is not familiar with the insider shorthand of quoting Torah. Akiba and Ben Azzai are holding an internal Jewish conversation, but with an eye to ever-expanding circles of social contact (and perhaps also to the growing Christian movement).

The point of this brief comparison is not to argue for the superiority of one over the other. It is, rather, to suggest that we should not make assumptions about which Jewish teachers were speaking to Jews and which to Gentiles. Each of these passages reports part of an

---

[4] David Flusser, "Jesus, His Ancestry, and the Commandment of Love," in *Jesus' Jewishness: Exploring the Place of Jesus in Early Judaism*, ed James H. Charlesworth (New York: Crossroad, 1991), 169.

ongoing conversation about questions that continue to concern us: What are the essential teachings of Torah? What does God expect of us? What do we expect of each other? How far do my obligations extend?

How far indeed? It seems likely that by the first century there was already an oral tradition that viewed "Love your neighbor as yourself" as a central teaching of the Torah. The discussion may then have been about who is included in the category of neighbor. But one might wonder why Leviticus 19:18 would be considered so central: Why not a few verses further on in the same chapter, where we are taught, "When a stranger resides with you in your land, you shall not wrong him. The stranger who resides with you shall be to you as one of your citizens; *you shall love him as yourself,* for you were strangers in the land of Egypt: I the Lord am your God" (Lev. 19:33-34 NJPS)?

In the Talmud it is pointed out that warnings against oppressing the stranger are repeated at least thirty-six times (*B. Baba Metzia* 59b). But the term "stranger" is usually understood by the rabbis as referring to the convert to Judaism (i.e., the naturalized citizen in contrast to the home-born), and a verse such as Leviticus 19:34 is understood as cautioning against taking unfair advantage of one who is a newcomer to the community. Nevertheless, it seems clear that the Torah has already set in motion a trend in the direction of ever-wider circles of obligation. Jesus' understanding of "neighbor" is in keeping with that trend.

In the twentieth century, the Jewish philosopher and teacher Emmanuel Levinas placed the principle of "Love the stranger as yourself" at the center of his ethical understanding. Like Hillel in the story above, Levinas in his philosophical writings did not generally quote directly from the Torah or other Jewish sources. But in his explicitly Jewish essays, it is quite clear that this principle is of fundamental importance: "The welcome given to the Stranger which the Bible tirelessly asks of us does not constitute a corollary of Judaism and its love of God . . . but it is the very content of faith. It is an undeclinable responsibility."[5]

Judaism back in the first and second centuries was a work in progress, and it still is today. More and more Christians now realize

---

[5] Emmanuel Levinas, "Religion and Tolerance," in *Difficult Freedom,* trans. Seán Hand (Baltimore: Johns Hopkins University Press, 1990), 173.

that Christianity cannot be understood without an appreciation for its roots in Judaism. And a Jewish understanding of Jesus would see him not as one who sought to overcome the Jewish teachings of his day, but as one who was fully engaged in the Jewish questions of that time. For Jews, insofar as we are able to recover and reclaim Jesus as a Jewish teacher, he may have something to teach us as well. At the very least, we should now be open to hearing him—not, certainly, as having the last word, but as part of the ongoing conversation of Torah.

16

Fresh Eyes

Current Jewish Renewal Could See Jesus as One like Themselves

MICHAEL LERNER

M ANY EARLY CHRISTIANS perceived themselves to be a Jewish renewal movement. Like members of earlier renewal movements, they saw Jewish institutions being dominated by elites who had often seemed to be using Jewish ritual as a substitute for spiritual involvement. Accommodating to the Hellenistic spirit of the times, many Jewish intellectuals distanced themselves from the spirit of Torah in order to better immerse themselves in the letter of Torah. Others saw their task as "nation building," worried more about the survival of the Jewish body and the Jewish community than about the Jewish soul. There were among the early Jewish-Christians many who felt that they were critiquing these distortions of Judaism and helping to restore the basic intuitions that had originally animated Judaism.

Jesus appears to have been motivated by a distaste for the ways that the Jewish establishment of his time had become excessively fixated on religious ritual at the expense of remaining true to the heart of Jewish spirituality and Jewish love. In innovative and forceful ways he tried to confront that establishment and to validate the experiences and needs of some of the most oppressed elements in Roman-occupied and Roman-dominated Judea. He may not have had an adequate understanding of the ways that the distortions in Jewish life were themselves the product of the attempts by some to accommodate and others to resist the Roman occupation. But nevertheless he had insights and ways of formulating Torah truths that could have served as an inspiration for many Jews. His insistence upon ethical and spiritual integrity, his message that in our individual lives and in the ways that we relate to whoever is the most downcast of the society, we must embody Torah's message of compassion, and his challenge to ritual separated from ethical sensitivity could easily have found a place in Jewish tradition, had it not been joined to the metaphysics of messianism and then to a religion that oppressed Jews. Indeed, as we move away from the historical period in which Christians oppress and demean Jews, it will be possible for Jews to look at Jesus' teaching with fresh eyes and to reclaim the Jewish Jesus as an honored teacher without having to reject everything he said merely because of the ways it was subsequently used to hurt us.

A healthy appropriation of the Jewish Jesus will avoid the kind of reverential tones that one sometimes hears from Jews who want to emphasize interreligious dialogue so much that they talk of Jesus as a prophet and healer in order to show Christians that now we can be nice to him. More appropriate to treat him like other Jewish teachers, subjecting him to the same rough-and-tumble scrutiny, recognizing his limitations in the same way that we recognize the limitations of other teachers of the talmudic age, learning the parts that seem good, rejecting the rest, and not allowing an internalized conception of how this will impact our relations with Christians to affect what is accepted or what is rejected. When we can come to that point, Jesus will regain his rightful place as a respected and sometimes insightful teacher of the Jewish people.

17

Yehoshua and the Intact Covenant

DREW LEDER

FOUNDATIONAL TO THE JEWISH PEOPLE are two experiences. The first is that of the covenant. "And I will take you to be my people, and I will be your God" (Exod. 6:7). The Jews are the chosen people, or, perhaps more aptly, the *choosing* people, who made a sacred deal: to follow the commandments of their Maker and receive in turn divine protection.

The second foundational experience of the Jews seems directly contradictory to the first. That is the fact of *suffering*. From the destruction of the Temple to the crematoria of Auschwitz, the history of the Jewish people has been riddled with bloodshed and persecution, ghettos and pogroms, mockery and exile. One can imagine a Jew saying of God, "Oy, with friends like this who needs enemies?" From the book of Job to Elie Wiesel's *Night*, a universal question of theodicy takes a distinctively Jewish form: Why do the good suffer in a covenantal world?

Two answers seem possible, even obvious, unavoidable. The first is that the Jew has shattered the covenant. Did not the prophets time and again remind the Jewish people of their profound failures of justice and mercy? Did not Moses smash the tablets at his followers' idolatry? When trouble rains down upon Job, his friends must assume that Job has grievously sinned. The alternative seems unthinkable.

But let's think it through: perhaps it's God who falls down on the job—falls down on Job, so to speak. Job himself can locate no pertinent offense he has committed. And, leaping across the millennia, Elie Wiesel can find no Jewish sin commensurate with the horrors visited upon his people. In the death camps, where was God? Or we might say, "*Where in hell was God?*" for it was a living hell for the inmates. The covenant seems like a mockery, or a product of wishful thinking, in a world ruled by ignorance and malice.

It is in this context that the life of Yehoshua can have special meaning for Jews. Was he a messiah, an *avatar*—a divine incarnation—a prophetic figure, reform rabbi, radical insurgent, a spirit-filled holy man? Whatever. Set aside for a moment the theological debates. Simply imagine that in some way he came, as he himself asserts, first and foremost to speak to his fellow Jews. Imagine too that he came, as so many experienced, bearing a God-message of great importance. Imagine finally that the circumstances of his life and death were part of that message in a way that he, himself, may not have fully understood. What would the message be? What might God have said to the Jews through Yehoshua's life and death?

Simply this: in the midst of suffering *the covenant is intact*. A good man can be subjected to horrifying deprivations: pain, mockery, abandonment, cruel death. Yet it need not mean that he has broken the covenant. "This is my Son, the Beloved, with whom I am well pleased" (Matt. 3:17). Nor does it mean that God has forgotten the covenant, though it may for a time so appear: "My God, my God, why have you forsaken me?" (Mark 15:34). We know these words are from Psalm 22, and preliminary to that psalm's ringing affirmation: "For He did not scorn, He did not spurn the plea of the lowly: He did not hide His face from him; when he cried out to Him, He listened" (Ps. 22:24). In Christianity this affirmation of God's love was found in the Easter experience and the theology of redemption.

But leaving Yehoshua a Jew, the message still resonates: suffering is compatible with the intact covenant. Even in the midst of physical agony, social ostracism, the dark night of the soul, God is profoundly *with us*—Emmanuel. Suffering need not mark our deficiency, nor God's duplicity. Beyond these two answers lies a third: Abba's love is with us unto eternity. That love may not register in the form of good fortune—health, wealth, and other worldly delights. Instead, we are offered the pearl of great price: relationship with the divine. The pearl retains its value, may even glow brighter, when set against the darkest of backgrounds.

To the Jew, Yehoshua's life and death must thus finally speak of Auschwitz. We do not arrive at the Christian theology that proclaims, "Jesus died for our sins." On the contrary, Yehoshua's death proclaims that the victims of Auschwitz *did not* die for their sins—or for

God's sins. The covenant is intact. This Hitler could not destroy any-more than could Pilate. The Jew throughout history has had occasion to cry out, "My God, my God, why have you forsaken me?" But it remains "*My* God," the God of the covenant, even in the midst of our crucifixions.

18

Jesus

A Prophet of Universalistic Judaism

LEWIS D. SOLOMON

TWO THOUSAND YEARS AGO Jesus walked the face of the earth, of that there is no doubt. To this day, however, the quest for the historical Jesus continues. Specifically, what did Jesus teach?

If you were to travel back in time to the first century C.E., you would discover that much, but not all, of Jesus' teachings were within the ethical boundaries of Judaism. Jesus grew up as a Jew and observed many Jewish traditions as well as the precepts of ethical monotheism. He read or heard the Torah, the Prophets and the Proverbs; he sang the Psalms.

Jesus' insistence on a universalistic, spiritually oriented Judaism echoed the great Hebrew prophets. Focusing on our need to love and forgive others, Jesus emphasized the universality of his message, not the separatism characteristic of Palestinian Judaism of his era. He was involved with all of humanity and urged others to be the same.

Stressing ethical principles and rejecting many traditional Jewish legalistic rules and practices that suffocated not only the Sabbath but also life more generally, Jesus followed the prophet Isaiah, who quoted God as follows: "Those people come near to Me with their mouth and honor Me with their lips, but their hearts are far from Me. Their worship of Me is nothing but human rules and traditions which they have simply memorized" (Isa. 29:13).

As summarized in this essay, the essence of Jesus' teachings is sevenfold: The Vision of God's Sovereign Rule; God's Attributes;

Personal and Social Human Virtues; Social Status and the Marginalized; Critique of Religious Rules and Rituals; Reversals of Normal
Expectations; and Life and Death.

THE VISION OF GOD'S SOVEREIGN RULE

Jesus focused on God's sovereign rule, a region where God's dominion is immediate and absolute, although not observable. Jesus asked
us to look to two ultimate questions: what is the purpose for creation
and why is each of us here. Like Buddha, another great sage, Jesus
wanted us to look beyond the illusory, the deceptive landscape of the
familiar, material world and focus on the way things really are—the
real world of God's domain—where the Eternal always watches over
and takes care of each of us.

In the saying on God's sovereign rule (Luke 17:21), Jesus indicated that God's domain, the Eternal's righteousness and love, is
imminently expected, if not already present. According to Jesus, "You
won't be able to see the coming of God's sovereign rule. People will
not say, 'Look, here it is!' or 'Over there!' On the contrary, God's
sovereign rule is right there in your presence, but people don't see it"
(*Gospel of Thomas*, Logion 113).

God's sovereign rule results in the manifestation of the Holy One's
power throughout the world and a divinely governed global reign,
relegating the particularistic, materialistic elements to the universalistic, spiritual aspects. The notion of God's sovereign rule permeated
Jesus' teaching. He did not suggest that the permanent new age
required an intermediary, such as seeking salvation through a belief in
Jesus. Personal repentance and virtuous conduct would achieve its
establishment. God's presence dominates our existence; thus, we
should honor the Eternal in all that we do and strive to emulate the
Holy One's ways.

Although the concept of God's reign appears in numerous biblical
sources, what was unique in Jesus' teachings on God's sovereign rule
was its implementation. Gone were the bloody final battles led by the
Eternal as a warrior. For instance, the ancient Hebrew prophet
Ezekiel imagined God as the Great Conqueror (Ezek. 39:3-5). God's
domain does not require the intervention of angels and archangels, as
depicted in the Dead Sea Scrolls. In the *War Scroll* (1QM 17:6-7),
the victory over the "forces of darkness" and the establishment of
God's rule resulted from a battle fought by the combined armies of

the angelic and human forces of light under the leadership of the heavenly prince Michael.

Jesus took a universalistic stance. He saw the critical role humans would play in the implementation of God's sovereign rule. Each person must devote himself or herself to the implementation of God's reign. In the parable of the pearl (Matt. 13:45-46), a merchant, presumably quite wealthy, after searching fearlessly, invested everything he had in a single, priceless pearl. On a material level, the pearl was a symbol for something precious; on a spiritual level, it was a symbol for a special type of wisdom, namely, that of God's domain. The pearl thus represented a new treasure, a splendid discovery, something of superlative wealth much more valuable than all of the merchant's earthly goods. According to Jesus, humans must deliberately concentrate their efforts and sacrifice to achieve the implementation of God's sovereign rule.

Beyond his vision of God's domain, where God's power and beneficent attributes would be apparent to all, Jesus brought to our attention two key relationships: first, between God and humans, and, second, among humans.

GOD'S ATTRIBUTES

Jesus explained God's relationship to humanity. He stressed the nearness and the presence of God. We have immediate access to God's concern, goodness, and providence. Jesus advised us to trust and have faith in the divine, who is merciful and beneficent to all.

Jesus' admonition "ask—seek—knock" (Matt. 7:7-8; Luke 11:9-10) represented the unconditional promise of a response to each of three requests. Jesus taught: "Ask—it'll be given to you. Seek—you'll find. Knock—it'll be opened for you. Rest assured: everyone who asks receives; everyone who seeks finds; and for the one who knocks, the door is opened." These absolute assurances reflected Jesus' serene confidence and trust in God's goodness and providence. Jesus sought our complete surrender to God.

Don't be afraid to ask, seek, and knock continually. Persistently pray to God, who hears and cares for each of us. If you bring your needs to the Holy One, trust that you will be satisfied. Maybe not immediately, but if you trust in the Eternal you'll receive, find, and experience an open door. According to the Psalmist, God declared: "Open wide your mouth and I will fill it" (Ps. 81:10).

"Ask," recalled a biblical verse: "Ask of Me, and I will give you . . ." (Ps. 2:8). As we read: Appearing to Solomon during the night in a dream, God said, "Ask for whatever you want Me to give you" (1 Kings 3:5). "Seek" has biblical parallels. According to the writer of Proverbs, God stated: "I love those who love Me, and those who seek Me find Me" (Prov. 8:17). In a letter to the Jewish exiles in Babylonia, the Hebrew prophet Jeremiah wrote: "You [the Jews] will seek Me [God] and find Me when you seek Me with all your heart" (Jer. 29:13). "Knock" echoed: It is the voice of my beloved who knocks, saying "Open to me . . ." (Song of Songs 5:2).

Jesus also used two rhetorical questions, "Who among you would give your son a stone when it's bread he's asking for? Who among you would give him a snake when it's a fish he's asking for? Of course no one would!" These responses of parents, who may not have been perfect, to their children's requests for good gifts (Matt. 7:9-11) show us how God treats humanity. The Holy One, who is pure goodness and an understanding, loving, and caring parent, will graciously provide good gifts to those who ask.

God was viewed as a parent in the Hebrew Bible. The author of the book of Deuteronomy asked: "Is the Eternal not your parent, your creator, who made you and formed you?" (Deut. 32:6). According to the Psalmist: "As a parent has compassion on his or her children, so God has compassion on those who revere the Eternal" (Ps. 103:13).

Later, noncanonical biblical materials also focus on God, as the loving protector of each individual. In the Apocrypha, Ben Sira noted: "I will praise you, O my God, my salvation, I will thank you my God, my parent" (Ecclus. 51:1). Thus, for Jesus and in earlier Hebrew materials we see the parental image of a loving, providential God, a near and approachable Holy One.

PERSONAL AND SOCIAL HUMAN VIRTUES

At the heart of Jesus' teachings were human relationships built on certain personal and social virtues and modes of conduct. Following the Eternal as a model, Jesus wanted us to adhere to the principles of love, compassion, and nonviolence. Furthermore, one receives forgiveness only after forgiving, that is, letting go of another's offense. He was critical of those who were judgmental as well as of the pompous and the self-righteous. Jesus also advised us to be tranquil and not to worry, rather placing our faith in God.

Loving. The saying "Love your enemies" (Matt. 5:44, 46; Luke 6:27, 32) was one of the keys to the teachings of Jesus. Jesus asked, "If you love only the people who love you, why should you be commended for that? Even sinners love those who love them!" For Jesus, this was a shorthand way of summarizing the Hebrew Bible's basic commandment regarding human relations.

The word "love" represents a genuine concern for someone else irrespective of his or her attractiveness or any prospect of reciprocation. Love means a desire for others' well-being; it connotes being good to them. An "enemy" is one's persecutors. Jesus asked us to love everyone no matter what their attributes, including our enemies. It takes no special effort to love those who are kind to us. However, the admonition of offering unconditional love, disinterested and uninfluenced by any expectation of return, represents a paradox. If you love everyone, you won't *have* any enemies! For Jesus, the love of enemies represented its own reward.

Jesus built upon the biblical admonition: "Do not take revenge or bear a grudge against one of your people, but love your neighbor as yourself" (Lev. 19:18) and "the stranger as yourself" (Lev. 19:34; also Deut. 10:18-19).

The general commandment to love one's neighbor, more generally, other human beings, encompasses specific actions demonstrating love: leaving some harvest for the poor, not lying, cheating, or stealing, not oppressing one's neighbor, paying a worker's wages promptly, caring for the deaf and the blind, being impartial in judgment, and not slandering others (Lev. 19:9-16). It is also derived from biblical statements requiring the giving of aid to one's enemy: "If you come across your enemy's ox or donkey wandering off, be sure to take it back to him or her. If you see the donkey of someone who hates you fallen down under its load, do not leave it there, be sure you help him or her with it" (Exod. 23:4-5).

We are told not to rejoice when your enemy is in trouble. We read: "If your enemy is in trouble, give him or her food to eat; if he or she is thirsty, give him or her water to drink" (Prov. 25:21-22). The author of the book of Proverbs also reminds us: "Do not gloat when your enemy falls; when your enemy stumbles, do not let your heart rejoice, or God will see and disapprove and turn the divine wrath away from your enemy [a wicked person] to you" (Prov. 24:17-18).

Noncanonical, biblical works develop a similar theme. In the Apocrypha, we are told: "Do not do to anyone what you yourself would hate" (Tobit 4:15). Ben Sira advised: "Be as friendly to your neighbor as to yourself, and be attentive to all that you hate" (Ecclus. 31:15).

For Jesus, we must strive to love all of humanity, reflecting the Holy One's attributes. As the author of the book of Leviticus (19:2) tells us, "Be holy because I, the Eternal Your God, am holy." Reflecting our Godlike nature and divine mercy, human love should be disinterested, seeking nothing in return.

Compassionate. The "giving and lending" sayings (Matt. 5:42; Luke 6:30) are paradoxical. Jesus taught, when someone asks you for something, give it to him; when someone wants to borrow something, lend it to her even if you won't get it back. Literally following these admonitions would result in financial disaster. Therefore, these sayings reflect an ancient dictum to engage in charitable acts and put others' needs before your own. Being compassionate enables us to be Godlike.

Jesus built on the advice offered by the author of the book of Deuteronomy, where we are told: "Be openhanded and freely lend what a poor person needs" (Deut. 15:8; also Lev. 25:35-36). Further, in the Apocrypha, Ben Sira advised us not to despise the supplication of the poor or turn away an afflicted soul (Ecclus. 4:4).

Furthermore, Jesus stood for faith in God's sovereign rule to the point of knowing you would be fully supplied by God. If you have that kind of trust, you will not experience any disaster. If you give with that kind of connection and with love and compassion, you will only receive more. If you're compassionate toward others, they will be compassionate toward you. You receive in order to give and then you will receive even more.

Forgiving. In the parable of the Prodigal Son (Luke 15:11-32), Jesus told of something lost and found as well as the importance of forgiveness. In dealing with different reactions to the prodigal son, the parable showed what God is like—abounding in love and expressing boundless mercy—and what humans should aspire to be.

Jesus had a reputation for fraternizing with willful and unrepentant "sinners," represented by the prodigal son, who cannot experience the joy of returning until he has departed. For Jesus, the departure of a beloved family member and his risk-taking preceded his return. After the younger son demanded and immediately received a portion of his father's property that would otherwise come ultimately to him on his father's death (one-third, in accordance with Deut. 21:17), he squandered his fortune and got a job feeding pigs, an animal Judaism regards as unclean (Lev. 11:7-8; Deut. 14:8). Coming to his senses, to his truer self, this son, having sufficient self-esteem yet aware of his moral corruption, took the initiative, acknowledging his sinful behavior (paralleling Ps. 51:4), completely relying on his father's mercy.

The reconciliation of son and father followed language of the biblical reconciliation of two brothers, Jacob and Esau. Although fearing what was ahead, Jacob was well received. We are told, "Esau ran to meet Jacob and embraced him; he threw his arms around his neck and kissed him, and they wept" (Gen. 32:10-11; 33:4). Likewise, in Jesus' parable, the father ran to his son, an unusual action for an older person in ancient times.

Forgiveness plays an important role in the Jewish tradition, reflecting the divine attribute of mercy. In the celebrated words of the Hebrew prophet Isaiah: "I [God] have swept away your offenses like a cloud, your sins like the morning mist. Return to Me for I have redeemed you" (Isa. 44:22) and "Though your sins are like scarlet, you shall be as white as snow, though they are red as crimson, you shall be as white as wool" (Isa. 1:18).

Jesus' parable illustrated God's love and the Eternal's willingness to take back repentant sinners. It is never too late to repent and receive divine compassion. God holds no one unworthy. Rather, the door is open, at any hour, to all who repent.

In Jesus' parable, in addition to the father, symbolizing a compassionate and forgiving God, totally and immediately forgiving the prodigal son with great kindness, the father invited the elder brother to join in a celebration to show the reconciliation of family. There were to be no grudges. The prodigal son was to be reabsorbed into the family.

So too God, in love and with patience, accepts the outcasts of society who turn to the Eternal with open arms. The father tried to make the elder brother understand that it was also his party if the older sibling, a homebody who never left home, was able to find it within himself to join in the celebration. The older brother, however, a pious but not righteous person, evidenced a grudging, rather sour attitude. He resented his father's generosity toward his younger brother and the paternal forgiveness. Although he had done everything right, particularly obeying his father's commands, he believed he had been treated unjustly. He felt alienated at the prodigal son's return.

The older son's anger was, however, consistent with Deuteronomy 21:18-22, where we read that if a parent had a stubborn and rebellious son who did not obey his parents and would not listen to them when they disciplined him, his parents needed to take hold of him and bring him to the elders at the gate of his town. They shall say to the elders, "This son of ours is stubborn and rebellious. He will not obey us. He is a profligate and a drunkard." Then all the men of his town would stone him to death.

Nonjudgmental. The sayings about the speck and the log (Matt. 7:3-5) use striking images, a rather grotesque comparison, to call attention to the irony of faultfinding and condemnation. Jesus taught, "Why do you notice the speck in your friend's eye but overlook the log in your own eye? How can you say to your friend, 'Let me get the speck out of your eye' when you have a log in your own eye? You phony! First get the log out of your own eye and then you'll be able to see clearly to remove the speck out of your friend's eye!"

Negative, faultfinding individuals, for Jesus, must first focus on correcting their own shortcomings before spotting defects in others. Once you remove a log from your eye then you have the responsibility of helping another remove his or her speck. Stated positively, Jesus recommended that we hesitate to judge others and give everyone the benefit of the doubt. If we see a person doing what appears to be "wrong," we ought to try to take a favorable view of his or her action. Try to stand in his or her shoes. Look on all of humanity with the nonjudgmental eye of love. Because we are all children of God, keep your heart open to everyone. Somewhere the innocence in each of us is alive.

Nonviolent. In the parodies—comic exaggerations—of the other cheek and the coat and the cloak (Matt. 5:39-40; Luke 6:29), Jesus challenged his listeners to react differently from our natural inclination to acts of aggression. Jesus declared, "Don't take revenge against someone who wrongs you. When someone slaps you on the right cheek, offer the other one as well. When someone takes your coat, don't prevent that person from also taking your cloak."

In Jesus' time and our own, a blow from the back of another's hand shows the greatest possible contempt. In addition, in the ancient world, one's cloak, an expensive garment, was an extremely valuable possession. Each of these parodies represented a possible mode of action. When struck, although we would want to strike back, it is possible to turn the other cheek. It is possible to offer your cloak when someone takes your coat, to which a Jew had an inalienable right in the Hebrew Bible (Exod. 22:26). If you had only two garments, that meant going naked. We can answer aggression with non-violent restraint.

According to Jesus, those who suffer, whose natural impulse is to hit back, need self-control. Being indifferent to personal injury, they need to focus on God's sovereign rule, turning their backs on a desire for revenge or retaliation. Jesus' admonition has parallels in the Hebrew Bible, where we are told to be forbearing and not seek revenge. According to the Second Isaiah: "I offered my back to those who beat me and my cheeks to those who pulled out my beard" (Isa. 50:6). The author of the book of Proverbs tells us: "Do not say, 'I'll do to others as they have done to me'" (Prov. 24:29).

When someone hurts you by deeds or words, your first reaction is to get even. However, in dealing with interpersonal conflicts and offenses, don't return a blow for a blow or repay anger with anger. Don't physically fight or verbally berate others to settle wrongs inflicted on you or to protect your possessions. In the face of an unprovoked assault or insult, be forbearing, long-suffering, and patient. Give up much and endure even more to avoid strife. Submit to wrongs and be long-suffering rather than create quarrels.

Humble. The parable of the Pharisee and the tax collector (Luke 18:10-14) contrasted the prayers and the demeanor of two men: the righteous (at least in terms of traditional Jewish religious practice), respected, prideful, and ostentatious Pharisee—an ancestor of pious Jews—and the outcast tax collector, regarded by the Pharisees as unrighteous, dishonest in business dealings, and derelict in religious duties.

The tax collector, who stood in the background, far from the other worshipers, offered a humble, personal, heartfelt prayer, "God, have mercy on me, sinner that I am," seeking God's mercy and compassion. It was an expression of despair echoing the Psalmist's cry: "For I know my transgressions, and my sin is always before me. . . . The sacrifices of God are a broken spirit; a broken and contrite heart, O God, you will not despise" (Ps. 51:3, 17).

In speaking against self-righteous pride, Jesus' parable commended the virtue of humility, a key virtue in the Jewish tradition. Moses is spoken of as "exceedingly humble" (Num. 12:3). According to the Second Isaiah, God states: "This is the one I esteem, one who is humble and contrite in spirit" (Isa. 66:2).

Tranquil. In a series of pronouncements on worrying and anxieties as immobilizing us (Matt. 6:25-31; Luke 12:22-29), Jesus emphasized serene trust and confidence in God. Because the divine cares for all creatures, the Eternal will provide for our basic needs—food, clothing, and shelter.

Jesus told us:

> Don't worry about your life—about what you're going to eat, or about what you're going to wear. Remember, there's more to living than food and clothing. Think about the birds: they don't plant seeds or gather a harvest; they don't have storerooms or barns, yet God feeds them. You're worth a lot more than birds! Can any of you add an hour to life by worrying about it? Why worry about clothes? Think about how the wild lilies grow: they don't work or make clothes for themselves. Let me tell you, not even Solomon at the height of his glory had clothes as beautiful as one of these flowers. If God dresses up the wild lilies in the field, flowers that are here today and tomorrow tossed into an oven, it is surely more likely that God cares for you. What little faith you have! So don't worry.

Worrying accomplishes nothing. Because of the harmful impact of worrying, it's more likely to shorten life than to prolong it. Jesus advised us not to worry about our fundamental needs. All that we have comes from God, who provides for our sustenance. Don't fret. Remember, Jesus told us, you will always have enough.

For Jesus, God provided food and clothing not only for birds and flowers but also for humans. This notion ties back to several biblical sources including the book of Job ("Who provides food for the ravens when its young cry out to God and wander about for lack of food?" [Job 38:41]) and the Psalmist ("and Who gives food to every creature?" [Ps. 136:25]; "The eyes of all look to You and You give them food at the proper time. You open your hand and satisfy the desires of every living thing" [Ps. 145:15-16]; "God provides food for the cattle and for the young raven when they call" [Ps. 147:9]).

We are reminded to trust in God, who will sustain us. As the

Psalmist advises: "Cast your cares on God, who will sustain you; the Holy One will never let the righteous be defeated" (Ps. 55:22).

SOCIAL STATUS AND THE MARGINALIZED

Jesus was an astute socioeconomic commentator. He wanted us to tear down dividing walls, for instance, those separating the rich and the poor. He expressed a deep feeling for the oppressed and foresaw woes for the complacent, oppressive rich.

In three sets of blessings (Matt. 5:3-4, 6; Luke 6:20-21), Jesus offers congratulations to the poor, the hungry, and those who weep. "Poor" may refer to those who are economically destitute—their outward conduct—or to those who are humble in spirit—their inward quality. Similarly, the hungry may be those who are deprived of food or those who hunger for righteousness. Those who weep carry not only the burden of personal grief but also societal hurts. Because they all are innocent and thus are in God's favor, they gain relief from their difficult circumstances. The poor can rejoice, even in the midst of destitution, because they currently partake of God's domain. Those who are hungry and weep must wait until a future time. However, Jesus told us, "These who are hungry will have a feast! Those who weep now will laugh."

The first blessing follows the Psalmist: "Who is like you, O God, who rescue the weak from those too strong for them, the poor from the oppressor" (Ps. 35:10). And the Second Isaiah says, "This is the one I esteem: he or she who is humble and contrite in spirit . . ." (Isa. 66:2).

The second blessing mirrors the words of the Second Isaiah: "Come, all of you who are thirsty, here is water; and you who have no money, come, buy grain and eat! Come, buy wine and milk without cost" (Isa. 55:1).

The third blessing, to those who weep, parallels the words of the Second Isaiah, who proclaims: "[A] year of the Holy One's favor and a day of vindication by God; to comfort all who mourn, and provide for those who grieve in Zion—to give them joy and gladness instead of sorrow and the spirit of despair. They will be called oaks of righteousness, a planting of the Holy One for the Eternal's glory" (Isa. 61:2-3). The Psalmist writes: "They that sow in tears shall reap in joy" (Ps. 126:5).

The Dead Sea Scrolls (Beatitudes 4Q525), looking primarily at what people can do in the present, how to live in the here and now, offer the following series of blessings, which, unlike Jesus' sayings, offer no mention of any reward: "Blessed are those who have a pure heart and do not slander with their tongue. Blessed are those who hold to your precepts and do not follow the ways of iniquity. Blessed are those who swear by your Torah and do not burst out in ways of folly. Blessed are those who seek it with pure hands and do not seek it with a treacherous heart. Blessed is the person who has attained wisdom and walks in the Law of the Most High."

In the saying about the eye of the needle (Matt. 19:23-24; Mark 10:23-25; Luke 18:24-25), Jesus cautioned, on one level, that wealth served as an impediment to entering God's domain. Jesus told his listeners, "It is very difficult for rich people to enter God's domain. I repeat: it's easier for a camel to squeeze through the eye of a needle than for a rich person to enter God's domain."

Because Jesus probably did not mean that all of us should embrace a life of poverty and a complete detachment from our worldly possessions, the saying should not be taken literally. Thus, Jesus may refer to how "rich" some people are in self-importance, pride, and ego. It happens that many wealthy people feel self-important and self-reliant. Fame and riches are huge spiritual tests that many fail. A person's wealth may become a deficiency inclining one to pride, self-indulgence, love of the material world, and the pursuit of earthly comforts. It's all a matter of the heart a wealthy person has, how much love, compassion, forgiveness, and humility he or she has. The image of the camel, the largest animal in ancient Israel, trying to squeeze through the eye of a sewing needle represents Jesus' quite memorable use of a graphic exaggeration, of hyperbole.

CRITIQUE OF RELIGIOUS RULES AND RITUALS

Jesus provided a sharp critique of traditional Jewish religious purity rules that delineated (and continue to delineate) the boundaries between the sacred and the profane. Observing these codes, according to traditional Jewish sources, maintained the holiness of Jews and furthered their separation from Gentiles. Jesus advised us to ignore these rules. We could eat foods deemed impure, share meals with those who do not observe purity standards, and come in contact with and even touch certain people considered ritually unclean. Seeking a religion of the heart, not a religion of form—the unimportant externals—Jesus also set human needs above the observance of religious ceremonies, for instance, the observance of the Sabbath.

In a couplet, "The Sabbath was made for the good of human beings; they were not made for the Sabbath. The members of the human race are preeminent, not the religious rituals, on the Sabbath" (Mark 2:27-28), Jesus gave humans dominion over religious rites, including observance of the Sabbath day—a way to honor God's holiness—one of the most widely practiced rituals among traditional Jews. In Exodus 20:10 and Deuteronomy 5:14 we read: "You shall not do any work [on the Sabbath], neither you, nor your son, nor your daughter . . ." (also Exod. 34:21; 35:2; and Lev. 19:3). There is also a positive commandment "to sanctify" the day, to make it "holy," to "remember" it, to "observe" it, to "rest" on it (Exod. 23:12).

Sabbath observance became an important and distinctive feature of Jewish life during and after the captivity in Babylon six centuries before Jesus (Ezek. 20:12-24; Neh. 10:31; 13:15-22). Most major ancient Jewish groups strictly observed the Sabbath. The way of life of the Jewish community in Palestine at the time of Jesus centered on the Sabbath.

For Jesus, human needs and a concern for individuals took priority over the need for people to conform to legalistic requirements and restrictions. The Sabbath could be an occasion to do good, to be loving, compassionate, and forgiving, to help and serve others, not to put humans in a ritualistic straightjacket.

In the saying about what goes in (Matt. 15:10-11; Mark 7:14-15), Jesus taught: "Listen to me, all of you, and try to understand. It's not what goes into a person from the outside that can defile you and make you ritually unclean; rather, it's what comes out that defiles you and makes you unclean." In so teaching, Jesus challenged the traditional Jewish laws regulating ritual purity.

Relying on various passages in the Hebrew Bible, ancient Jewish groups emphasized special food laws and diligently sought to keep them. In chapter 11 of Leviticus, the entire section lists what may and may not be eaten (see also Deut. 14:3-21). Exodus 23:19, 34:26, and Deuteronomy 14:21 state: "Do not boil a young kid in its mother's milk." In terms of the daily practice of Judaism, the food laws stood out in Jesus' time, together with Sabbath observance, as the defining aspects of the Jewish tradition. Any transgression of the dietary laws was quite obvious; therefore, keeping the food laws identified individuals as observant Jews. However, Jesus ran counter to these fundamental Jewish laws. In teaching that nothing taken into the mouth can defile, Jesus transgressed the established Jewish purity rules regarding foods fit for human consumption. Religious impurity and uncleanness caused by things, such as food, animates the Five Books of Moses and the teachings of the rabbis throughout the ages, who viewed nonobservance of these rules as defiling God's Law. An observant Jew who ingested foods deemed unfit for consumption or ate with non-Jews defied traditional Jewish codes and practices. He or she needed to be ritually purified, through various techniques, usually by means of immersion in a ritual bath, before being able to participate in Jewish religious observances. These purity concerns served as boundary markers and as a means of promoting Jewish identity.

However, observance of the dietary laws may lead to hypocrisy and self-righteousness. Outward "purity" may mask inner corruption.

Although literally applicable to foods, the saying applies also to all types of pollutants. For Jesus, a person was defiled by what he or she expelled—deeds as well as words, by his or her "bad" qualities, such as evil conduct, envy, or pride. Speaking on many levels, Jesus left ambiguous what orifice he was referring to. But perhaps the most important level is what you speak. What comes out of your mouth, representing the wickedness of your heart—is what defiles you. What "comes out" is probably the words that are spoken. Jesus realized that words were energy. When you speak negatively, you create poisonous, negative energy around yourself and others. Thus, what makes a person unclean comes from within, radiating out of one's heart and connoting what one says as well as what one thinks and does.

Reflecting a spiritual, not a ritualistic, perspective, Jesus was concerned with internal impurity. He followed the prophet Hosea who states: "For I [God] want your love, not your animal sacrifices" (Hos. 6:6). In the Pseudepigrapha's *Testament of the Twelve Patriarchs,* we read: "As the sun is not defiled by shining on manure and mud, but rather dries up both and drives away the unpleasant smell; so also the pure mind, though encompassed by the defilements of the earth, rather becoming a source of strength cleanses them and is not itself defiled" (*Testament of Benjamin* 8:3).

Jesus repeatedly challenged the classification of persons and things into pure and impure. He rejected religious practices designed to set some apart from or above others.

REVERSALS OF NORMAL EXPECTATIONS

Reversals of normal expectations played an important role for Jesus. Rewards were not necessarily dispensed according to time devoted or merit accumulated. The poor, among other marginalized groups, would assume a key place in God's domain, not the self-important.

The saying "The last will be first and the first will be last" (Matt. 20:16) represented a reversal of expectations. According to Jesus, those who think they will be first, presumably in the afterlife—the somebodies who enjoy worldly prominence—will be last; while those occupying the last position—the nobodies—will come out on top.

In the parable of the vineyard laborers (Matt. 20:1-15), emphasizing the equality of reward, two groups get what they do not expect. Jesus' parable focused on goodness, generosity and, ultimately, divine grace. The vineyard owner went into the marketplace, the city's public square where business was done and casual labor hired beginning at daybreak, and continued to hire workers for the harvest until the eleventh hour of a twelve-hour workday. In ancient times, the day was divided from sunrise to sunset into twelve hours. The eleventh hour was 5 P.M.

The vineyard owner continued hiring workers to complete a job in one day, seemingly because the pressing of the grapes had to be completed before the onset of the rainy season. Thus, the task was urgent. He needed more workers who would toil until sunset when light no longer remained in the fields. He promised to pay the additional workers what was proper. It's not clear whether the laborers who worked for a shorter time were at fault because they arrived later or were blameless. However, they all did their best during the hours they worked.

At sunset, the workers were called to collect the day's wages so they would not go hungry. As the author of the book of Leviticus (19:13) tells us, "Do not hold back the wages of a hired worker overnight." And in the book of Deuteronomy (24:15), we read, "Pay the workers each day before sunset because they are poor and are counting on it."

Those hired at the beginning of the day, who worked under the broiling sun the entire day, might have expected to be paid something more than what they were hired for despite their agreement with the owner. Although the owner did not shortchange these seemingly deserving workers, they grumbled. In contrast, the owner rewarded those hired last, who got much more because they were paid a full day's wage for an hour's work. There was inequality of service, yet the reward was the same.

Jesus may be telling us that rewards may not be handed out in God's domain in relation to time devoted or merit accumulated. God rewards according to the divine concepts of equity. The Holy One works in a different way. God's gracious, merciful love is bestowed equally on those the Eternal chooses. We should not be jealous or envious; however, no one will receive less than what he or she expected. In addition to the notion of divine reward, this parable reflected also the principle of grace, which was so important to Jesus. Even if one does not repent, there is the divine grace, which will overcome the divine wrath. God's mercy will prevail over God's anger.

LIFE AND DEATH

Jesus provided us with his reflections on life and death, particularly the impermanence of life. In the parable of the rich man or "you can't take it with you" (Luke 12:16-20), Jesus commented on the difficult, even the sad, life of the wealthy, who often focused only on earthly things. The man in this parable had to decide what to do with his overflowing harvest. By failing to consider the impermanence of life and the shallowness of living only for creature comforts, the farmer failed to respond appropriately to his very favorable situation. He treated wealth as the object of his ultimate concern. He would not share his abundance. He felt no responsibility to others. He hoarded his possessions out of a conviction that this life and the material world are all that there is. According to Jesus, God said to the farmer, "You fool! Tonight your life will end. Who will get all these things you've kept for yourself?"

In the man's hour of greatest need, his wealth proved useless. Despite his wealth, he had no control over his destiny. He would have no use for earthly riches when he died, nor will we on our demise.

In Ben Sira, we read a similar comment: "There is a man who is rich through his diligence and self-denial, and this is the reward allotted to him. When he says 'I shall enjoy my wealth!' he does not know how much time will pass until he leaves it to others and dies" (Ecclus. 11:18-19). This notion of the unpredictability of life builds on Psalm 39:6 ("We are mere phantoms as we go about; we bustle about, but only in vain; we gather wealth, not knowing who will get it") and more generally, on the book of Ecclesiastes. There the author advises: "I have seen another injustice under the sun, and it weighs heavily on people. God gives a person wealth, possessions and honor, so that one lacks nothing one's heart desires, but God does not enable the individual to enjoy them, for a stranger enjoys them instead" (6:1-2). Further, in the book of Job, we read, "[H]e will have no respite from this craving [for wealth]; he cannot save himself by his treasure" (Job 20:20).

The self-centered, rich man, according to Jesus, was a fool in the biblical meaning of the term, who practically denied God's existence (Ps. 14:1). Not fearing death, his priority should have been, according to Jesus, the development of genuine relationship with God and an emphasis on spiritual, not material, concerns through love, compassion, and service to others. As the prophet Jeremiah warns: "Let not the wise person boast of wisdom, or the powerful of strength, or the wealthy of riches, but let them boast about this, that they understand and know me, that I am God, the Holy One, who exercises kindness, justice, and righteousness on earth, for in these I delight" (Jer. 9:23-24).

Jesus' parable also built on biblical prudence cautioning against over-optimism. The book of Proverbs states: "Do not congratulate yourself on tomorrow, for you do not know what a day may bring forth" (Prov. 27:1).

Jesus sought a universalistic, nonlegalistic, nonritualistic religion of inner and outer spiritual perfection, based on ethical monotheism. He believed in the existence of one God, the Creator and Sustainer of us all, and wanted us to focus on how we live our lives as well as the words and deeds we express toward others, not the slavish adherence to a multiplicity of details, rule upon rule, ritual upon ritual.

Jesus' ethical teachings did not depart from those of Judaism. His bottom line was unconditional love for others and faith in divine love, which guides and protects us. Nor should we worry as we're led and loved by God. All will be well. Jesus' teachings were devoid of legal prescriptions. He saw his role as educational and inspirational. He sought to promote the concept of Judaism as a universal teaching valuable to all humanity.

19

Listening to Jesus with an Ear for God

RAMI M. SHAPIRO

"RABBI, YOU'RE WRITING about Jesus? You don't believe in him, do you?"

Well, do I?

Do I believe Jesus lived? Yes, Jesus was from Galilee, son of Mary and Joseph the stonecutter, who lived in the early years of the first century.

Do I believe Jesus was a Jew? Yes, Jesus lived and taught totally within the framework of Judaism; his aim was not to invent a new religion but to reform the one he had.

Do I believe Jesus was God-intoxicated and filled with *Ruach haKodesh*, the Holy Spirit? Yes, from the moment of Jesus' baptism in the Jordan at the hands of John the Baptizer, Jesus was awake to the presence of God in, with, and as all reality.

Do I believe Jesus was crucified by the Romans? Yes. Jesus drew large crowds, and crowds made the Romans nervous. They were the occupying army and much hated by the Jews. There was always the possibility that a crowd could riot.

Do I believe that the Jewish authorities colluded with Pilate to end the threat of violence that Jesus' crowd drawing posed? Yes. To maintain the integrity of the Temple the priests had to compromise with Rome. I think the motive of the Jewish leadership was political and not theological as the Gospels claim. First-century Palestine was rife with messianic pretenders, and Jesus would have been seen as just another in a long line of claimants to the throne of David. What worried them was the threat Jesus posed to national survival.

Do I believe that the Jewish people rejected Jesus and traded his life for that of Barabbas? Absolutely not. First of all, Roman law and custom did not allow for the freeing of a criminal. Second, the story of Barabbas is most likely a deliberately twisted version of the true event. The name "Barabbas" is Hebrew for "Son of the Father." The fact that Barabbas's first name was Jesus strongly suggests that the Jews came to Pilate demanding the release of Jesus bar Abbas, Jesus who is the Son of the Father. The story was deliberately inverted to shift the blame for Jesus' death from the Romans to the Jews, and thus ease the propagation of Christianity among the Romans.

Do I believe Jesus was literally resurrected on the third day? No. I believe that the resurrection is symbolic of the continued presence and power of Jesus in the lives of those for whom he is the Messiah.

Do I believe Jesus was the only-begotten Son of God through whom comes redemption from original sin and eternal life in the world to come? No. As a Jew I do not believe in original sin and have no need of a Messiah's redemption. As a Jew I continue to await the coming of a Messiah whose kingdom is of this world, and who will do what the prophets said he would do: bring peace to Israel and the world.

Given all of this, do I believe it is worthwhile for Jews to study Jesus? Not only worthwhile, but vital. Jesus is the most famous Jew who ever lived. To ignore him or to allow others to lift him out of his Jewishness and historical context in order to define him as a god-man is to give up an important part of our legacy as Jews.

I understand Jesus as a God-intoxicated Jew, a mystic suffused with *Ruach haKodesh*/Holy Spirit. This Jesus becomes an important teacher of a Jewish expression of the perennial philosophy mystics of every faith have taught for thousands of years. Reading Jesus as a Jewish mystic of the perennial philosophy reclaims him as a Jew and frees his deepest message from both Jewish rejection and Christian adulation.

In the pages that follow I will attempt to articulate Jesus' perennial message by interpreting selections of the Gospel according to John, the most theological of the Gospels. In so doing I hope to recover Jesus' message, and to give him a new hearing among Jews.

WHAT IS THE PERENNIAL PHILOSOPHY?

The perennial philosophy is the mystical core of all spiritual wisdom. Existing in virtually every culture across time and space, this philosophy has been articulated in many ways. Despite cultural differences, all teachers of this philosophy agree about its core elements:

1. Divine Reality exists. Call it God, Allah, Tao, Dharmakaya, Brahman, Yahveh, Shiva—there is one Reality that is the source and substance of all.

2. This divine Reality is our true nature. Just as a wave is not other than the ocean, we are not other than God.

3. We do not realize our true nature, because our perception of reality is clouded by self-centered and dualistic thinking.

4. Meditation is a way of seeing through dualism and awakening to the supreme identity of woman, man, nature, and God.

5. Awakening to this supreme identity replaces selfishness and fear with a loving commitment to justice and compassion, transforming not only our own lives but, through us, the life of all the world.

Given this philosophy, it is my contention that Jesus articulated a Jewish version of the perennial philosophy; that Jesus saw God not as himself only, but as all selves; that Jesus' references to himself were aimed not at his person but at the level of God-consciousness he had attained; that Jesus' call to follow him was not a call to submit to him as master, but to follow his lead and discover God for ourselves.

READINGS FROM THE GOSPEL
ACCORDING TO JOHN

In the beginning was the Word and the Word was with God, and the Word was God. He was in the beginning with God. All things came into being through him, and without him not one thing came into being. What has come into being in him was life, and the life was the light of all people. The light shines in the darkness, and the darkness did not overcome it. (John 1:1-5)

There is nothing in John's statement that is not Jewish. In the beginning was God and the word of God was the means of creation. All life comes from God. Recognizing that all life comes from God is the first step to seeing all life as a manifestation of God. And this is what Jesus and all perennial philosophers proclaim: God is not separate from creation. While God is certainly greater than nature, nature is not other than God.

All of Jesus' teachings must be understood in this light. In the beginning was God and creation is the manifestation of God, and men and women have the capacity to raise their awareness to the point of seeing the kingdom of God in everyone and everything. This is what Jesus did for himself and what he wanted to teach everyone else to do as well.

> He was in the world, and the world came into being through him; yet the world did not know him. (John 1:10)

When you look into a mirror whom do you see? Your outer self, the self you call "I," the self that seems separate from all other selves? Or do you see God, the "I AM" revealed to Moses, the true I behind all the little I's of personality, persona, and ego? Do you see the part or the Whole? Chances are you see the little self, the temporary self, the self that is born and dies. Chances are you imagine that this self is all you are. And so you worry: What will happen to me after I die? It is from this fear of death that all theology arises.

Jesus did not fear death because Jesus did not mistake his ego for the Self. Jesus knew that he was God—not the All of God as those who worship him claim—but a manifestation of God, the image and likeness of God of which Torah speaks, charged with bringing godliness to bear on the plane of creation. Jesus did not fear death because he identified with that which is timeless, birthless, deathless. Jesus, the part, identified with God the Whole and Holy.

> And the Word became flesh and lived among us, and we have seen his glory, the glory as of a father's only son, full of grace and truth. (John 1:14)

Christ-consciousness, the awareness that we are each and all manifestations of the One True Reality, is not alien to us. It dwells within us. It can be nurtured and cultivated by us until we achieve what Jesus achieved: the knowledge that the self and God—the "I" and the I AM—are one. The fact that John speaks of God's "only son" is simply John's inability to understand the fuller message of his Messiah.

> From his fullness we have all received, grace upon grace. The law indeed was given through Moses; grace and truth came

through Jesus Christ. No one has ever seen God. It is God the
only Son who is close to the Father's heart, who has made him
known. (John 1:16-18)

There are two manifestations of God: the relative and the absolute.
They are two sides of a single reality, for God is all and always One.
When we seek to reveal the absolute of God we speak of truth. When
we seek to apply the principles of godliness in the relative world of
men and women, we speak of law. To separate the two and to pit each
against the other is a betrayal of the wholeness of God. The law
applies the truth to the everyday situations of our lives. The truth
reveals that our lives are not ours at all, but God's; that we are not
separate selves but unique and temporary manifestations of the One
Self, the I AM behind everyone who says "I am."

This awareness of God as the source and substance of all things
requires a radical shift in consciousness. It requires us to see the One
who is also the many. It is this radical shift in consciousness that Jesus
attained, and which so many of his official interpreters failed to attain.
Jesus awoke at the hands of John the Baptizer to the truth that he was
one with God. He then returned to the world of his fellow Jews and
tried to teach them that they too contain the kingdom of heaven, that
they too are both human and divine.

For God so loved the world that he gave his only Son, so that
everyone that believes in him may not perish but may have eternal life. (John 3:16)

God's love is what makes God-realization possible. God's love
speaks to the intimacy of matter and spirit. They are not opposites,
but twin sides of a God who cannot be restricted by or reduced to
one or the other. God is bigger than our dualities. If we would but
trust in God's love, we could look beyond the self and discover the
Self; we could look beyond the lone and lonely ego and discover the
original face of the Son, the child of God that is our truest self. It is
not that we are to believe in Jesus, but to believe in and surrender to
that which Jesus revealed: the fact that I and the Father are one; that
every I is also the I AM that is God.

Those who believe in him are not condemned; but those that do
not believe are condemned already. . . . And this is the judgment, that the light has come into the world, and people loved

darkness rather than light. . . . For all who do evil hate the light.
. . . But those that do what is true come to the light. (John 3:18-
21)

The insistence on Jesus' uniqueness renders this passage a condemnation of all those who are not Christians. But look at it again.
Condemnation is continued dwelling in the darkness of ignorance.
Ignorant of our original self, we dwell in the dark loneliness of the
separate self. The darkness is our sense of alienation and existential
loneliness, which haunts all who insist they are apart from rather than
a part of God. The light of truth is revealed only when we abandon
our self-centered point of view, and realize the truth that we are all
the light, and all our deeds done with the Whole in mind are done IN
GOD; that is, they reveal the profound and simple fact that we are
always in God.

THIS KNOWLEDGE HAS
TRANSFORMATIVE POWER

But what is the impact of this knowledge? What difference does it
make in the world? The meeting at the well between Jesus and the
Samaritan woman is a beautiful model of the transformative power of
divine awakening. To understand the story you have to remember
that both women and Samaritans posed a problem to Jewish men
loyal to the conventional Judaism of their day. Women were a source
of temptation, and Samaritans a source of heresy. Contact with the
former was highly regulated. Contact with the latter was avoided as
much as possible.

But Jesus does neither. Jesus sees beyond gender and ethnicity,
beyond arbitrary codes of proper conduct that separate people from
one another. Jesus looks at the woman and sees a daughter of God, a
manifestation of the One who is not other than himself. Once awake
to the divinity manifest as all humanity, Jesus no longer put stock in
labels or the divisions that such labels are meant to support.

This is the first lesson of the story. The God-realized do not fall
victim to the arbitrary divisions of humankind.

Jesus then reveals to the woman that while she may have access to
nature's water, he has access to "living water." He says to her that the
thirst slaked by her well water will return, but that the thirst
quenched by what Jesus has to offer is quenched forever. Jesus is talk-

ing about the thirst we all have for meaning, for purpose, for truth. No matter how we try to quench this thirst, it returns. Why? Because there is nothing external to ourselves that can quench the thirst that comes with the insistence that we are separate selves cut off from God. The thirst is ended only when the self is shown to be a manifestation of God, only when the part realizes it is one with the Whole, only when the thirst is seen to be the creation not of the truth of our oneness but of the delusion of our otherness.

Jesus does not point to yet another distraction, another external remedy that works for a short time, but which in the end always fails. Jesus offers the woman an inner spring always "welling up for eternal life" (John 4:4-16). Within ourselves is the wellspring of God. Do not turn to others for your salvation, turn within, for only in turning within are you truly turning to God.

The Samaritan woman goes on to ask Jesus about the proper place to worship God. The Jews insist that worship be restricted to the Temple in Jerusalem. The Samaritans insist that it be restricted to their holy mountain. Which, the woman asks, is the true place of God?

Jesus the Jew knows that one of the holy Hebrew names of God is *HaMakom*, The Place. Jesus the Jew knows that God is the place of the world, the foundation of all creation. Jesus the God-intoxicated mystic cannot imagine that The Place is meant to be limited to one physical place. God is the Place of all places; God is infinite; the whole world is filled with divine glory—How can one place be more holy than another, or one person more godly than another?

So Jesus says: "Woman, believe me, the hour is coming when you will worship the Father neither on this mountain nor in Jerusalem . . . [but] in spirit and truth" (John 4:21, 23). And these are available everywhere. The worship of God cannot be restricted to one place, or legislated by one people or priesthood. God is realized when we open ourselves to the *Ruach haKodesh*, the Holy Spirit that is the deepest essence of each of us. When we awake to the *Ruach haKodesh* we know the truth: we are one in, with, and as God. This opening to Spirit is completely without boundaries and borders. The Holy Spirit is not Jewish or Samaritan; it is not Christian or Muslim; the Holy Spirit is the very breath of God breathed into each of us as it was breathed into Adam, the first of us. Jesus knew the artificiality of boundaries and refused to be coerced by them.

As the story progresses, Jesus reveals his true identity to the Samaritan woman, thus making it crystal clear that truth is not limited to any one people.

The woman said to him "I know that Messiah is coming. When he comes, he will proclaim all things to us." Jesus said to her, "I am he. . . ." (John 4:25-26)

Remember that Jesus is a Jew. The phrase I AM carries a deep and profound meaning for him. Jesus is not saying "I am the Messiah." Jesus is articulating the revelation of God's true nature: God is I AM, pure Being, manifest as the little "I am" that each self is.

Jesus reveals to the Samaritan woman the very same Godhead that God revealed to Moses at the burning bush: the I AM that is the real identity of all. The revelation that God is the I AM, the true self who manifests as the multitudinous selves of the world, is the deepest revelation of all. It is not limited to one people, nor can it be restricted to one person. The I AM is you and I; the true I that makes our temporary I's possible.

Thus Jesus says in Matthew 16:24: "If any want to become my followers, let them deny themselves." That is to say: One who would follow me and learn to become like me, a realized child of God, must let go of the delusion of a separate self, for it is this delusion that keeps you in the darkness of ignorance, blind to the light that is God's universal truth. Understanding this is crucial to understanding the message of Jesus the Jewish mystic of the perennial philosophy.

THE NAME OF GOD: I AM

When Moses encounters God at the burning bush he tells God that the Hebrew people will not believe that he has been sent to them by God. Moses needs to tell them who sent him. Moses asks God to tell him his name.

In Israelite culture a name reflected one's essence. Moses is asking God to reveal what it is to be divine. God says to Moses that the people knew him in the past as the Almighty, a power over and above anything they themselves could imagine or pretend to be. Now it is time to liberate them from bondage, not simply the bondage of physical slavery, but the bondage of ignorance. Now it is time to reveal the deeper truth of God, not only the Cosmic One, but the intimate I AM that is at the heart of each who is.

So God says to Moses: *Ehyeh asher Ehyeh*, I am what I am, and will be what I will be. In other words God says to Moses: "I am the unconditioned and unconditional state of pure Being that manifests as all conditioned reality. I am the sun that manifests the sunlight; I am the ocean that swells up as waves; I am the One who is the many. Tell them I AM sent you so that they might discover the true freedom that comes with knowing that who they are is who I AM."

All this the mystic Jesus knew. And he knew it not as some abstract idea but as his most intimate self. "I AM," he says to the Samaritan woman. I AM, not I am the Messiah, or I am the one for whom you wait. Simply I AM.

What Jesus is doing is mirroring for this woman her true nature as I AM. He is saying to her: "I AM! Can you see yourself in me? Can you see your 'I' reflected back as the I AM it is? Look! Look! Right now as I am speaking, can you see the truth? You are not only a Samaritan. You are not only a woman. You are the One Who Is. You are the I AM. Know this and be set free."

Knowing who we are, knowing the I AM to be our truest self, is profoundly liberating. There is no slavery more damning than slavery to the ego as separate self. There is no more powerful ball and chain than that forged by the endless cravings of a deluded self. We are enslaved to our hunger for meaning, our thirst for knowledge. We enslave ourselves to any teaching or teacher that promises to end our craving. We give over our truth and our freedom to one who is not less deluded than ourselves, but who yet convinces us that he or she has what we all so desperately seek.

When messiahs point to themselves rather than to our hearts, when religions turn our attention toward ritual and away from our Self, when ideologies demand blind obedience rather than seeing into the truth, then they are all false and dangerous. The true Messiah points beyond self to God; true religion is a means not an end, a vehicle for God-realization, not a path to institutional piety; true ideology is one that transcends itself in the knowledge that God cannot be reduced to catechism.

How sad, then, that Jesus the messenger is mistaken for the message. Jesus says: "I can do nothing on my own. . . . I seek to do not my will but the will of him who sent me" (John 5:30). The God-realized person is not inventing something new, but rather mirroring something timeless. She is not projecting her own ego; she is manifesting That Which Is. In effect Jesus is saying: "Do not think that I, Jesus, am doing any of this. I am not the judge, my ego is not willing what is happening. I am a vehicle for godliness, I am a manifestation of I AM. My willful self is set aside and the divine acts through me.

Do not mistake me, the self called Jesus, for the selfless One Who Is."

The God-realized person knows that the small self, the ego, is not the ground upon which to build a godly life. Indeed, the knowledge that I and the Father are one reveals that it is only when the godly in us is allowed to act that we rise above the limits of selfishness. Jesus makes it plain that it is not Jesus who is God, but God who is Jesus.

It is his insight into the true nature of self and God that moves Jesus to say, "My kingdom is not from this world" (John 18:36), meaning that the spiritual revolution he experienced and wishes others to experience is an essential inner one and only phenomenologically an outer one. While certainly a problem, Rome is not the root problem. The scribes and Pharisees are not the problem. The Samaritans are not the problem. The root problem is that we each dwell in dark ignorance of our true nature as holy beings manifesting the image and likeness of God.

OUR ORIGINAL SELF IS NOT
THE HUMAN NAME

When we awake to our true nature as manifestations of God, we become the "bread of life that came down from heaven" (John 6:41) and put an end to the gnawing hunger that reducing self to ego inevitably creates. When we know the I AM who is our original self, we suddenly discover that our thirst for wholeness is gone. It is not that we have been given that which we lacked, but that we have discovered we never lacked at all—I and the Father are One. Or as King David sang in Psalm 23: "Lord, my Shepherd, for what can I lack? You are with me." While the physical body of the enlightened still needs care, the soul of the enlightened never goes hungry again.

They were saying: "Is this not Jesus, the son of Joseph, whose father and mother we know? How can he now say 'I have come down from heaven?'" (John 6:42)

The Jesus who speaks in this way is not the son of Joseph but the self-realized son of God. When Jesus lays claim to I AM he is not imagining that he and he alone is the incarnate God, but that the I AM itself is alive in him and can be awakened in each of us. The Jews are right to question the egotism of Jesus claiming to be sent from heaven, but it isn't Jesus speaking this, it is God manifest in him. It is the consistent mishearing of Jesus that leads Jews to reject him and Christians to deify him. Neither response is true to the message Jesus brings: "I am not God," Jesus says. "God is acting through me as me; my ego is not divine, my will is not divine, but ego and will are not my truest self, my original self—the Self that is each of us—that Self is God. It is this that speaks through me. Do not mistake the messenger for the message."

Jesus says to the Jews: "You will search for me, but you will not find me; and where I am you cannot come" (John 7:34). If we are looking for the man Jesus in the divine, we will not find him. He is totally subsumed in God. His will has surrendered to God's will. His "I" is nothing before God's I AM. When we look for the Truth external to ourselves, we will never find it. Where Jesus is, the place of absolute unity with God, no separate self can go. As long as we insist on being other than God we cannot experience the I AM that is us.

Jesus tries in so many different ways to reveal the true nature of his realization. One of the most puzzling, and yet most revealing, is this: "Before Abraham came to be, I AM" (John 8:58). Jesus makes this assertion during a confrontation with the Jewish leaders in the Temple. This encounter between Jesus and his fellow Jews is just another in a long string of misunderstandings.

Here in the Temple Jesus appears to make the claim that he predates Abraham. His listeners object, saying, Jesus is not yet fifty, how can he be older than Abraham? But they are mixing realities. Jesus is speaking from the point of view of the absolute. His listeners are hearing from the perspective of the relative.

In the world of the absolute there is no time, no birth, no death, no change. God was, is, and will be the I AM of all. God transcends any manifestation of God. Jesus the man is not older than Abraham; neither is I AM "older than" Abraham. I AM is timeless.

But his listeners hear only the relative Jesus, the Jesus son of Mary and Joseph, who was born and who will die. They have lost touch with the I AM that is all and cannot see that Jesus is trying to mirror It for them that they may find It within themselves: "The Father and I are one" (John 10:30). That is to say, the True I, your True I-dentity, is not the time-bound mortal ego you mistakenly assume yourself to be but the timeless I AM that is God. Look at the Father in me and see your Self!

Jesus uses himself to illustrate the Self in each of us. "I am the resurrection and the life" (John 11:25). Death is only for the personality, the true you is eternal. "Those who believe in me, even though they die, will never die" (John 11:26); all you have to do is see that I AM who you are, and the death of the personality will not be the end of life because the I AM is birthless, deathless, and timeless—and the I AM is all.

And just in case we still mistake Jesus for God as opposed to seeing that God is Jesus: "Whoever believes in me believes not in me but in Him who sent me. And whoever sees me sees Him who sent me" (John 12:44-45). Jesus tries to make clear the distinction between Jesus the man and the state of God-realization that he has reached. It is not the man Jesus who is of value but the I AM of which he became aware.

So again: "I am the way and the truth and the life" (John 14:6a); I AM is the way to truth and life. "No one comes to the Father except through me" (John 14:6b); unless you do as I have done, unless you see your self as a reflection of the Self, you cannot discover the supreme unity of Father and Son. "I am in the Father and the Father is in me" (John 14:11); I AM is both Father and Son, the absolute and the relative—this is the essential truth that all sages of the perennial philosophy come to teach.

Conventional Jewish thinking has it that Jesus is setting himself up as an intermediary between people and God, something Judaism says is not needed and does not exist. In this way conventional Judaism can reject Jesus and ignore the radical awakening he embodied.

Conventional Christian thinking has it that Jesus is in fact the intermediary between humans and God, and that only by calling on the Son can we contact the Father. In this way conventional Christianity can erect Jesus as a buffer between self and Self, between the I of ego and the I AM of God, and ignore the radical awakening he embodied.

That is what conventional religion always does: it denies the supreme identity of Creator and creation and seeks to sell us a bridge to cover a gap that exists only in its own imagination. There is no gap between creation and Creator. There is no separation between the ray and the sun, between the wave and the ocean. There is no gulf between the relative I and the absolute I AM.

From the perspective of the absolute order we can each say as Jesus says: I AM is the way, the truth, and the life; I AM is the essence of all that is. You cannot reach the Infinite except by discovering that the finite is the Infinite. And when you do, the unity of Father and Son is revealed to be seamless.

CONCLUSION

Jesus said to the Jews of his time:

Listen to me! You are splitting your world into warring camps:
holy and unholy, tax payer and tax collector, scholar and sinner,
men and women, Jew and Samaritan. All this division only per-
petuates fear and your sense of separation from God. I have realized the I AM that each of us is, and I no longer live in a world
of competing camps. I am not bound by the divisions of custom
that narrow our concerns to petty purity rather than transcendent holiness. My way is the way of unity, the way God intended
the world to be. Look to me only to see reflected the nature of
your True Self. Do not mistake the mirror for the image it
reflects. I am not what you see. What you see in me is I AM.
Look deeply into yourselves and see the I AM that you are.
Realize this as your True Self and the Light you will see will illu-
mine the unity of all in God.

There is a level of Reality beyond self and ego. It is the kingdom of heaven and it is within you. To reach it you need not go
anywhere or follow anyone. All you need is to do as I have done:
put down the illusion of ego; recognize that the self you imagine yourself to be is nothing but a pasting together of fleeting
images, thoughts, feelings, and sensations. Stand back from
these and this self fades, revealing the One Self who manifests as
all selves: God the Father who is in each of us, even as each of
us is in Him. Do not follow me, follow my example. Do not see
me as God, see the God Who is me.

I AM is the Way—walk It!

I AM is the Truth—realize It!

I AM is Life—live It.

And in this way shall you manifest the kingdom of God
within and without.

Epilogue

I T HAS BEEN A GREAT EXPERIENCE working with these contributors. They are all highly creative people with impressive lists of
accomplishments behind them. I enjoyed getting to know them,
almost all of them only by telephone, and found them warm and
friendly, humorous, and very cooperative. We have had a good time
together, and I want to take this opportunity to thank them.

Did we accomplish what we set out to do? I think we made a good
start on opening up the "new conversation." It will be extremely
interesting to see where it goes from here. Of course, there are a
number of other people also working on the same thing. And that is
all to the good. For the amount of damage that quarreling over Jesus
has caused, we can't have too much effort expended on trying to set
matters right if and where they are wrong and especially on trying to
heal and prevent hurts in every way we can. I feel that what has been
said here is a valuable contribution in that direction.

What one hopes, of course, is that something further will come of
this effort. I would like to see it move in three directions.

I hope that other people will write—and collect—pieces such as
these, or give lectures on this topic: scholarly, theological, pastoral,
personal, spiritual, whatever. I am thinking of doing another collection like this, maybe organizing a national conference.

I am especially interested in seeing studies—or speculations—on
what Jesus' practical program may have been. We have a good deal of
material on his religious views, spiritual principles, and moral opinions. Did he also have social and economic suggestions for the people of his time, place, and circumstances? If so, is there anything in
those ideas that we could usefully adapt to our own situation?

Another line of development would be to move from the scholarly
level to the congregational level and the family level. Scholars seem to
operate in a world in which the same language is spoken, the same criteria of judgment are applied, and diverse opinions are welcomed and
respected. But the people in the pews are living in a different set of
contexts. The Jesus issue, when it impacts them, is connected not to

the interpretation of texts but to what's happening to their children. Will a fresh look at Jesus be of value to them? Would easing bad feelings toward him personally—as distinguished from the struggle with the majority culture—and letting him have his merits and demerits the same as any other ancient figure in the tradition make enough of a difference that we should try to open up the opportunity for anybody who wants to go into that? For instance, what would leaders of Hillels think of making some experiments in this direction?

There are many interfaith activities going on now. Probably every American city of any reasonable size has at least one. One event in this area that seemed to me especially encouraging was the initiative of "A Jewish Statement on Christians and Christianity," published by the Institute for Christian and Jewish Studies as a full-page ad in the *New York Times* and the *Baltimore Sun* on September 10, 2000. The statement is further elaborated in a book entitled *Christianity in Jewish Terms* and is expected to be a foundation for years of exploration by study groups all over the country. The idea is that Jews ought to understand their neighbors, but they need to approach that understanding in their own terms.[1]

I hope that what the contributors to this volume have done can be seen as another such initiative, undertaking to look at Jesus "in their own terms." And, to the extent that such an initiative is successful, perhaps he can be drawn again into the family's discussions, into a new conversation.

---

[1] The editors say in their preface: "We believe it is time for Jews to learn about Christianity in Jewish terms: to rediscover the basic categories of rabbinic Judaism and to hear what the basic categories of Christian belief sound like when they are taught in terms of this rabbinic Judaism. To hear Christianity in our own terms is truly to understand it, perhaps for the first time" (*Christianity in Jewish Terms*, edited by Tikva Frymer-Kensky, David Novak, Peter Ochs, David Fox Sandmel, and Michael A. Signer [Boulder: Westview, 2000], xii).

Resources for Further Conversation

Ben-Chorin, Shalom. "The Image of Jesus in Modern Judaism." *Journal of Ecumenical Studies* 11 (1974): 401-30.

Cohn, Haim H. *The Trial and Death of Jesus.* New York: Harper & Row, 1971.

Cook, Michael J. "The Death of Jesus: A Catholic–Jewish Dialogue [opposite Raymond Brown]." In *No Religion Is an Island: The* Nostra Aetate *Dialogues.* New York: Fordham University Press, 1998.

———. "Jesus and Christian Origins through Jewish Eyes." In *Proceedings of the Klutznick Colloquium,* edited by Leonard Greenspoon. Omaha, Neb.: Creighton University Press, 2001.

Hagner, Donald. *The Jewish Reclamation of Jesus.* Grand Rapids: Zondervan, 1984.

Jocz, Jakob. *The Jewish People and Jesus Christ.* Reprint, Grand Rapids: Baker, 1981.

Rivkin, Ellis. Review of *The Trial and Death of Jesus,* by Haim H. Cohn. *Saturday Review* (June 19, 1971): 22, 61-62.

Sandmel, Samuel. *We Jews and Jesus.* New York: Oxford University Press, 1965.

Schwartz, G. David. "Is There a Jewish Reclamation of Jesus?" Response to Donald Hagner, *The Jewish Reclamation of Jesus. Journal of Ecumenical Studies* 24, no. 1 (winter 1987).

Internet Resources

Institute for Christian and Jewish Studies: http://www.icjs.edu

Jewish Christian Relations: http://www.jcrelations.net/index.htm

Internet Resources for the Study of Judaism and Christianity: http://ccat.sas.upenn.edu/rs/resources.html

Contributors

RABBI HOWARD ADDISON was ordained by the Jewish Theological Seminary and earned his Doctor of Ministry from the Chicago Theological Seminary and a Ph.D. in Theological Studies from the Graduate Theological Foundation. He is also certified in leading contemplative groups by the Shalem Institute and is the author of *Show Me Your Way: The Complete Guide to Exploring Interfaith Spiritual Direction*. He is the rabbi of Temple Sinai in Dresher, Pennsylvania, and has contributed to *Emet Ve'Emunah*, the Conservative movement's defining theological work of the last two decades. He leads retreats and workshops on Jewish liturgy and meditation, men's issues, and personal spiritual development, in both Jewish and interfaith settings.

LAURA BERNSTEIN holds a master's degree from the University of Chicago and a certificate in Child Psychotherapy from the Chicago Institute for Psychoanalysis. She studied rabbinics at the Hebrew Seminary of the Deaf in Skokie, Illinois. She is a frequent presenter at Common Ground, an interfaith study center in Deerfield, Illinois, and was a contributor to *Finding a Way: Essays on Spiritual Practice*. Her articles have appeared in *The American Vedantist, Sacred Journey*, and *Schola*. Her current interest is interfaith sacred chant, and she leads chanting in a variety of settings, including workshops, retreats, churches, and synagogues.

RABBI HERBERT BRONSTEIN is Senior Scholar of North Shore Congregation Israel, a leading metropolitan Chicago congregation, where he served as Senior Rabbi for over a quarter of a century. He has served as the President of the Chicago Board of Rabbis. He has lectured and taught history and philosophy of religion at the University of Rochester, at Northwestern University, and at the University of Illinois at Chicago, and as visiting scholar at Oxford University in England. At present he teaches comparative religion at Lake Forest

College and accepts invitations to speak at churches and synagogues across the country. He is the editor of "a modern classic" of Jewish liturgy, the Haggadah of Reform Judaism, and served many years as Chairman of Liturgy of the Central Conference of American Rabbis and Chairman of the Commission on Worship of Reform Judaism.

RABBI MICHAEL J. COOK is the Sol and Arlene Bronstein Professor of Judaeo-Christian Studies at Hebrew Union College–Jewish Institute of Religion, Cincinnati Campus. He was educated at Haverford College, Hebrew University, Jerusalem, and HUC-JIR, New York, where he earned an M.A. in Hebrew Literature and Ordination. His doctoral work at the Cincinnati campus focused on the Second Temple period and concentrated on the New Testament. He has served on advisory boards of several institutes for Jewish/Christian studies and on the Joint Commission on Interreligious Affairs of the Central Conference of American Rabbis, the Union of American Hebrew Congregations and HUC-JIR. He travels widely, addressing Jewish and Christian audiences, academicians, and clergy, including leading scholars of the Southern Baptist Convention and the Episcopal Presiding Bishop's Advisory Committee on Christian-Jewish Relations. Dr. Cook has published extensively in his area of Jewish–Christian relations and is currently writing a major book entitled *Removing the Veil: Modern Jews and the New Testament*.

RABBI LAURENCE EDWARDS serves the Congregation B'nai Abraham in Beloit, Wisconsin. He is a graduate of the University of Chicago, ordained by Hebrew Union College–Jewish Institute of Religion, and is a doctoral candidate at Chicago Theological Seminary. He has a long-standing interest in interreligious dialogue. As Hillel Director and Jewish Chaplain at Dartmouth College and at Cornell University, he was deeply involved in interfaith ministry. Currently he teaches in fourteen Catholic high schools in the Chicago area, through the Catholic-Jewish Educational Enrichment Project of the American Jewish Committee. He also serves as Associate National Director for Interreligious Affairs of the American Jewish Committee.

ANDREW VOGEL ETTIN is the spiritual leader of Temple Israel, Salisbury, North Carolina, and Professor of English at Wake Forest University. He is a graduate of Rutgers College (B.A.), Washington University (M.A., Ph.D.), and the Spertus Institute of Jewish Studies

(M.S.J.S.). His books include *Speaking Silence: Stillness and Voice in Modern Thought and Jewish Tradition.*

LANCE FLITTER is a computer scientist at a Navy research center (applied artificial intelligence, author of numerous technical papers and conference presentations) whose wife is a Christian. Because of his personal experience he has been actively involved in interfaith family groups for several years. He serves on the Board of Directors of the InterFaith Families Project of Greater Washington and is an active member of the Dovetail Institute for Interfaith Family Resources and contributes to their conferences and publications. He is also active in several Internet groups related to interfaith families and religion.

RABBI JOSEPH H. GELBERMAN is a modern Hassidic rabbi in the "way of Martin Buber" and also a psychotherapist. At present, he is the Rabbi of the New Light Temple and Director of the Mid-Way Counseling Center of New York City. Dr. Gelberman was the Founder and Rabbi of The Little Synagogue for twenty years. He also founded and led the Kabbalah Center, the Wisdom Academy, the Foundation for Spiritual Living, and The New Seminary. He is the editor of *Kabbalah for Today.* He is a member of the Association for Humanistic Psychology and an active member of the New York Academy of Sciences; he has authored seven books. He is currently active in The All Faiths Seminary International (branches in several countries), which ordains Interfaith Ministers and offers a doctoral program in conjunction with the International Institute of Integral Human Sciences (affiliated with the United Nations).

RABBI LAWRENCE KUSHNER is Rabbi-in-Residence at Hebrew Union College–Jewish Institute of Religion in New York City, where he teaches Jewish spirituality and mysticism and mentors rabbinic students. Prior to his present position, he served for twenty-eight years as the rabbi of Congregation Beth El in Sudbury, Massachusetts. He is a graduate of the University of Cincinnati, and was ordained rabbi from the Hebrew Union College. For over a decade he has served as a visiting lecturer at the HUC–JIR in New York and has been a commentator on National Public Radio's *All Things Considered.* His lectures and publications, including ten books, translated into five languages, have contributed to the present Jewish agenda for personal and institutional spiritual renewal. In this connection, he initated synagogue *havurot* (fellowship groups of families) and led his congregants to publish their own prayer book, the first gender-neutral liturgy. He has conducted over seventy-five *kalla* weekends for personal religious growth, and was the first Rabbinic Chairman of Reform Judaism's Commission on Religious Living.

DREW LEDER is a Jewish Quaker, with an M.D. from Yale and a Ph.D. from the State University of New York at Stony Brook, who is professor of Western and Eastern philosophy at Loyola College in Baltimore. In his book *The Absent Body* and elsewhere, he has published extensively on bodily experience and its impact within medicine. More recent books have focused on cultivating the sacred in everyday life. *Spiritual Passages* looks at the transformational possibilities inherent in the aging process and later life. *Games for the Soul* offers a playful approach to spiritual disciplines. *The Soul Knows No Bars: Inmates Reflect on Life, Death, and Hope* is based on his nationally recognized work with maximum security prisoners.

RABBI MICHAEL LERNER is founder and editor of *TIKKUN* magazine, a bimonthly Jewish critique of politics, culture, and society. Active as a Jewish liberation theologian, he is a disciple of the late Abraham Joshua Heschel and serves as rabbi of Beyt Tikkun Synagogue in San Francisco. He holds Ph.D.'s in philosophy and clinical psychology and is the author of *Surplus Powerlessness: The Psychodynamics of Individual and Social Transformation*. Recent publications are *The Politics of Meaning, Jewish Renewal,* and *Spirit Matters. Utne Reader* named him one of America's one hundred most visionary thinkers. He is currently working on a spiritual commentary on the Torah and creating a network of spiritually oriented professionals from all walks of life to implement the vision articulated in his books.

DANIEL MATT is the author of *The Essential Kabbalah, God and the Big Bang,* and *Zohar: The Book of Enlightenment.* He served as professor of Jewish spirituality at the Graduate Theological Union in Berkeley, California, and has also taught at Stanford University and the Hebrew University in Jerusalem. He is now at the Shalom Hartman Institute in Jerusalem, where he is composing an annotated English translation of the *Zohar,* the masterpiece of Kabbalah (the Jewish mystical tradition).

RABBI DANIEL POLISH is the Director of the Joint Commission on Social Action of the Union of American Hebrew Congregations and the Central Conference of American Rabbis. Educated at Northwestern University and Hebrew Union College, Cincinnati, where he was also ordained, he earned his Ph.D. in the history of religion from Harvard. He has taught at Harvard, Tufts, and the University of Maryland, as well as at Occidental College and HUC-JIR in Los Angeles. He has published widely, a good deal of his work being in Jewish–Christian relations. For instance, he edited two books with Dr. Eugene Fisher of the United States Conference of Catholic Bishops and contributed to *Issues of Jewish Christian Dialogue.* He writes regularly for the *Journal of Ecumenical Studies.* His editorial "A Painful Legacy: Jews and Catholics Struggle to Understand Edith Stein and Auschwitz," which appeared in *Ecumenical Trends,* was chosen by the Catholic Press Association as one of the best editorials in a Catholic publication.

STANLEY N. ROSENBAUM credits his marriage to his Catholic wife, Mary, with making a devout and observant Jew of him. The two of them have made a career of providing resources for interfaith families. They have written a book entitled *Celebrating Our Differences: Living Two Faiths in One Marriage* and, with others, co-founded the Dovetail Institute for Interfaith Family Resources. Mary Rosenbaum edits its journal. Stanley Rosenbaum earned a Ph.D. in Near Eastern and Judaic Studies at Brandeis and taught Judaic Studies for twenty-eight years at Dickinson College. They now live in Boston, Kentucky, and Stanley Rosenbaum teaches at the University of Kentucky at Louisville, Louisville Presbyterian Theological Seminary, and occasionally at the Trappist Abbey of Gethsemani. His most recent publication is *Amos of Israel: A New Interpretation,* and his history of biblical Israel will be published this year. He sees Jesus, who stands squarely within the Israelite prophetic tradition, as being easily among the five most important individuals who ever lived.

RABBI ALLEN A. SECHER heads a Jewish Renewal community, Congregation Makom Shalom in Chicago. Along with two priests, he is a counselor to the Jewish–Catholic Dialogue Group of Chicago, a 550-couple support and educational group for interfaith couples. He serves as an officer of the Dovetail Institute for Interfaith Family Resources. He is a board member of Aleph, the umbrella organization for Renewal Judaism. A graduate of Brandeis University with a degree in philosophy, he was ordained by Hebrew Union College, New York. Rabbi Secher has a second career in the media. For thirty years he was host of an internationally syndicated radio show, *East of Eden*. As a television producer he has won seven Emmys, the most recent for a PBS special on resistance in Auschwitz, hosted by Academy Award winner Ellen Burstyn.

RABBI RAMI SHAPIRO is president of Metivta Center for Contemplative Judaism in Los Angeles, California, and director of the Simply Jewish Foundation (www.simplyjewish.com). Ordained by the Hebrew Union College–Jewish Institute of Religion, and graduated from Union Graduate School with a Ph.D. in contemporary Jewish thought, he is the author of *Wisdom of the Jewish Sages*, *Minyan: Ten Principles for Living a Life of Integrity*, *The Way of Solomon*, and *The Book of Proverbs*. He is prominent in the Jewish Renewal movement and is a popular lecturer.

RABBI BYRON L. SHERWIN is the David C. Verson Professor of Jewish Philosophy and Mysticism at the Spertus Institute of Jewish Studies in Chicago, where he also serves as Dean of Faculties and Vice President for Academic Affairs and as Director of the Joseph Cardinal Bernardin Center for the Study of Eastern European Jewry. He holds degrees from Columbia University, Jewish Theological Seminary of America, an M.A. from New York University, and a Ph.D. from the University of Chicago. He was ordained at the Jewish Theological Seminary. His interfaith activities include teaching at Mundelein College (Catholic) and Chicago Theological Seminary (Church of Christ); he is a member of the Advisory Board of the Institute for Jewish-Christian Understanding. He is co-author and co-editor with Harold Kasimow of *No Religion Is an Island: Abraham Joshua Heschel and Interreligious Dialogue* and *John Paul II and Interreligious Dialogue*.

RABBI LEWIS D. SOLOMON is the Theodore Rinehart Professor of Business Law at the George Washington University Law School, where he has taught corporate and tax law for over twenty years and authored or co-authored more than forty legal volumes. He received his ordination as a post-denominational rabbi from the Rabbinical Studies Department of The New Seminary under the mentorship of Rabbi Dr. Joseph H. Gelberman. He also received clinical training in mind/body medicine from the Harvard Medical School, and has written *The Jewish Book of Living and Dying* and *The Jewish Tradition and Choices at the End of Life: A New Judaic Approach to Illness and*

Death. He has taught courses on Jewish bioethics, Jewish views of the afterlife, and Jewish spirituality. A recent book is *Jewish Spirituality: Revitalizing Judaism for the Twenty-First Century,* congenial to his concerns as President of the International Federation of Rabbis, a professional organization of rabbis united by a commitment to Jewish tradition and a desire to facilitate the Jewish spiritual growth and life-cycle needs of all. Another area of teaching and writing finds expression in his most recent book, *A Modern Day Rabbi's Interpretation of the Teachings of Jesus.*

RABBI ARTHUR WASKOW is one of the leading creators of theory, practice, and institutions for the movement for Jewish renewal. He is a Pathfinder of ALEPH Alliance for Jewish Renewal. In 1983 he founded and continues to direct the Shalom Center, a division of ALEPH that focuses on Jewish thought and practice to protect and heal the earth and society. Among his seminal works in Jewish renewal are *The Freedom Seder; Godwrestling; Seasons of Our Joy; Down-to-Earth Judaism: Food, Money, Sex, and the Rest of Life. Godwrestling—Round Two* received the Benjamin Franklin Award in 1996. He co-edited *Trees, Earth, & Torah: A Tu B'Shvat Anthology,* a major new volume in the classic series of Festival Anthologies from the Jewish Publication Society. His most recent publication is as editor of *Torah of the Earth: Exploring 4000 Years of Ecology in Jewish Thought.* In 1996 Rabbi Waskow was named by the United Nations one of forty "Wisdom Keepers," religious and intellectual leaders from all over the world who met in connection with the Habitat II Conference in Istanbul.

RABBI ARNOLD JACOB WOLF has been the rabbi of Illinois' oldest Jewish congregation, Kehilath Anshe Maarav Isaiah Israel, in Chicago, since 1980, emeritus beginning in 2000. Earlier he served Congregation Emanuel, Chicago, and was founding rabbi of the experimental, avant-garde Congregation Solel on Chicago's North Shore. He was educated at the University of Chicago, the University of Cincinnati, and Hebrew Union College, where he was ordained and awarded a Doctorate of Divinity. He taught at HUC-JIR, New York and Los Angeles, University of Chicago Divinity School, Loyola Marymount University in Los Angeles, Spertus Institute, and Yale University. He has lectured at Amherst, Harvard, Williams, Princeton, Colgate, Illinois, Cornell, Brandeis, Wisconsin, Dillard, Michigan, and many other universities, as well as at churches and synagogues. Rabbi

Wolf was the first official Jewish representative to the World Council of Churches Assembly in 1975. In 1962 he was honored with the National Conference of Christians and Jews Brotherhood Award. He has served as a board member of the Jewish Peace Fellowship, the Jewish Council on Urban Affairs, and the national Commission on Social Action of Reform Judaism. He was a founding editor of *Sh'ma: A Journal of Jewish Responsibility* and is presently theology editor of the quarterly *Judaism*. He has authored five books and more than two hundred fifty essays.